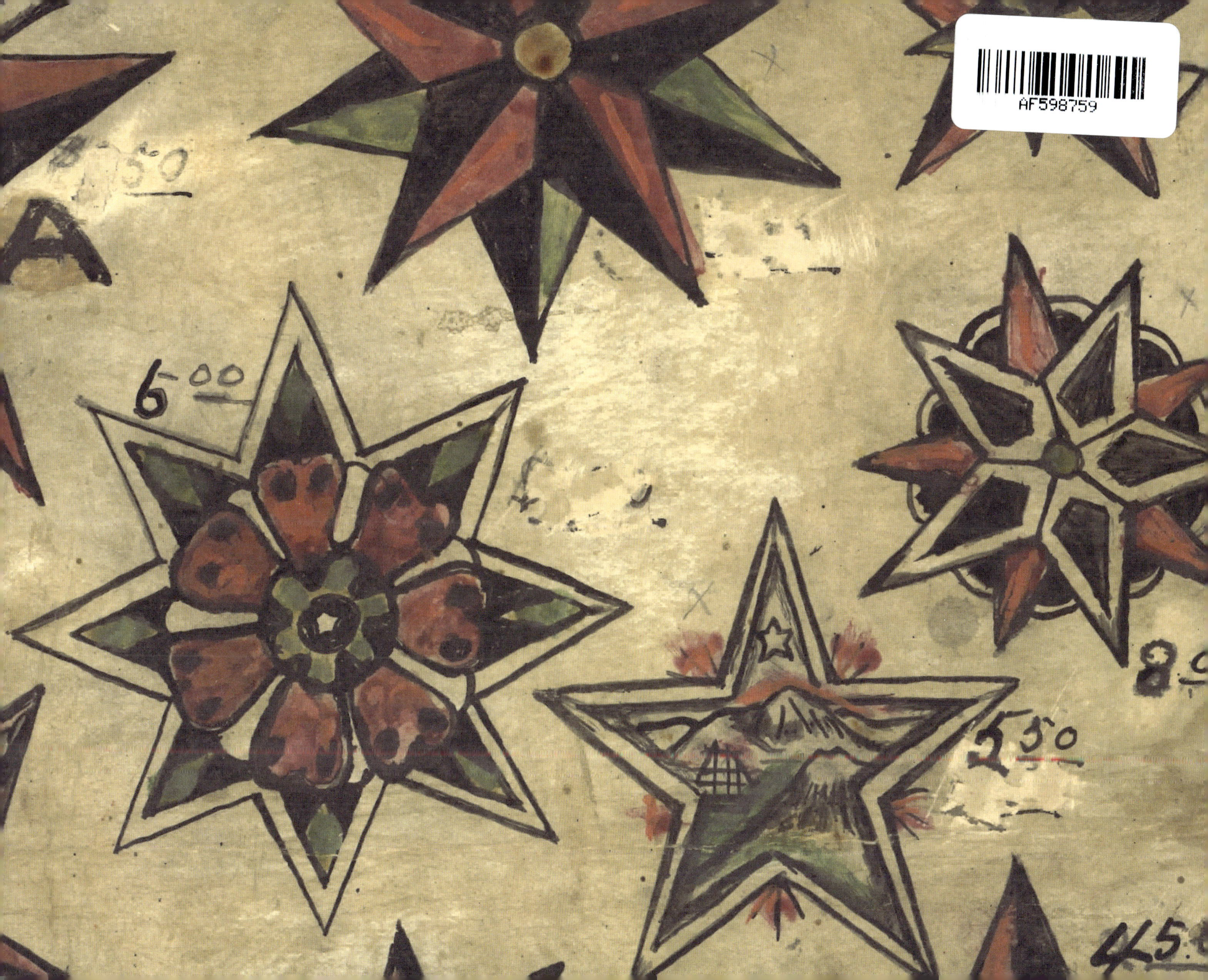
6-00
5 50
8
4 5

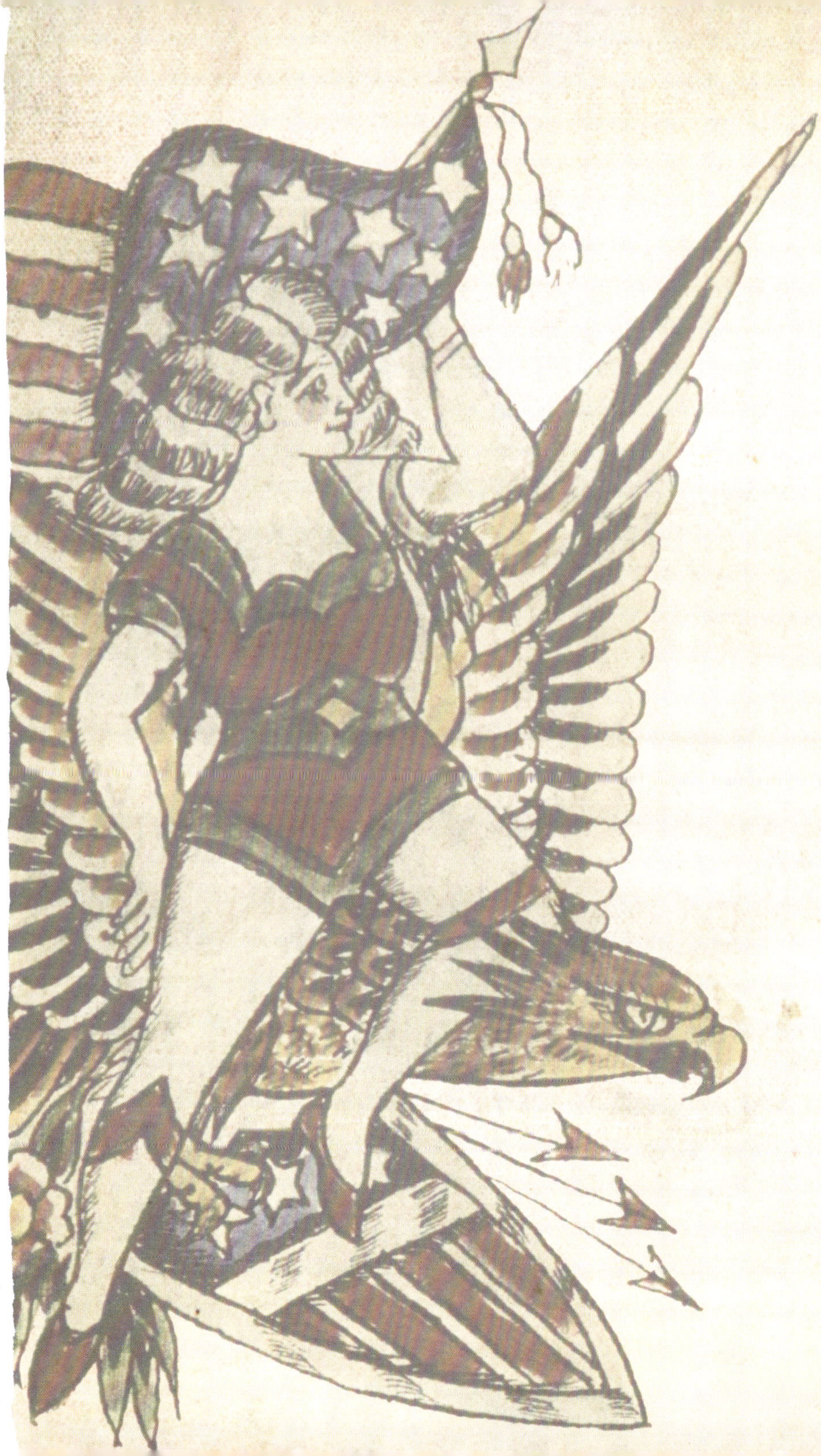

GUS WAGNER

GLOBE TROTTER

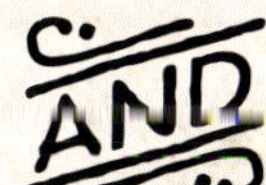

HAND TATTOO ARTIST

ALAN GOVENAR

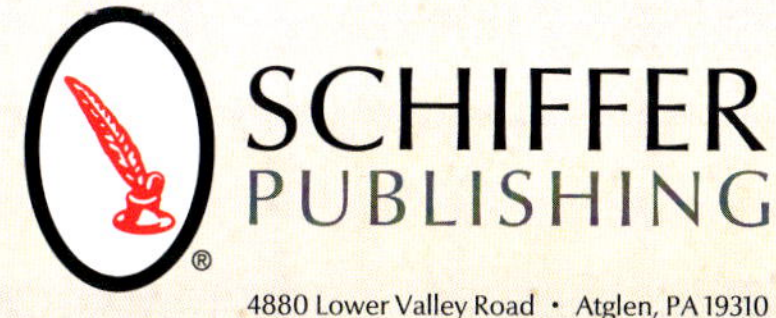

4880 Lower Valley Road • Atglen, PA 19310

Other Schiffer Books by the Author:
Stoney Knows How: Life as a Sideshow Tattoo Artist, 3rd Edition,
ISBN 978-0-7643-6400-6
The Early Years of Rhythm & Blues, ISBN 978-0-7643-1983-9
Anne Morgan: Photography, Philanthropy, and Advocacy,
ISBN 978-0-7643-6590-4

Library of Congress Control Number: 2023941027

Cover design by Molly Shields
Photographs, flash, ephemera, artifacts, and scrapbook pages, ca. 1897–1941, from the Alan Govenar and Kaleta Doolin Tattoo Collection, South Street Seaport Museum.
Photographs on pages 3 and 51, courtesy of Derin Bray.
Photograph on page 52, courtesy of Ben Krzykowski.

Type set in Citrus Gothic/Cambria

ISBN: 978-0-7643-6728-1
Printed in China

Published by Schiffer Publishing, Ltd.
4880 Lower Valley Road
Atglen, PA 19310
Phone: (610) 593-1777; Fax: (610) 593-2002
Email: Info@schifferbooks.com
Web: www.schifferbooks.com

For our complete selection of fine books on this and related subjects, please visit our website at www.schifferbooks.com. You may also write for a free catalog.

Schiffer Publishing's titles are available at special discounts for bulk purchases for sales promotions or premiums. Special editions, including personalized covers, corporate imprints, and excerpts, can be created in large quantities for special needs. For more information, contact the publisher.

We are always looking for people to write books on new and related subjects. If you have an idea for a book, please contact us at proposals@schifferbooks.com.

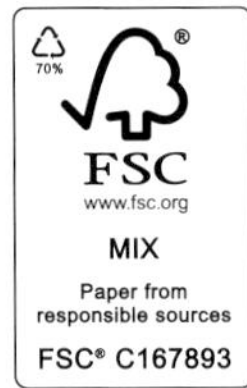

Gus Wagner as a merchant seaman, ca. 1897–1904

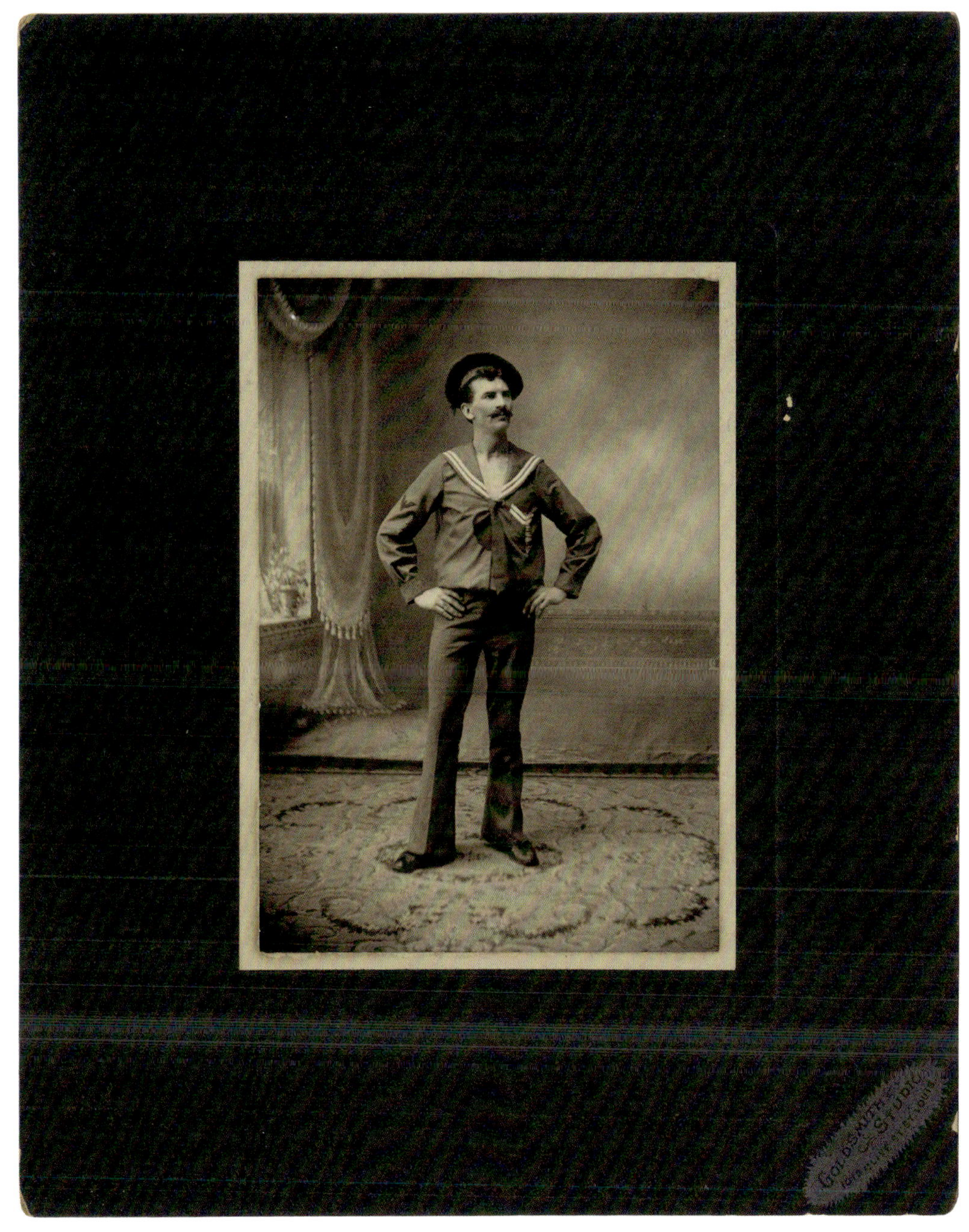

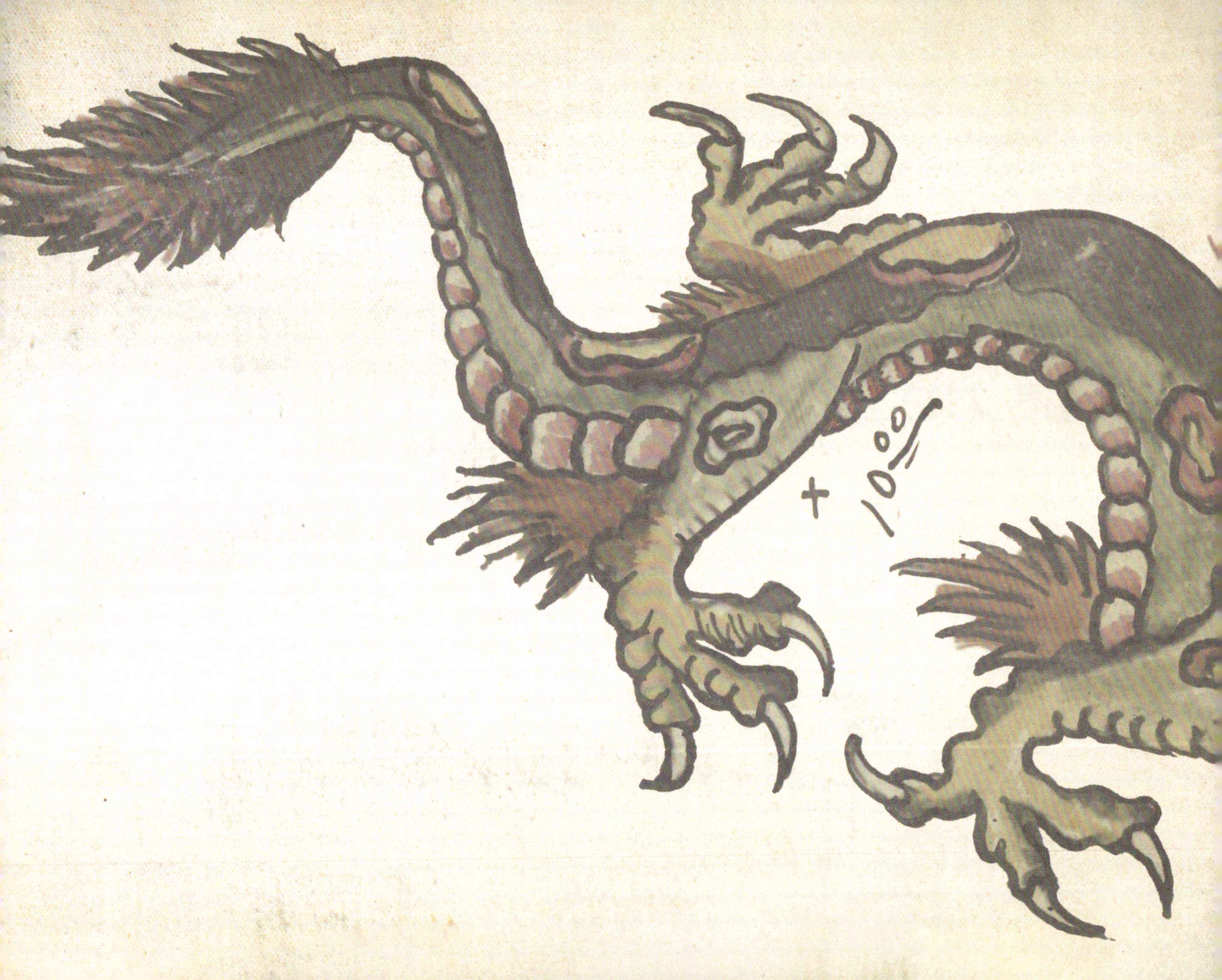

CONTENTS

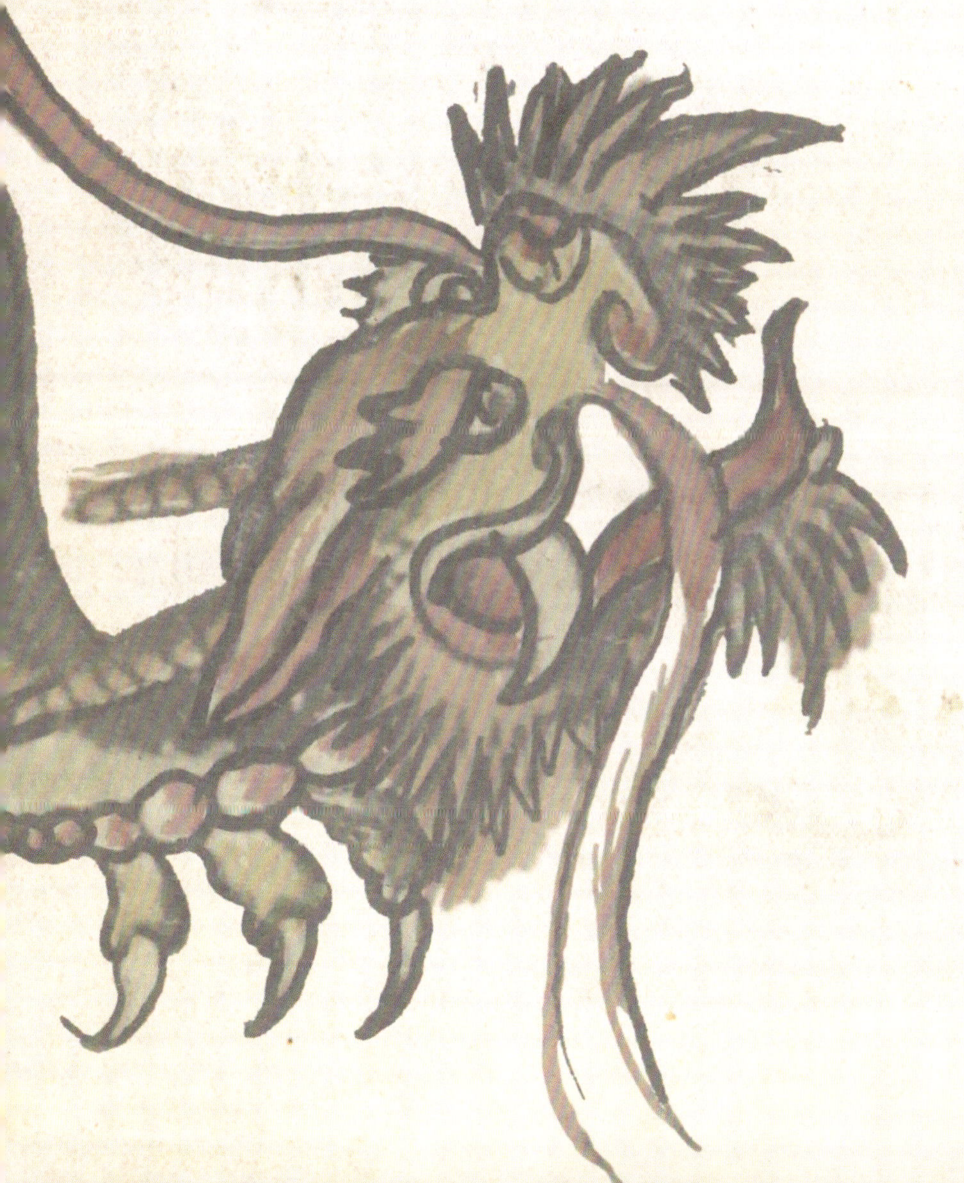

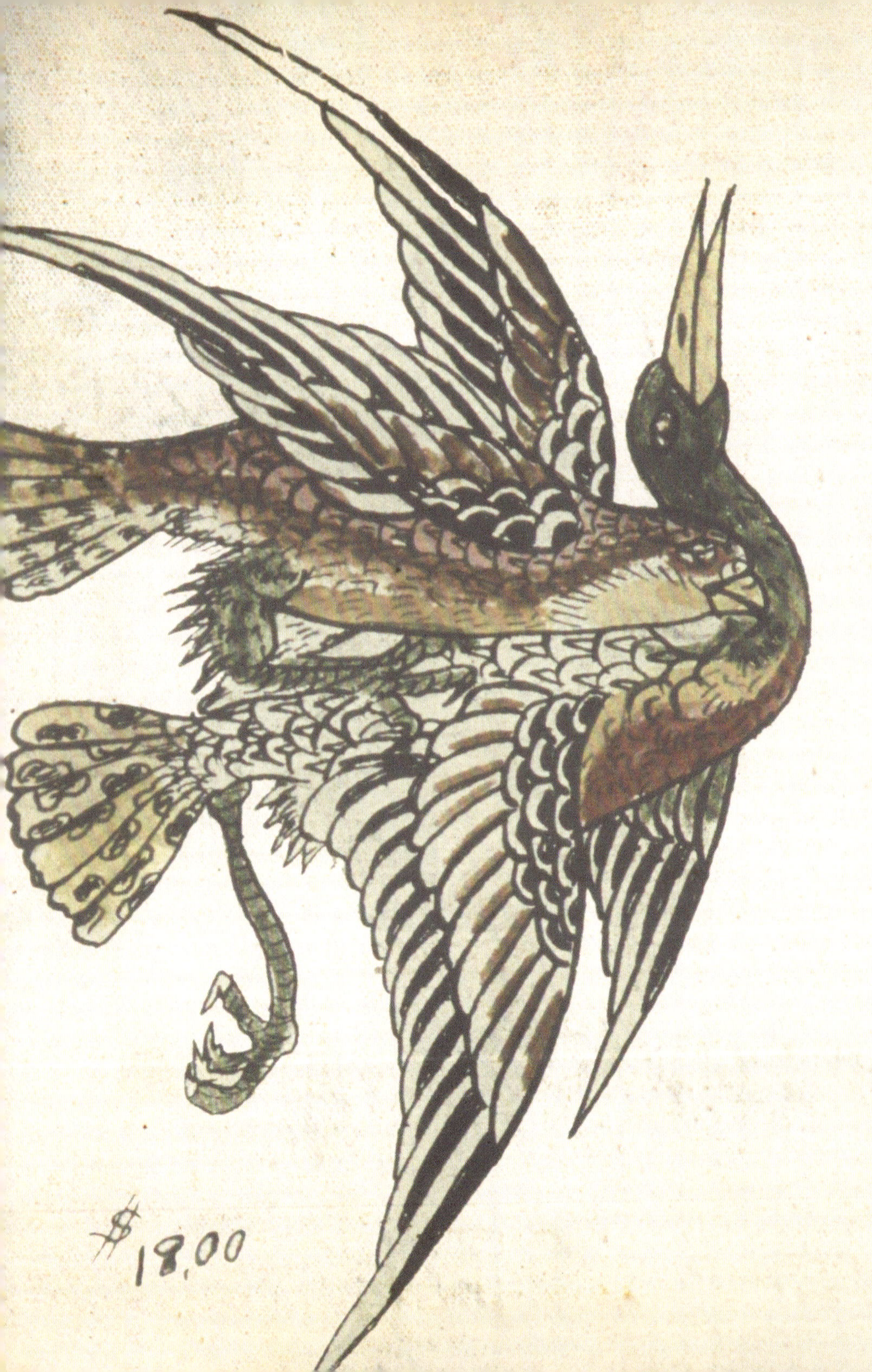

PREFACE

In 1989, I invited my wife, Kaleta Doolin, who I was dating at the time, to go with me to a tattoo convention in Arlington, Texas. My book and film about old-school tattoo artist Stoney St. Clair, both titled *Stoney Knows How*, were in active distribution. My doctoral dissertation, "Issues in the Documentation of Tattooing in the Western World," was controversial among some academics but highly regarded by the ever-expanding tattoo community and the contemporary art scene. *Stoney Knows How* premiered in 1981 at Film Forum in New York City, and in 1982, it was shown as part of the Museum of Modern Art's New Director series, followed by screenings at the Centre Pompidou in Paris and the London Film Festival, where it was selected as an Outstanding Film of the Year.

At the Arlington convention, I reconnected with Chuck Eldridge of the Tattoo Archive and Ed Hardy, who is featured in my film *Stoney Knows How*. Chuck and Ed were excited about meeting Lotteva Wagner Davis, who spoke to them at length about the legacy of her parents. Her father, Gus Wagner (1872–1941), a globetrotter and hand tattoo artist, met her mother, Maud Stevens Wagner (1877–1961), at the St. Louis World's Fair, where she was working as an aerialist and contortionist. Between 1904 and 1907, Gus tattooed Maud, and together they traveled around the United States making tattoos and exhibiting their full-body tattoos.

After looking at Ed's and Chuck's snapshots of Gus's tattoo *flash*, we started talking about the need to exhibit this amazing work. At that point, there had been no museum exhibitions of tattoo flash as an art form; the drawings and paintings of tattoo artists had long been overlooked, not only by folk art specialists but also by curators of contemporary art. John Slate, archivist and curator of collections at the Hertzberg Museum in San Antonio, helped us to organize an exhibition on the history of tattoo flash, and Ed and I collaborated on a book, *Flash from the Past: Classic American Tattoo Designs 1890-1965*.

As plans for the Hertzberg exhibition advanced, Ed began working with Ann Philbin, who was then director of the Drawing Center in New York City, on another exhibition, titled *Pierced Hearts and True Love: A Century of Drawings for Tattoos*, which he envisioned to be two-thirds on the work of contemporary tattoo artists and one-third on historical antecedents. Ultimately, however, the percentages changed, and when the exhibition opened in 1995, the majority of the drawings were historical and included numerous pieces by Gus Wagner.

At Ed's request, I had planned to meet with Lotteva at her home in Plainview, Texas, to see more of her father's flash and to assess which pieces might be suited for the Hertzberg and Drawing Center exhibitions. But in 1993, she died, and her son, Rockey Reisner, inherited the Wagner family collection.

Rockey lived in a house trailer near Plainview and told me he was a retired *carny* who traveled with the Wagners on various carnival and circus shows and was "adopted" because he said he was essentially an "orphan." Rockey revered Lotteva and didn't have enough money to give her a "proper" burial. But at the same time, he was reluctant to sell the tattoo collection he inherited because he was more concerned about the legacy of Gus, Maud, and Lotteva than in making a profit.

I explained to Rockey that Kaleta and I were interested in preserving the collection by donating it to a museum that would commit to its importance. Rockey seemed to like what I was saying, but he was skeptical. He was a volunteer policeman and firefighter in the small town where he lived, and he had his doubts about strangers.

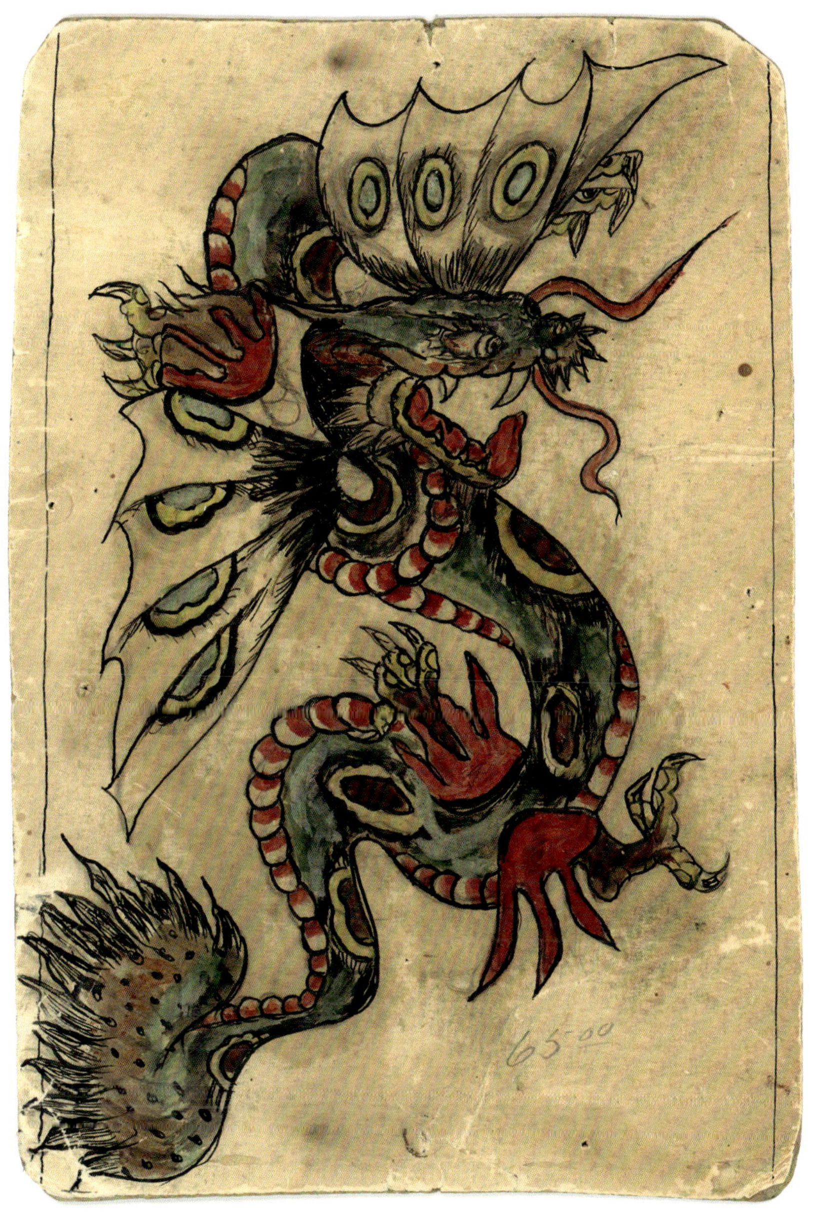

Gus Wagner flash

Sitting across from him in his house trailer, Rockey exuded a *carny* bravado, his handgun within easy reach on the little table in front of him. To introduce myself, I had brought a copy of my book *Stoney Knows How*, and while I sat watching him, Rockey thumbed through the book. After about ten minutes, he looked up and said emphatically, "This is the best damn book on the sideshow I've ever read." And he then proceeded to sell me the contents of overflowing boxes of flash, photographs, and ephemera, one item at a time.

After a few hours we were done, and I wrote Rockey a personal check from Kaleta's and my joint account, and as I started to prepare to load my car, he said that he had "forgotten" to show me the "really old stuff." He pulled a box out from under his bed. Inside were hand-carved tattoo instruments and flash books with oil paintings on canvas pages.

The value of what Rockey showed me was incalculable. I had written extensively about tattooing but was learning more than I could have ever imagined. Once again, Rockey priced each item one at a time, and when he finished, I told him I didn't have another check and I needed to go to an ATM. And Rockey looked up and smiled, "What's an ATM?"

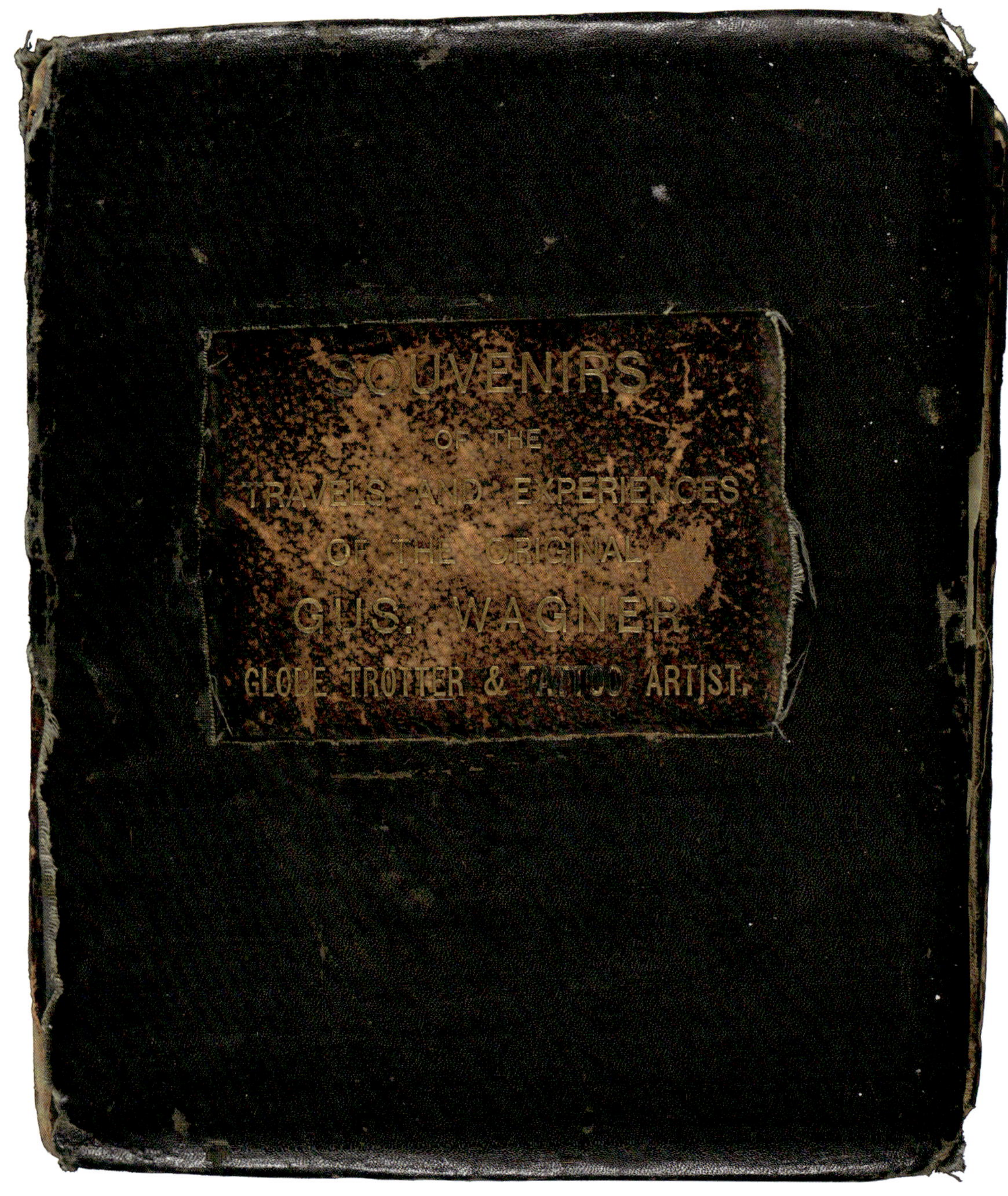
SOUVENIRS
OF THE
TRAVELS AND EXPERIENCES
OF THE ORIGINAL
GUS. WAGNER
GLOBE TROTTER & TATTOO ARTIST.

Rockey and I set off in my car, going from one local bank to another. The withdrawal limit at each was $200, which meant we had to go to different locations, but as we found out, we also had to go to places that were not somehow linked together with the same banking system.

By the time I gathered enough funds and loaded my car, it was past 10:00 p.m., and I was still a two-and-a-half-hour drive from Dallas. I called Kaleta and stayed in a motel. I needed to unload the boxes of Wagner materials and then load them back into my car before heading home the next morning.

One piece in the collection that Rockey held back was what he called Gus's "press book," a foot-thick, leather-bound, hand-embossed scrapbook with memorabilia from family photos, portraits, and snapshots to tattoo artists' business cards, letters, merchant seaman papers, and postage stamps. Rockey was considering "the Showman's Club" as a possible home for Gus's tome but said if he changed his mind, he would call me, and about a year later he reached out to me.

Finding the right museum for the Wagner collection was a challenge. In the end, Kaleta and I gifted the collection to the South Street Seaport Museum in New York City on November 13, 2001. Peter Neal, who was then the museum's director, had the strongest proposal—to organize an exhibition, preserve the collection, and start a tattoo institute to engage artists around the world and to potentially become a repository for their research and collections.

Gus Wagner: Globe Trotter and Hand Tattoo Artist is the first of three books in the *Last of the Hand Tattoo Artists* series and focuses on the period from 1872 to 1903. The second book explores Gus and Maud's life together, from their marriage in 1904 to their travels across America as tattoo artists and sideshow attractions to Gus's death in 1941. The third book features Gus and Maud's daughter, Lotteva Wagner Davis, her tattoo flash, and her work as a tattooist and graphic artist.

"Souvenirs of the Travels and Experiences of the Original Gus Wagner: Globe Trotter and Tattoo Artist," ca. 1897–1941

ACKNOWLEDGMENTS

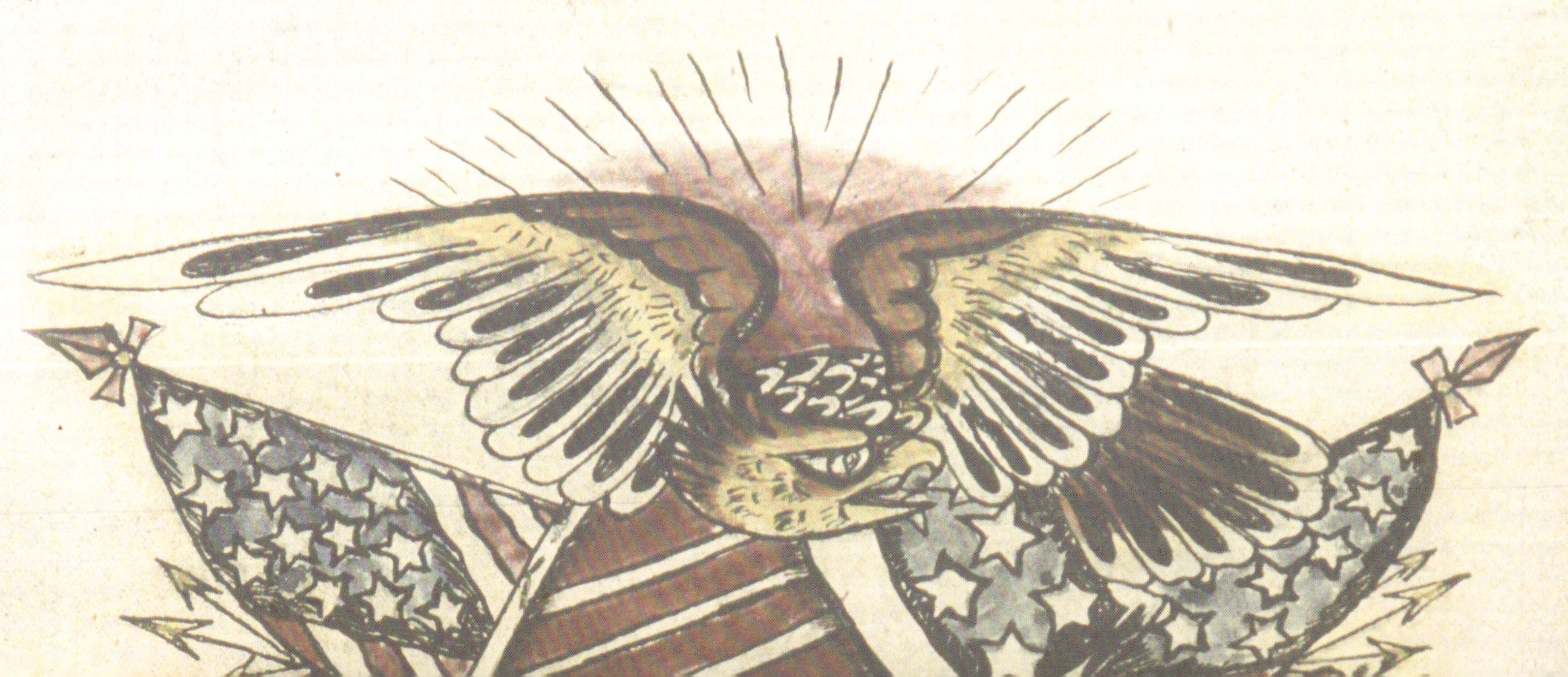

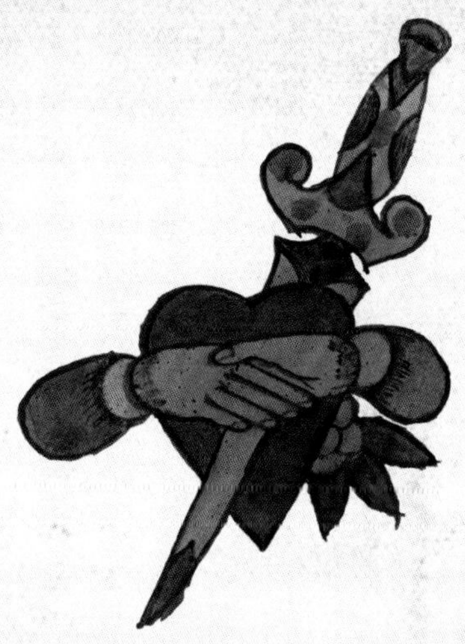

First and foremost, I am grateful to Rockey Reisner for entrusting me with his family treasures, and to my family for encouraging my work. Martina Caruso, director of collections at the South Street Seaport Museum, provided scans and documentation and has guided the preservation and conservation of the Alan Govenar and Kaleta Doolin Tattoo Collection. Ed Hardy and Chuck Eldridge offered good counsel as my work advanced. Michelle Myles and Michael McCabe shared their insights into the history of tattooing in New York City. Derin Bray, Ben Krzykowski, and Ron Dolacek loaned photographs from their collections. Jason Johnson-Spinos assisted with copyediting and the preparation of photographs and images for publication.

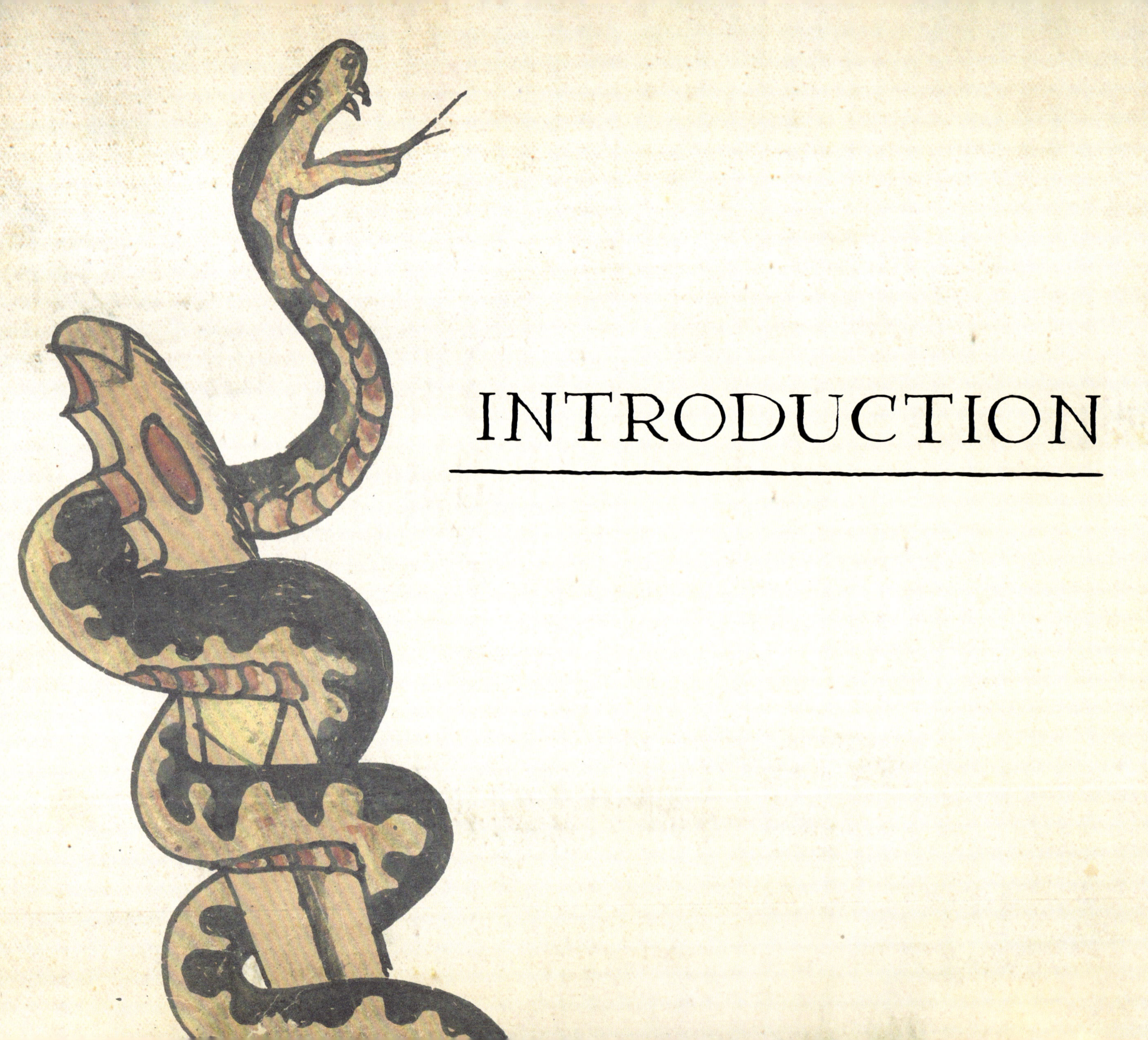

INTRODUCTION

Gus Wagner was a man of his own making. Self-reliant and industrious. Independent and hard-edged. A globe trotter who embraced the zeitgeist of the nineteenth century and defied the social mores of the Victorian era. A merchant seaman. Tattooed man. Sideshow attraction. The self-proclaimed "Globe Trotter and Hand Tattoo Artist."

Born in 1872 in Marietta, Ohio, at the confluence of the Muskingum and the Ohio Rivers, Gus was drawn to the maritime life at an early age. At twelve, he saw his first heavily tattooed man, "Captain Constentenus—the Greek Albanian" in a traveling sideshow. Standing before him, Gus was amazed and realized perhaps that he could become the person he was looking at.

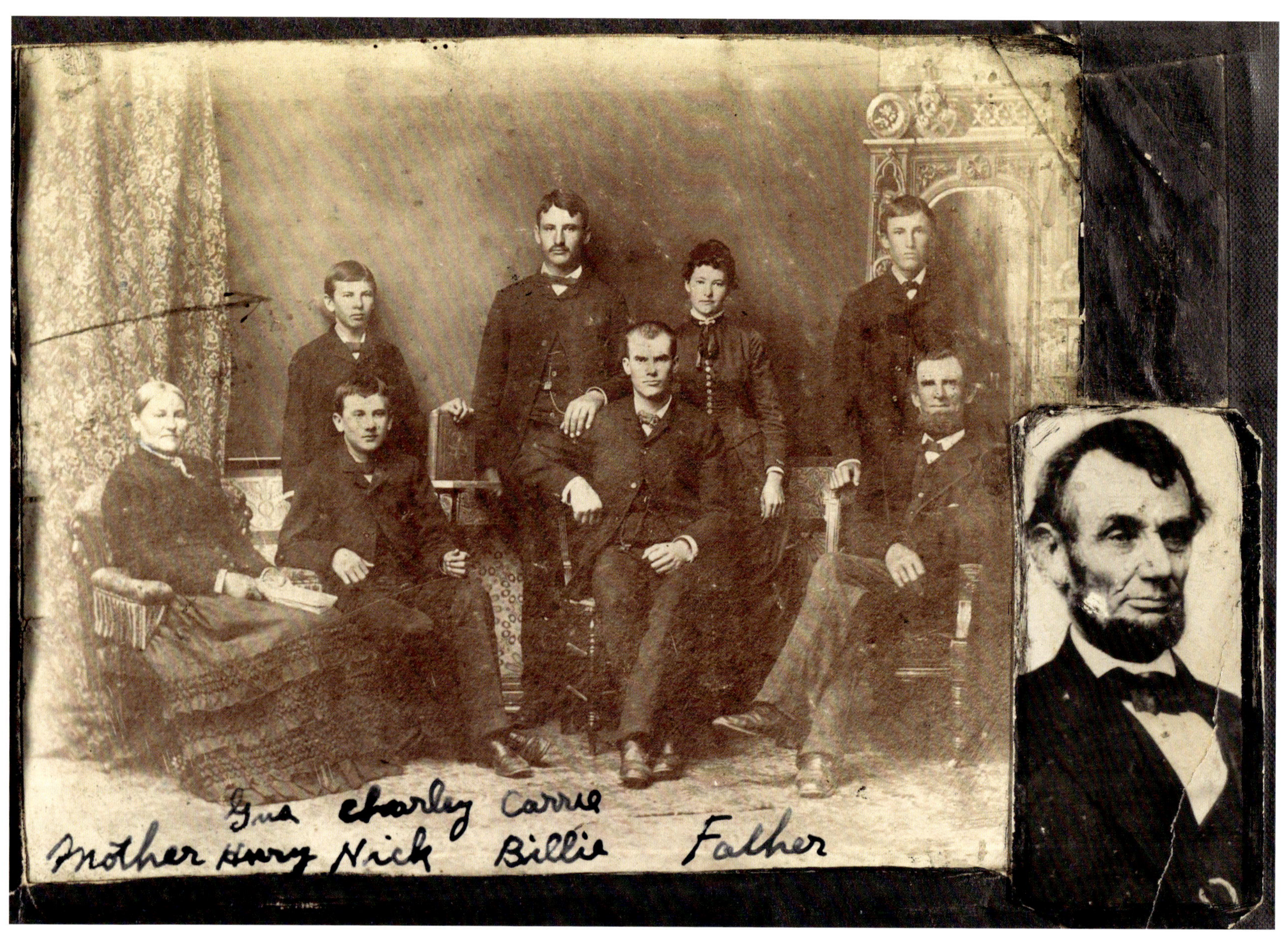

Gus Wagner with his family.
Detail from Gus Wagner's scrapbook

One can only wonder about what attracted Gus to Constentenus and what motivated Gus to get his entire body tattooed. Under Constentenus's iconic portrait on P. T. Barnum show poster was the text "Tattooed from Head to Foot, in Chinese Tartary as Punishment for engaging in Rebellion against the King."

Did it matter to Gus that Constentenus's tattoos were purportedly made against his will? Or was his tale of woe part of a sideshow bally that made people want to pay to see his tattooed body? Gus was a showman and was clearly committed to the time-honored, albeit cryptic, tradition of the heavily tattooed man, dating back to at least the sixteenth and seventeenth centuries.

In a counternarrative, Lotteva Wagner Davis, Gus's daughter, told Chuck Eldridge that Gus's father was born in Berlin and his mother in Alsace-Lorraine, France.

> When Gus was eleven years old, he ran off with Barnum's circus playing in Sousa's band playing the slide trombone. He went back home, started to study to be a doctor. His father passed away. He went to London. He wanted to travel the world and see what it was all about. He went to work in Scotland Yard and then started going by ship all over the country. He traveled in every country that had a flag and many that didn't at that time. While he was in London, where he made his home base, he met a man by the name of Professor Alfred South, a tattoo artist that tattooed the royal family, including Queen Victoria of England.

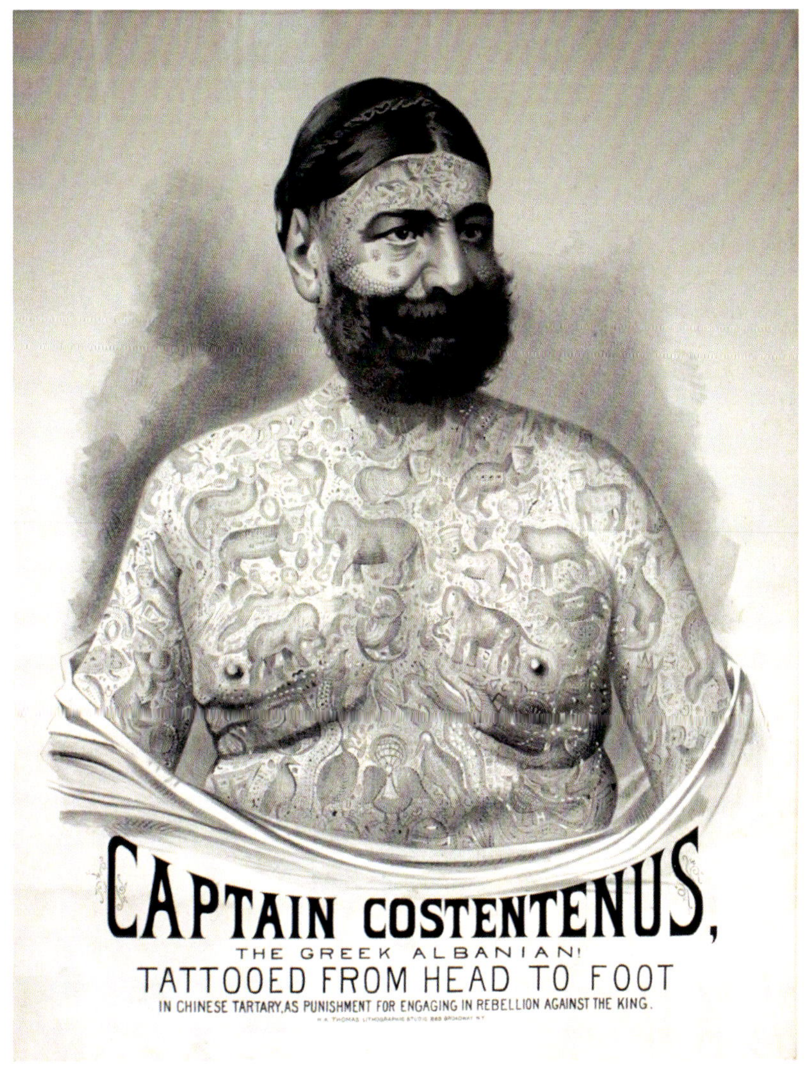

Poster advertising Captain Costentenus as a sideshow for the Great Farini or P. T. Barnum circus

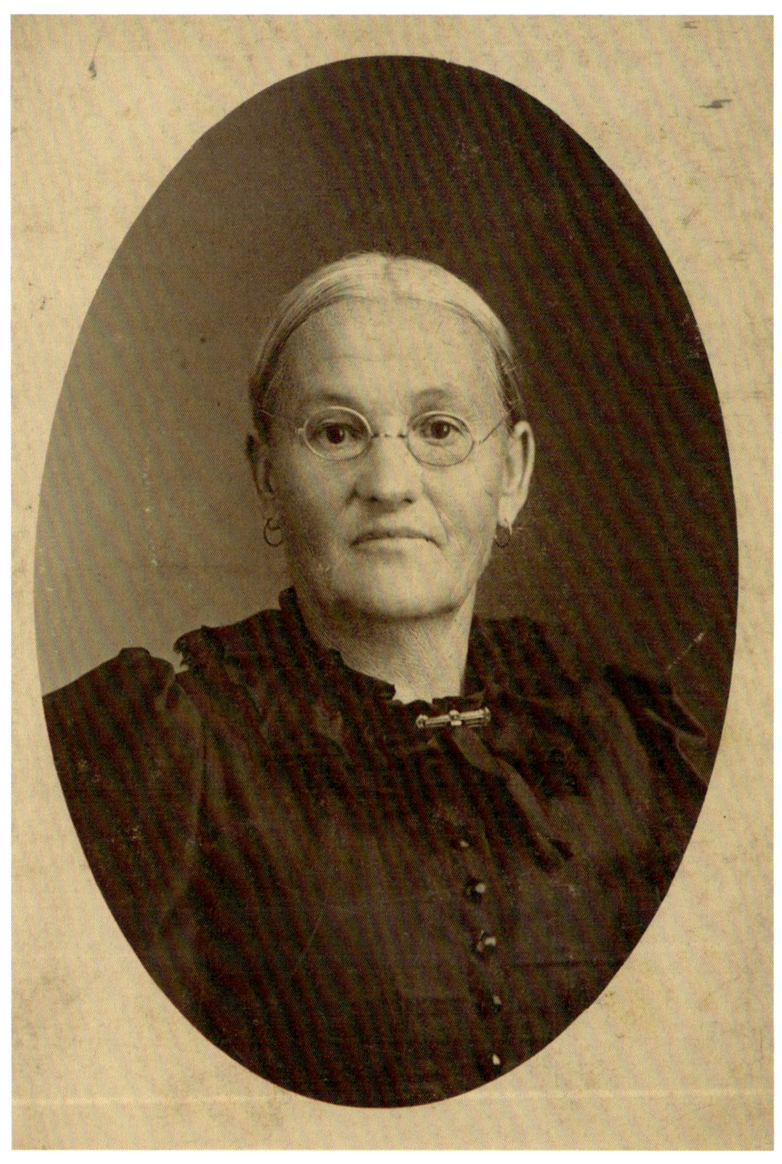

Gus Wagner's mother, Charlotte Wagner

> So, he got tattooed by South, several designs, and then he started to learn to tattoo, which he did learn on board ship. For a long time, I had one of his little books of designs that he drawed [*sic*]. The old hourglass ladies that Grandpa used to like, they were supposed to be in very naughty clothes and they was practically all covered. Frankly, yes.
>
> Gus tattooed sailors. And then every port he went into where there was a tattooer, he got tattooed. He was tattooed with bone needles, fish needles, bamboo. The only kind of tattoo he didn't have was where they cut the flesh and put in dry powder and burnt leaves. When it heals it's embossed, leaves knots in the skin. He didn't have that done because he said that was disfiguring to your body. As though the tattoos don't.
>
> Well, he traveled all over and got all kinds of tattoos and got completely covered. To run this long story short, he come back to this country, and started tattooing again.

In his twenties, Gus left home to see the world, determined to ferret out the ancient roots of tattooing, an art form that had invigorated him for more than a decade and propelled his passion to distinguish himself in a way that upended the values of the Western world. By 1901, Gus reportedly had 264 tattoos of his own, and over 800 by 1908. Gus traversed the United States by wagon and train, promoting himself as "the most artistically marked-up man in America." He appeared in circus and carnival sideshows and busked on street corners and in front of ice cream stands and barbershops, performing sometimes on the

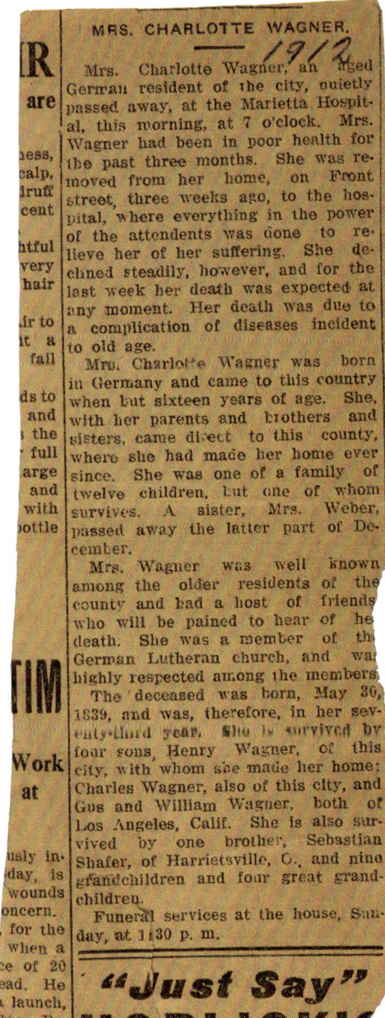

MRS. CHARLOTTE WAGNER.

1912

Mrs. Charlotte Wagner, an aged German resident of the city, quietly passed away, at the Marietta Hospital, this morning, at 7 o'clock. Mrs. Wagner had been in poor health for the past three months. She was removed from her home, on Front street, three weeks ago, to the hospital, where everything in the power of the attendents was done to relieve her of her suffering. She declined steadily, however, and for the last week her death was expected at any moment. Her death was due to a complication of diseases incident to old age.

Mrs. Charlotte Wagner was born in Germany and came to this country when but sixteen years of age. She, with her parents and brothers and sisters, came direct to this county, where she had made her home ever since. She was one of a family of twelve children, but one of whom survives. A sister, Mrs. Weber, passed away the latter part of December.

Mrs. Wagner was well known among the older residents of the county and had a host of friends who will be pained to hear of her death. She was a member of the German Lutheran church, and was highly respected among the members.

The deceased was born, May 30, 1839, and was, therefore, in her seventy-third year. She is survived by four sons, Henry Wagner, of this city, with whom she made her home; Charles Wagner, also of this city, and Gus and William Wagner, both of Los Angeles, Calif. She is also survived by one brother, Sebastian Shafer, of Harrietsville, O., and nine grandchildren and four great grandchildren.

Funeral services at the house, Sunday, at 1:30 p. m.

Charlotte Wagner's obituary

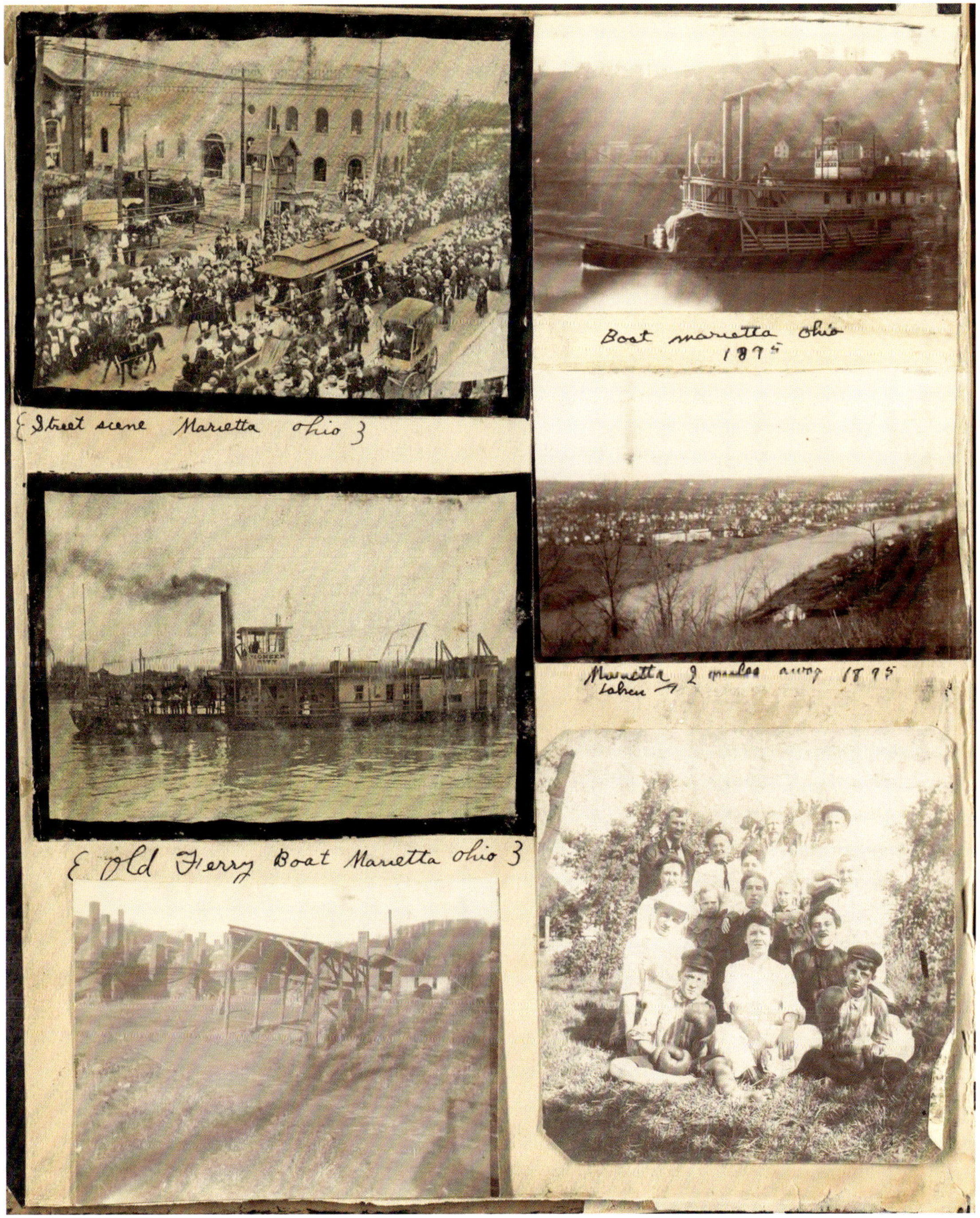

{Street scene Marietta Ohio}

Boat Marietta Ohio 1875

{Old Ferry Boat Marietta Ohio}

Images of Marietta, Ohio.
Page from Gus Wagner's scrapbook

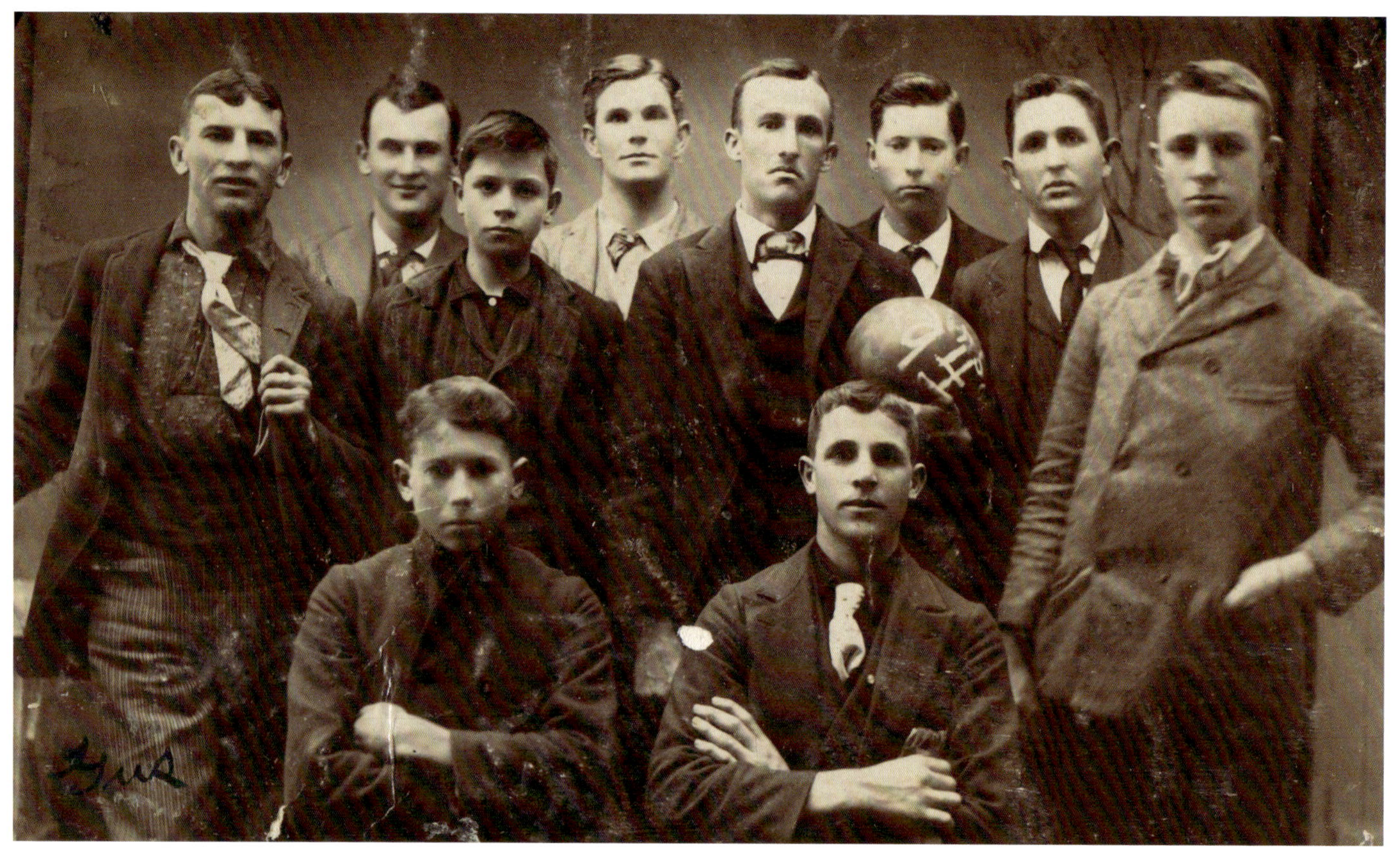

outdoor stage of county fairs. Over the course of his more than forty-year career, Gus was the subject of countless interviews and collected his memorabilia. This book is primarily a chronicle of Gus's life and career from quotations—excerpted from the answers he gave to the questions various newspaper reporters asked him. Gus Wagner was a figure of literary proportions in the way he lived and worked. Distinguishing fact from fiction in his interviews is complicated. He was prone to hyperbole but grounded in personal experience. Surely, to wander the globe at the end of the nineteenth century, when movement from place to place was time consuming and often difficult, encountering the "other" and non-Western practices, traditions, and beliefs was no doubt exhilarating but, at the same time, confounding and overwhelming.

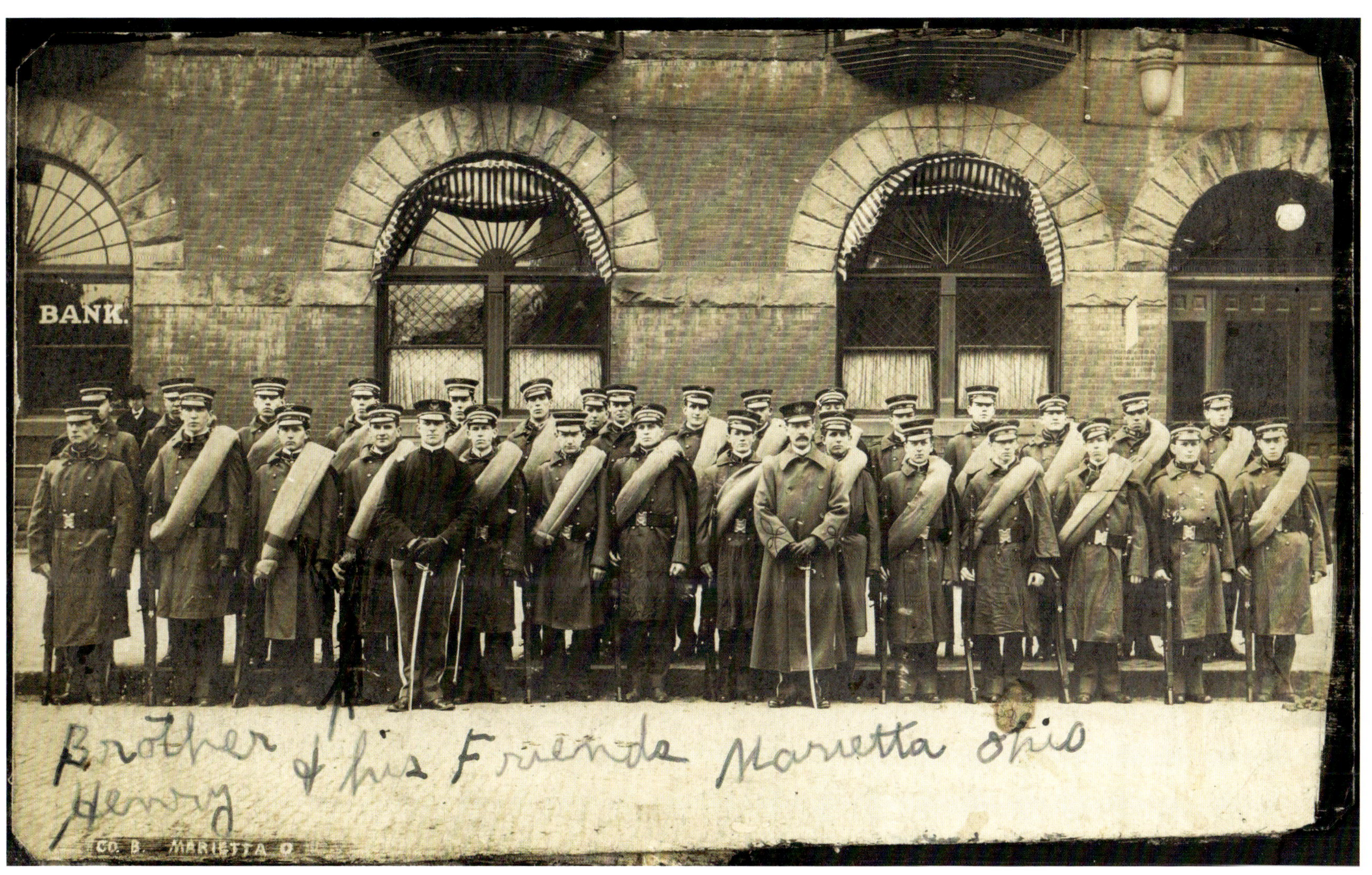

Opposite and above: Details from Gus Wagner's scrapbook

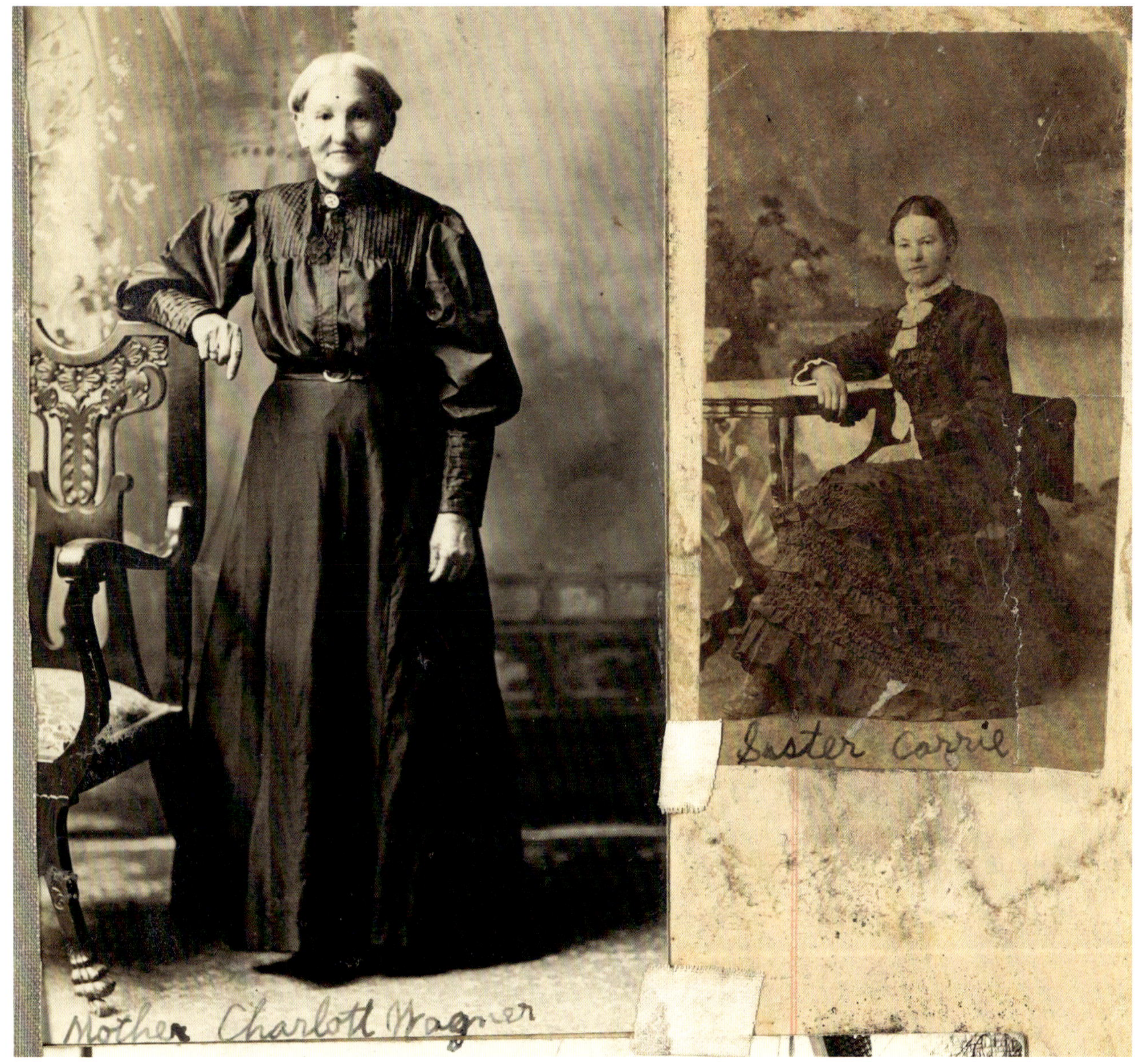

Gus Wagner's mother, Charlotte Wagner, and sister Carrie.
Detail from Gus Wagner's scrapbook

Detail from Gus Wagner's scrapbook

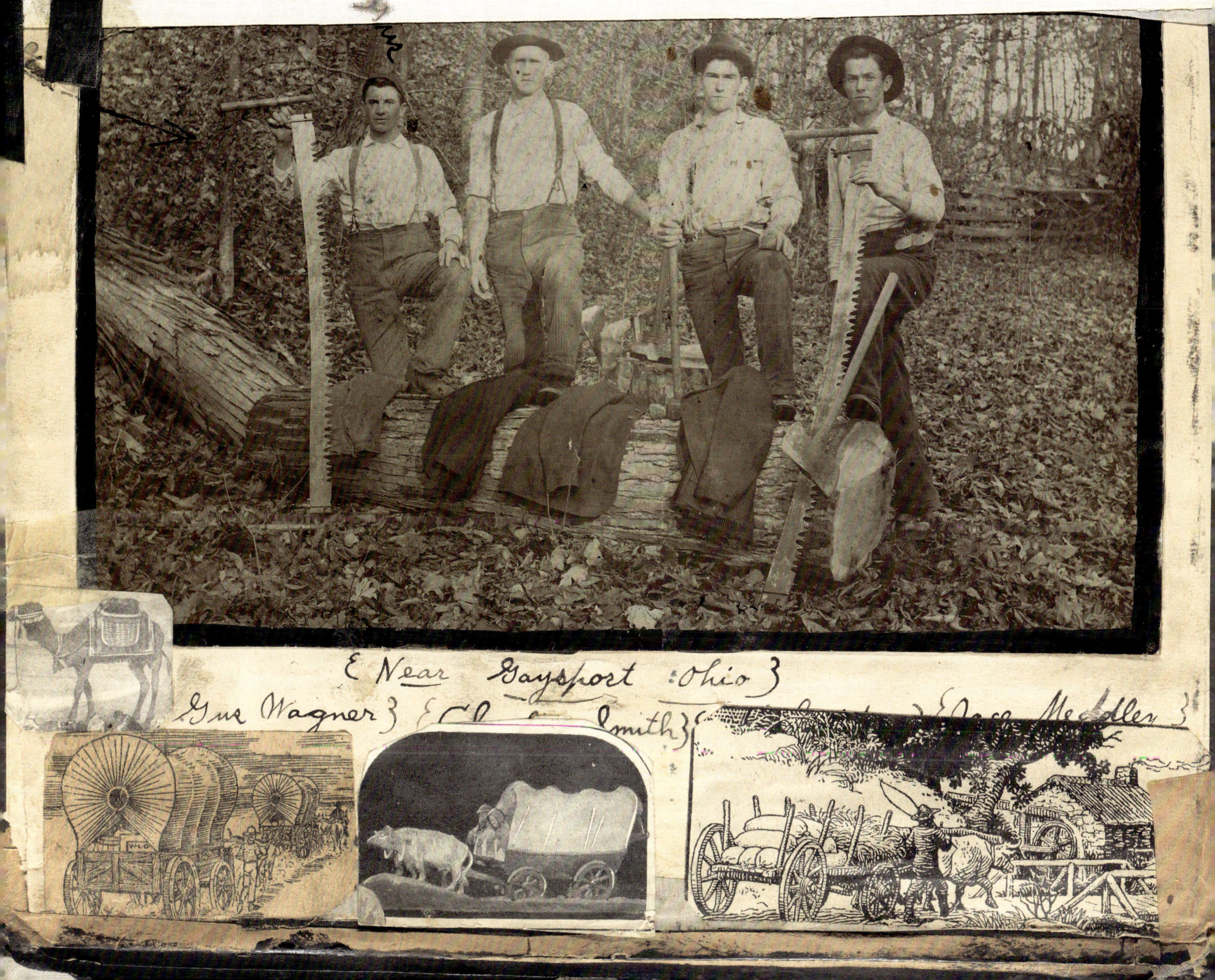
{ Near Gaysport :Ohio }
Gus Wagner }
Smith }
Meddler }

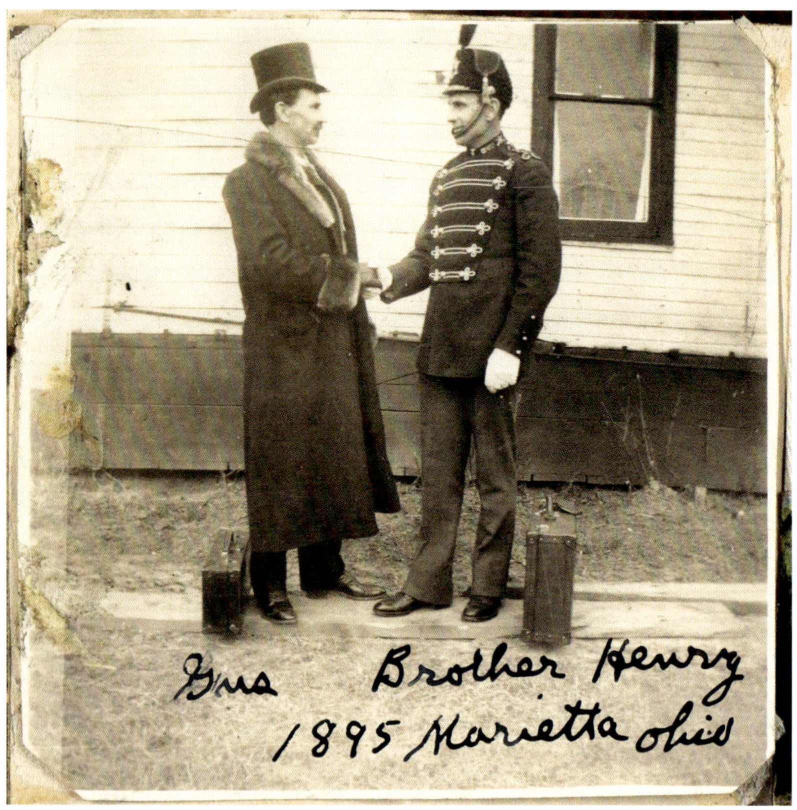

Gus Wagner and his brother.
Detail from Gus Wagner's scrapbook

Reading Herman Melville helps put Gus in perspective. While Melville's stories and ethnographic descriptions predate Gus's journey, they offer an unparalleled window on the significance of tattooing in the maritime life of the mid-nineteenth century. To illuminate the context of the oral history of Gus Wagner, there are selected passages from three of Melville's novels—*Typee*, *White Jacket*, and *Moby Dick*. Melville was an astute observer of hand tattoo artists and their clientele. One can only imagine Gus's presence among the panoply of Melville's characters. Clearly, *Typee* and *White Jacket* contain the most-vivid accounts of tattooing among sailors, while *Moby Dick* delves deeper into the meaning of the tattoo and its metaphysical and metaphorical power. For both Ishmael and Queequeg, the symbolism of the tattoo becomes profound.

For Gus Wagner, tattooing was a way of life. He was hellbent on challenging existing notions of savagery and civility, questioning whether either of them truly exists. As a man and artist, Gus Wagner was unique.

TYPEE:

A PEEP AT POLYNESIAN LIFE.

DURING A

FOUR MONTHS' RESIDENCE

IN

A VALLEY OF THE MARQUESAS

WITH NOTICES OF THE FRENCH OCCUPATION OF TAHITI AND
THE PROVISIONAL CESSION OF THE SANDWICH
ISLANDS TO LORD PAULET.

BY HERMAN MELVILLE.

PART I.

NEW YORK:
WILEY AND PUTNAM.
LONDON:
JOHN MURRAY, ALBEMARLE STREET

1846.

WHITE JACKET;

OR,

THE WORLD IN A MAN-OF-WAR.

BY

HERMAN MELVILLE,

AUTHOR OF "TYPEE," "OMOO," "MARDI," AND "REDBURN."

"Conceive him now in a man-of-war; with his letters of mart, well armed, victualled, and appointed, and see how he acquits himself."—FULLER's *Good Sea-Captain*.

VOL. I.

LONDON:
RICHARD BENTLEY, NEW BURLINGTON STREET.
1850.

GUS WAGNER IN HIS OWN WORDS

EDITED FROM NEWSPAPER CLIPPINGS
BY ALAN GOVENAR

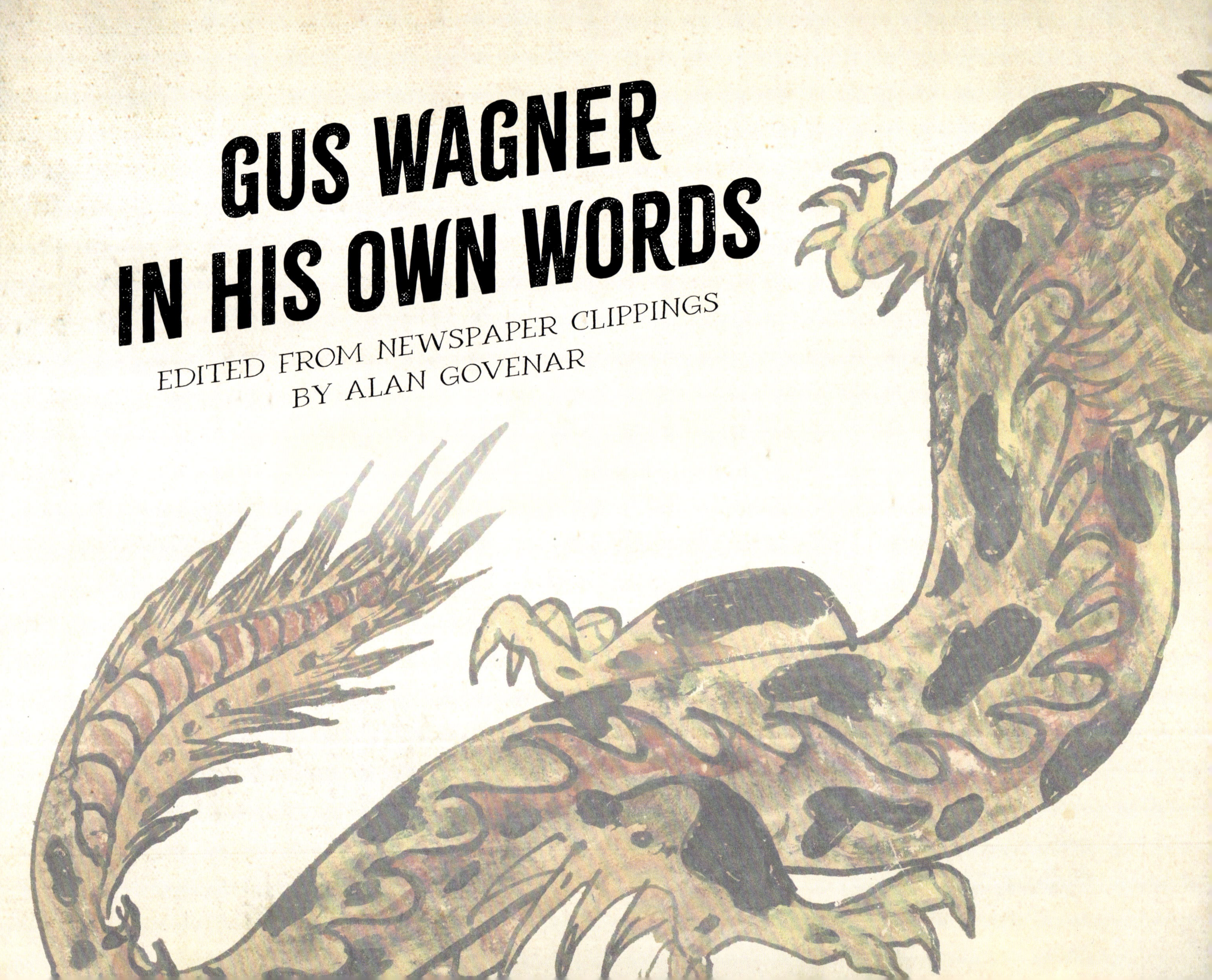

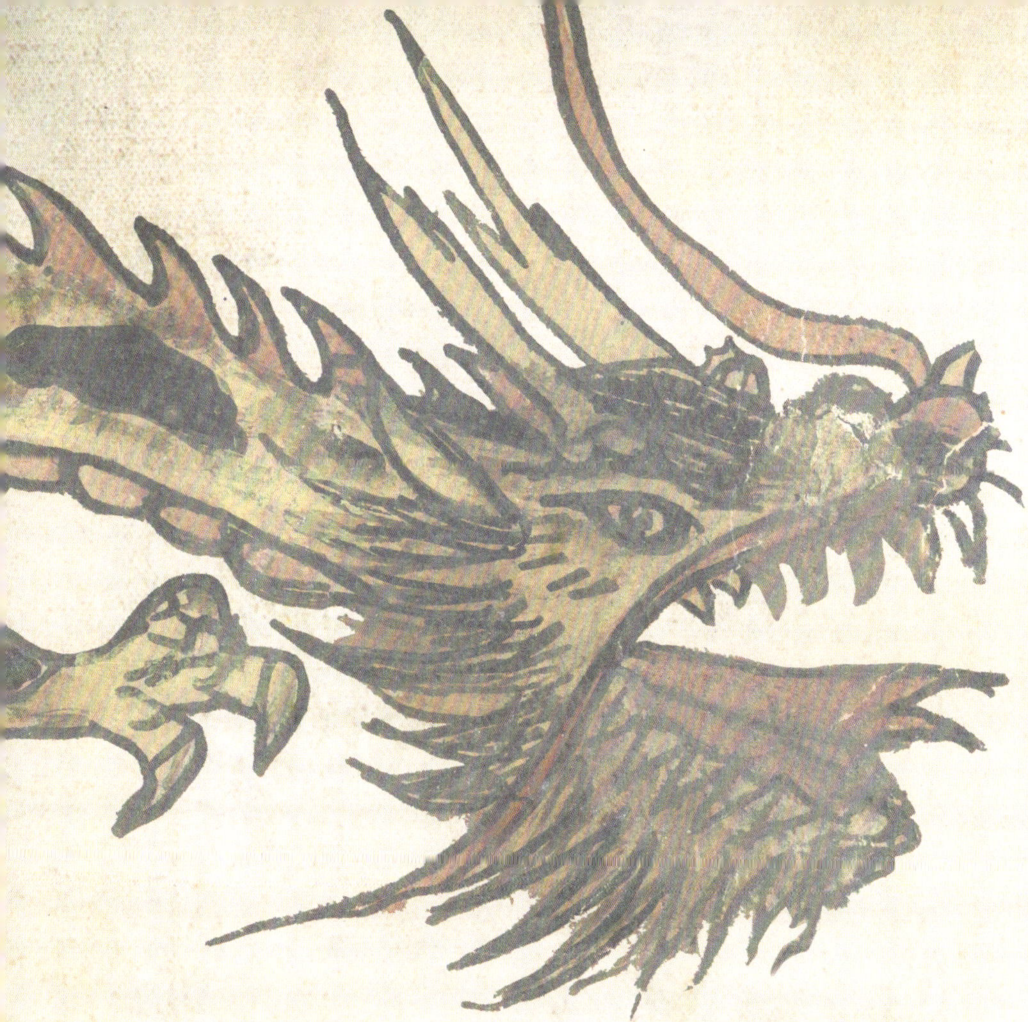

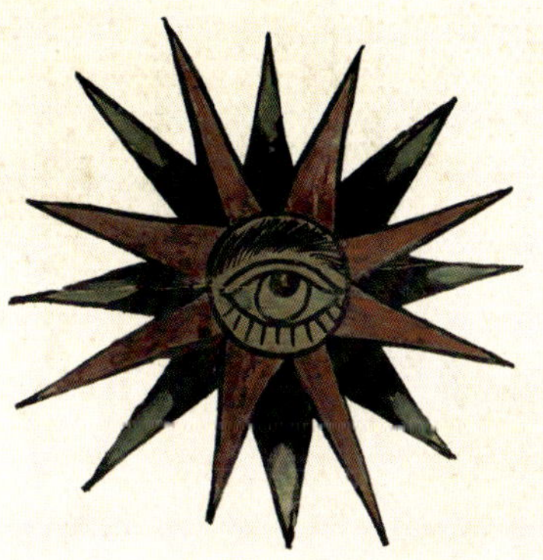

I was born in Marietta, Ohio. I am an American, although I have spent much of my time in foreign countries and in the show business. I have been to every civilized county on the globe and been tattooed and done tattooing in most of them; and I've been to a good many countries that were not civilized and have been tattooed there too. I've a history of my life on my breast, a history of America on my back, a romance of the sea on each arm, the history of Japan on one leg, and the history of China on the other. Here and there about my body, where the room was not needed for the big work, I have various bits of tattooing, done in Java, Australia, and the South Sea Islands and on shipboard.

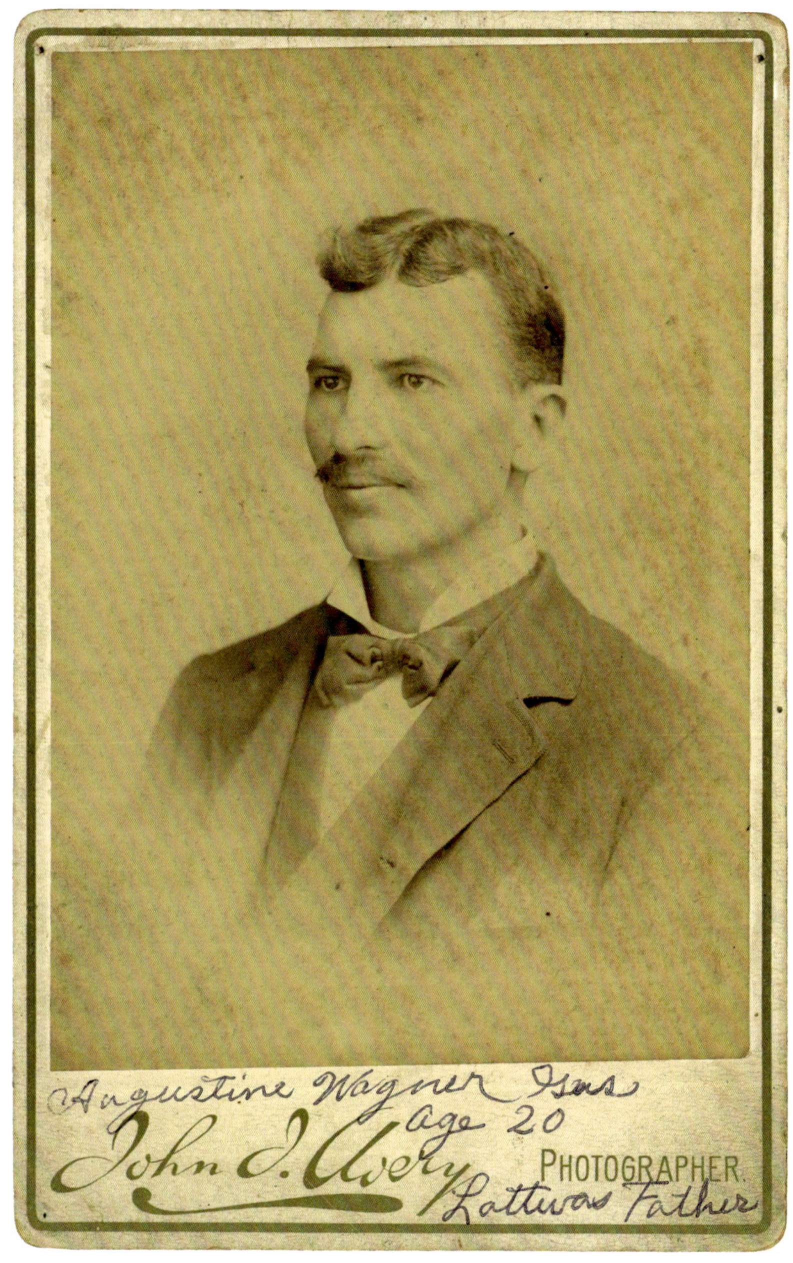

I got into the business while I was a sailor, and studied the old masters quite seriously—in Java, where I first became interested in Japan, and almost everywhere that tattooing has been brought to an unusual degree of perfection. While I was studying, I was practicing mostly on my myself and some of my shipmates. But I did a bad job on myself in many places and later had professional tattooers in Japan, Australia, Java, the South Sea Islands, and other places to do it over.

I took up tattooing as a profession about six years ago [1898], and my first work off shipboard was done in Marietta, O[hio], my old home. Among my patrons were thirty-one society women, and how they did have dogs, pet cats, lovers' hearts, clasped hands, birds, and butterflies—especially butterflies—tattooed on their arms. And I've tattooed a lot of them on arms that were not so fair, for negroes like to be tattooed. Where they are just yellow, it isn't hard to tattoo them, but where they are black, you can't find a color that will show.

Actors seem to take to tattooing as readily as sailors do. They give most of my business, as there are not many sailors in St. Louis. Lodge people are next, and they include many of the actors too. Lodge people want to have their lodge seals put on them.

Left: Gus Wagner at age twenty. *Opposite:* Verso of photo card.

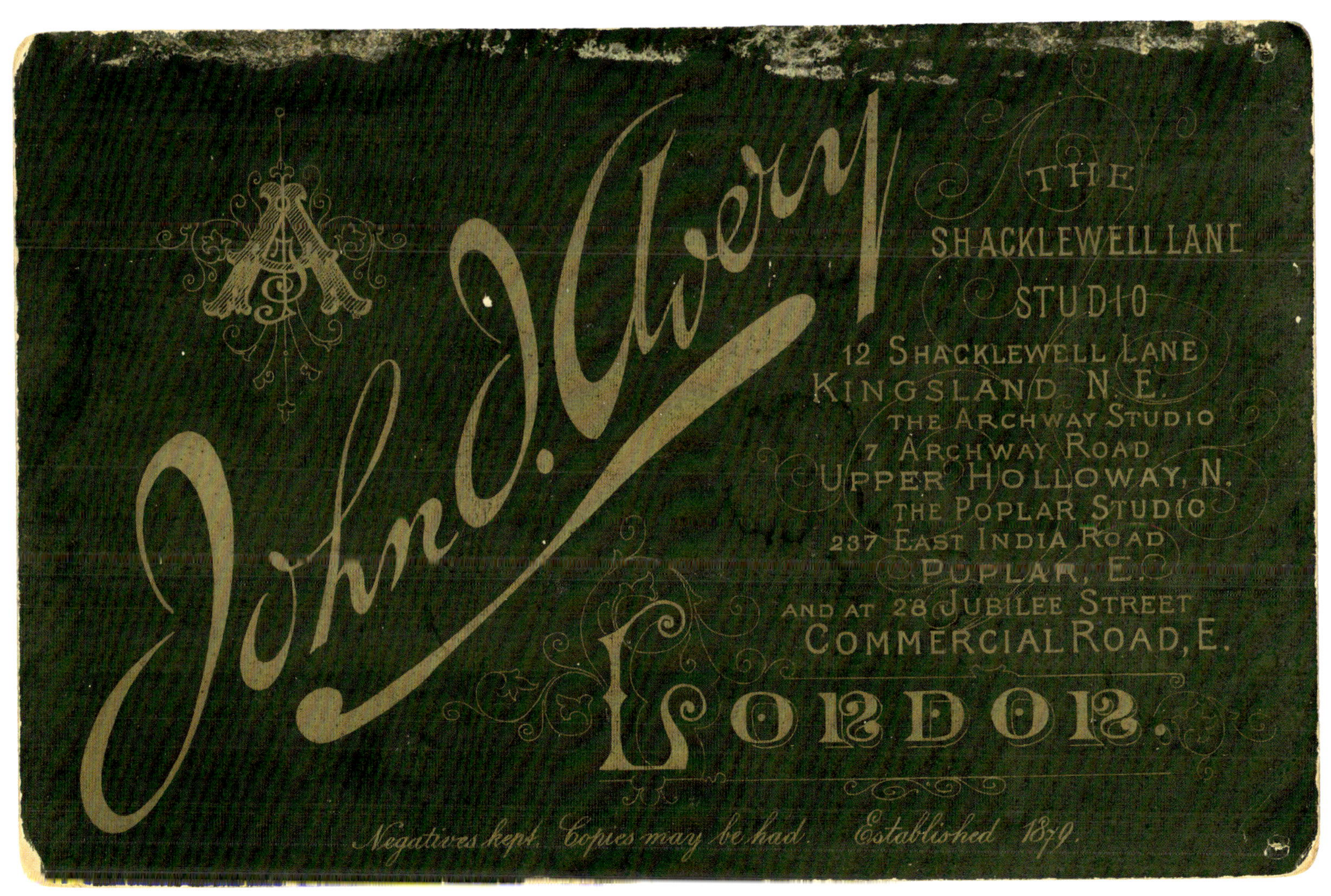
John J. Avery
THE
SHACKLEWELL LANE
STUDIO
12 SHACKLEWELL LANE
KINGSLAND N. E.
THE ARCHWAY STUDIO
7 ARCHWAY ROAD
UPPER HOLLOWAY, N.
THE POPLAR STUDIO
237 EAST INDIA ROAD
POPLAR, E.
AND AT 28 JUBILEE STREET
COMMERCIAL ROAD, E.
LONDON.
Negatives kept. Copies may be had. Established 1879.

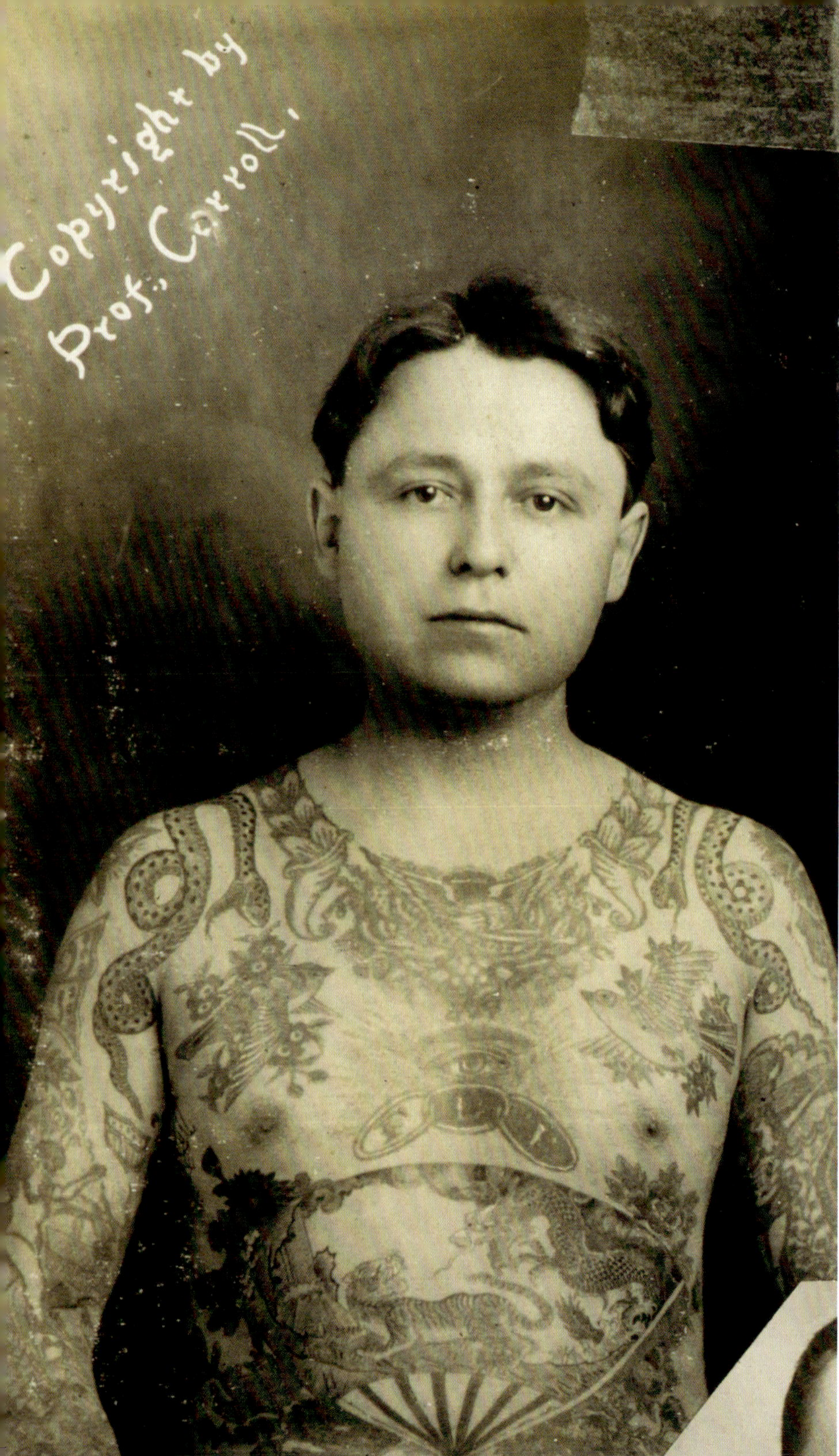

Man tattooed with the main symbol of the Independent Order of Odd Fellows: three chain links with the letters F, L, and T inside them (Friendship, Love, and Truth).
Detail from Gus Wagner's scrapbook

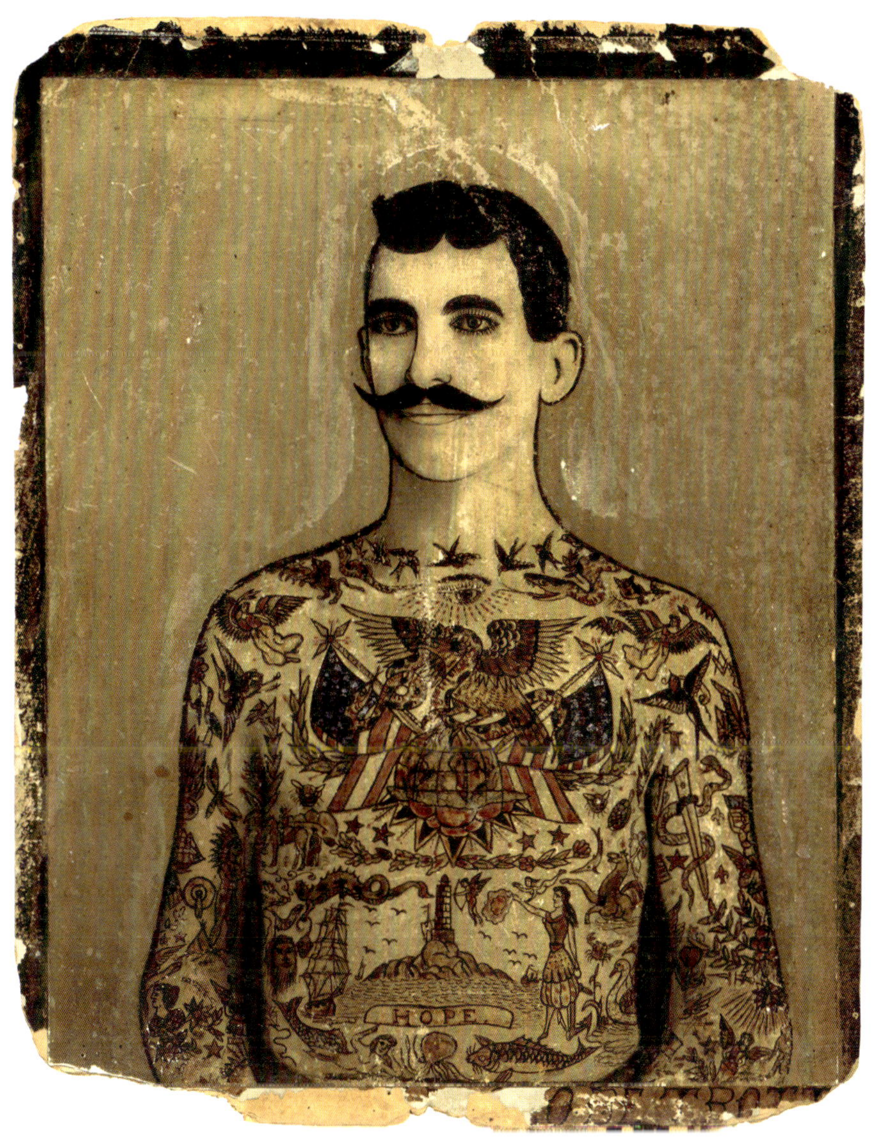

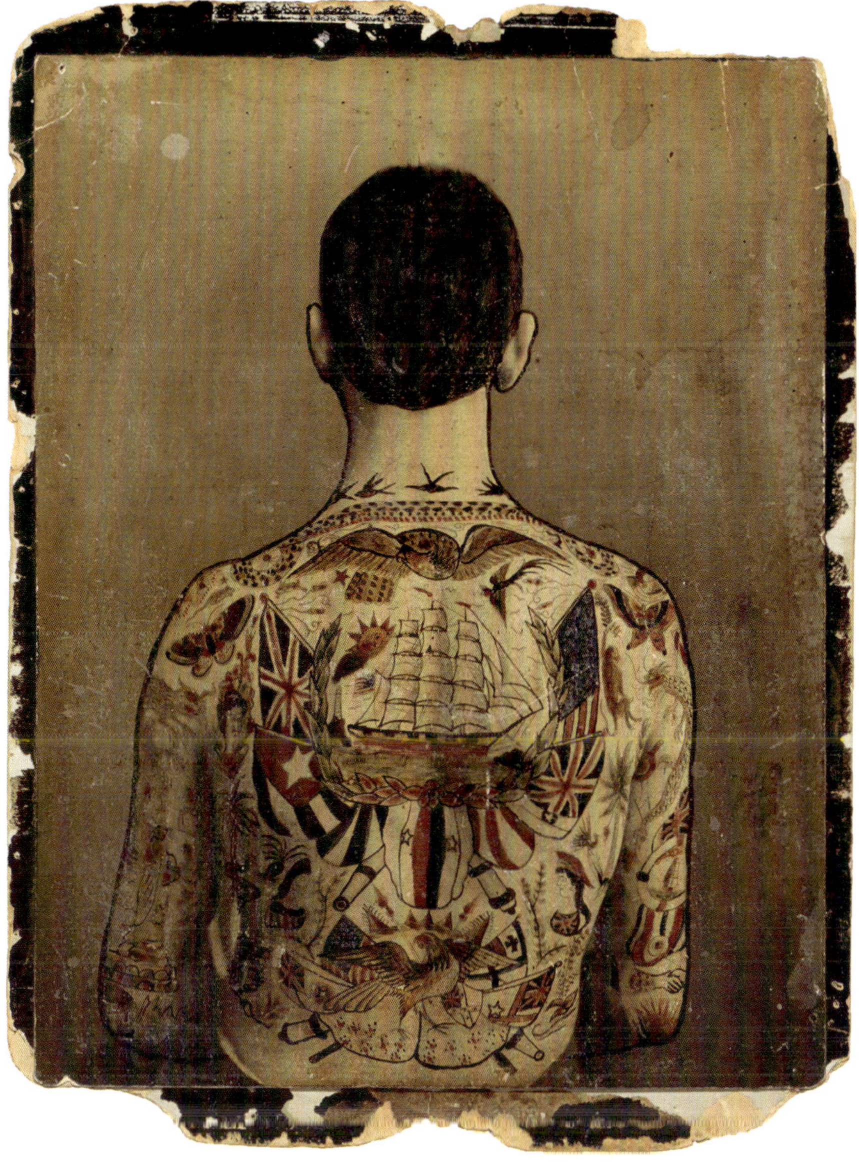

Illustration of Gus Wagner and his tattoos

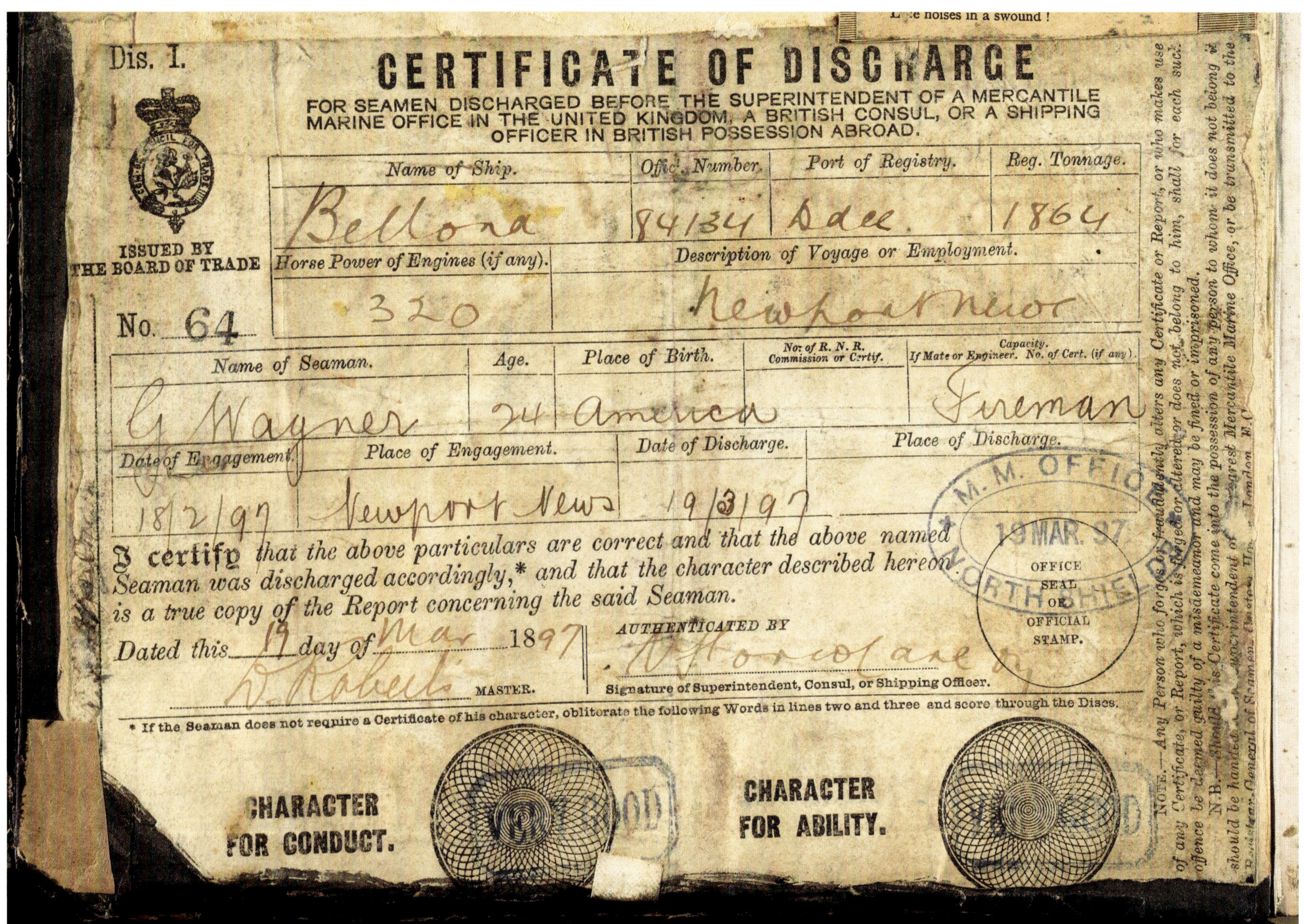

Dis. I.

CERTIFICATE OF DISCHARGE

FOR SEAMEN DISCHARGED BEFORE THE SUPERINTENDENT OF A MERCANTILE MARINE OFFICE IN THE UNITED KINGDOM, A BRITISH CONSUL, OR A SHIPPING OFFICER IN BRITISH POSSESSION ABROAD.

ISSUED BY THE BOARD OF TRADE

No. 64

Name of Ship.	Offic. Number.	Port of Registry.	Reg. Tonnage.
Bellona	84134	Adee	1864

Horse Power of Engines (if any).	Description of Voyage or Employment.
320	Newport News

Name of Seaman.	Age.	Place of Birth.	No. of R. N. R. Commission or Certif.	Capacity. If Mate or Engineer. No. of Cert. (if any).
G Wagner	24	America		Fireman

Date of Engagement.	Place of Engagement.	Date of Discharge.	Place of Discharge.
18/2/97	Newport News	19/3/97	

I certify that the above particulars are correct and that the above named Seaman was discharged accordingly,* and that the character described hereon is a true copy of the Report concerning the said Seaman.

Dated this 19 day of Mar 1897

D Roberts MASTER.

AUTHENTICATED BY

Signature of Superintendent, Consul, or Shipping Officer.

M. M. OFFICE 19 MAR. 97 NORTH SHIELDS

OFFICE SEAL OR OFFICIAL STAMP.

* If the Seaman does not require a Certificate of his character, obliterate the following Words in lines two and three and score through the Discs.

CHARACTER FOR CONDUCT. VERY GOOD

CHARACTER FOR ABILITY. VERY GOOD

NOTE.—Any Person who forges or fraudulently alters any Certificate or Report, or who makes use of any Certificate, or Report, which is forged or altered or does not belong to him, shall for each such offence be deemed guilty of a misdemeanor and may be fined or imprisoned.

N.B.—Should this Certificate come into the possession of any person to whom it does not belong it should be handed to the Superintendent of the nearest Mercantile Marine Office, or be transmitted to the Registrar General of Seamen, London, E.C.

Detail from Gus Wagner's scrapbook

Page from Gus Wagner's scrapbook

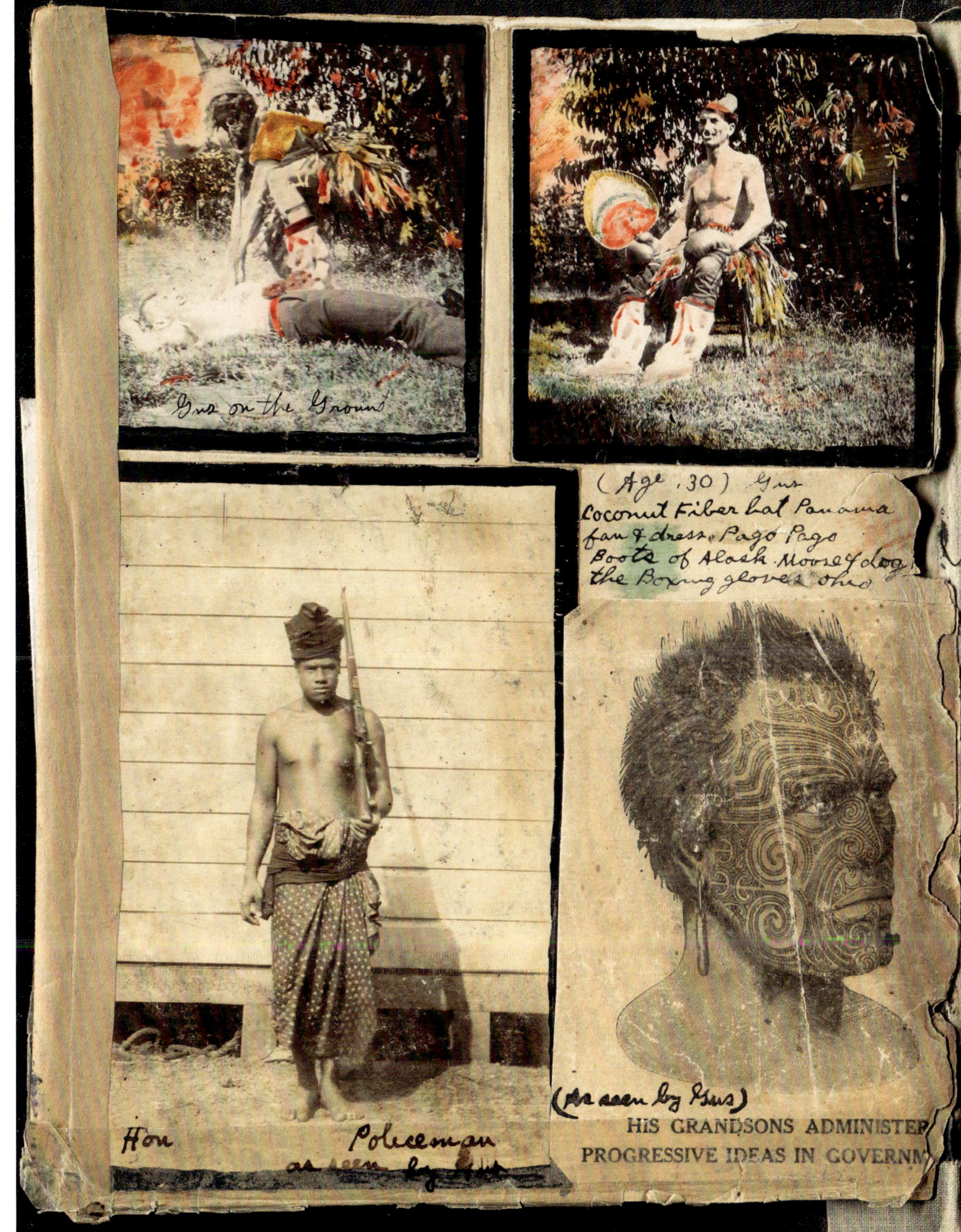

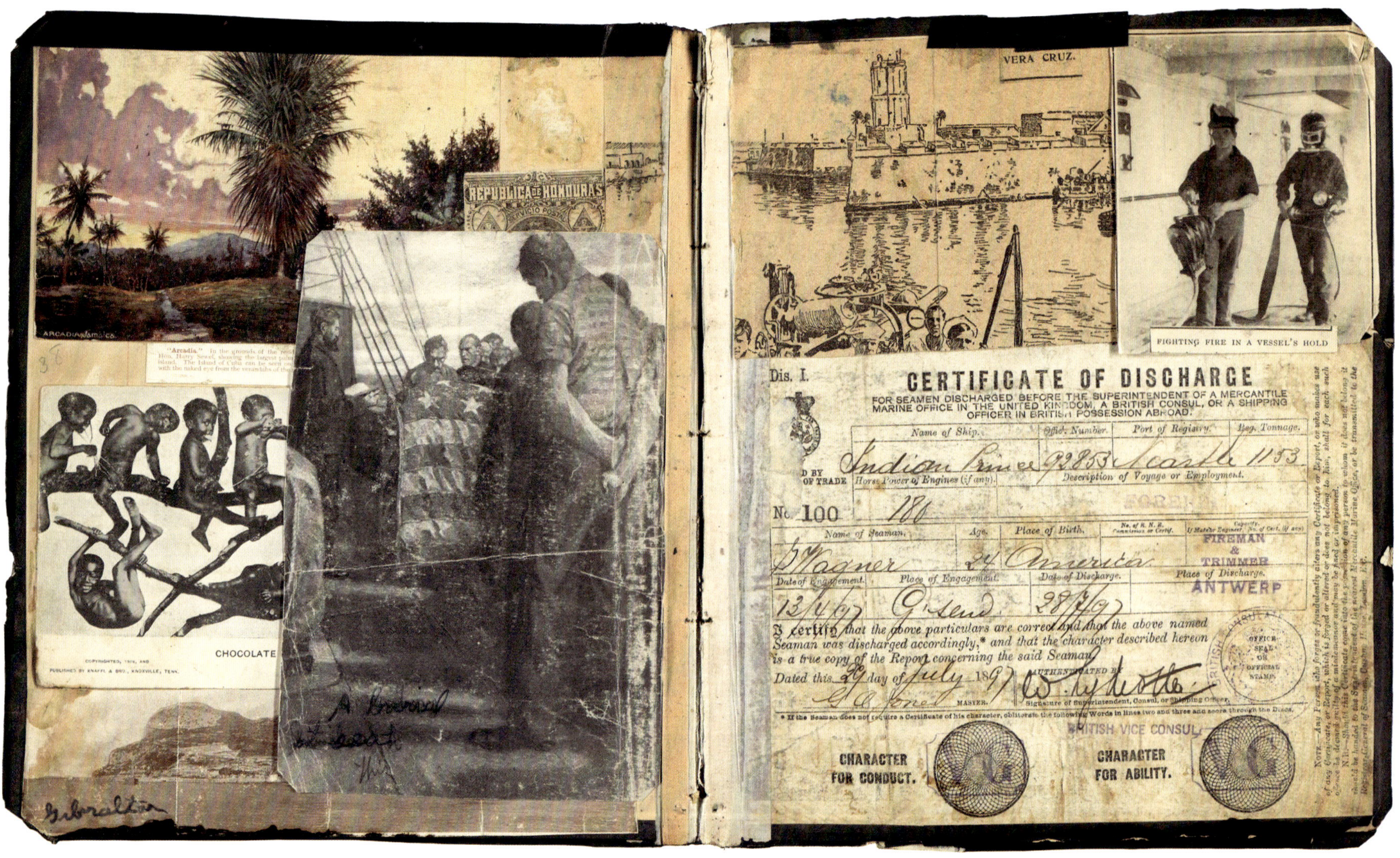

ARCADIA, Jamaica
REPUBLICA DE HONDURAS
CHOCOLATE
A burial at sea
Gibraltar
VERA CRUZ.
FIGHTING FIRE IN A VESSEL'S HOLD
Dis. I.
CERTIFICATE OF DISCHARGE
FOR SEAMEN DISCHARGED BEFORE THE SUPERINTENDENT OF A MERCANTILE MARINE OFFICE IN THE UNITED KINGDOM, A BRITISH CONSUL, OR A SHIPPING OFFICER IN BRITISH POSSESSION ABROAD.
Name of Ship. Offic. Number. Port of Registry. Reg. Tonnage.
Indian Prince 92853 Seattle 1153
Horse Power of Engines (if any). Description of Voyage or Employment.
No. 100 180
Name of Seaman. Age. Place of Birth.
G Wagner 24 America
FIREMAN & TRIMMER
Date of Engagement. Place of Engagement. Date of Discharge. Place of Discharge.
12/4/97 G'send 28/7/97 ANTWERP
I certify that the above particulars are correct and that the above named Seaman was discharged accordingly, and that the character described hereon is a true copy of the Report concerning the said Seaman.
Dated this 29 day of July 1897
MASTER.
Signature of Superintendent, Consul, or Shipping Officer.
BRITISH VICE CONSUL
CHARACTER FOR CONDUCT.
CHARACTER FOR ABILITY.

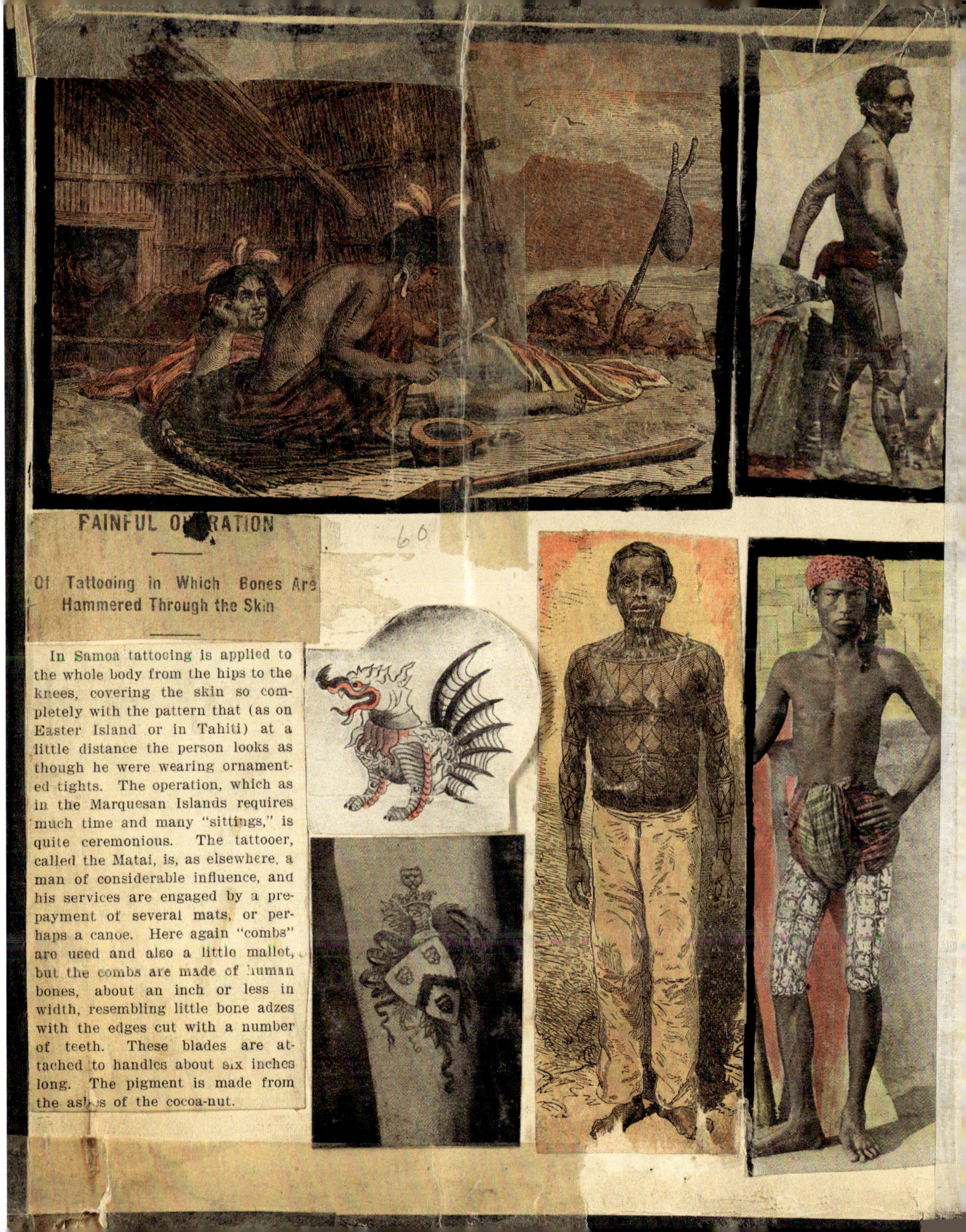

Pages from Gus Wagner's scrapbook

PAINFUL OPERATION

Of Tattooing in Which Bones Are Hammered Through the Skin

In Samoa tattooing is applied to the whole body from the hips to the knees, covering the skin so completely with the pattern that (as on Easter Island or in Tahiti) at a little distance the person looks as though he were wearing ornamented tights. The operation, which as in the Marquesan Islands requires much time and many "sittings," is quite ceremonious. The tattooer, called the Matai, is, as elsewhere, a man of considerable influence, and his services are engaged by a prepayment of several mats, or perhaps a canoe. Here again "combs" are used and also a little mallet, but the combs are made of human bones, about an inch or less in width, resembling little bone adzes with the edges cut with a number of teeth. These blades are attached to handles about six inches long. The pigment is made from the ashes of the cocoa-nut.

60

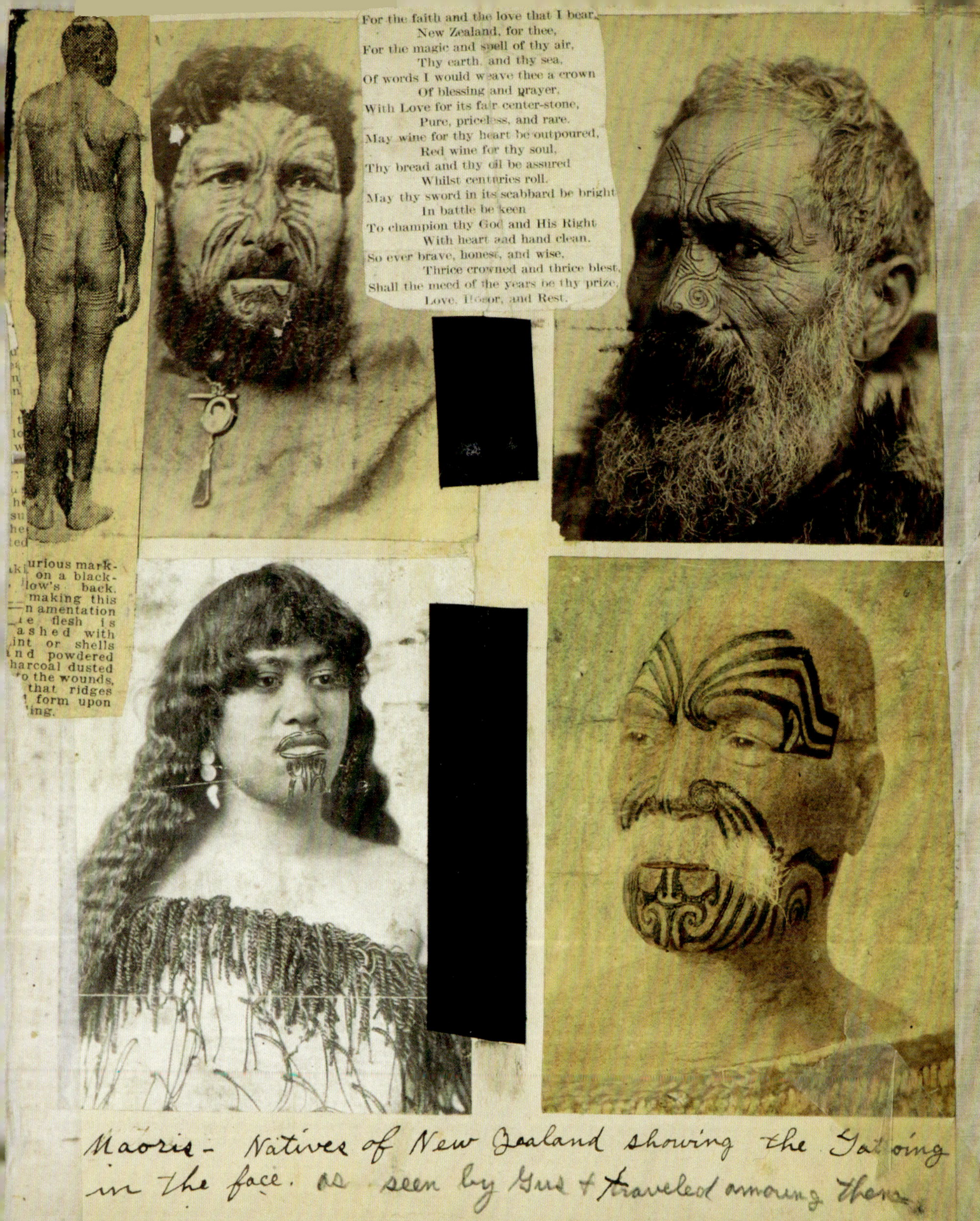

Pages from Gus Wagner's scrapbook

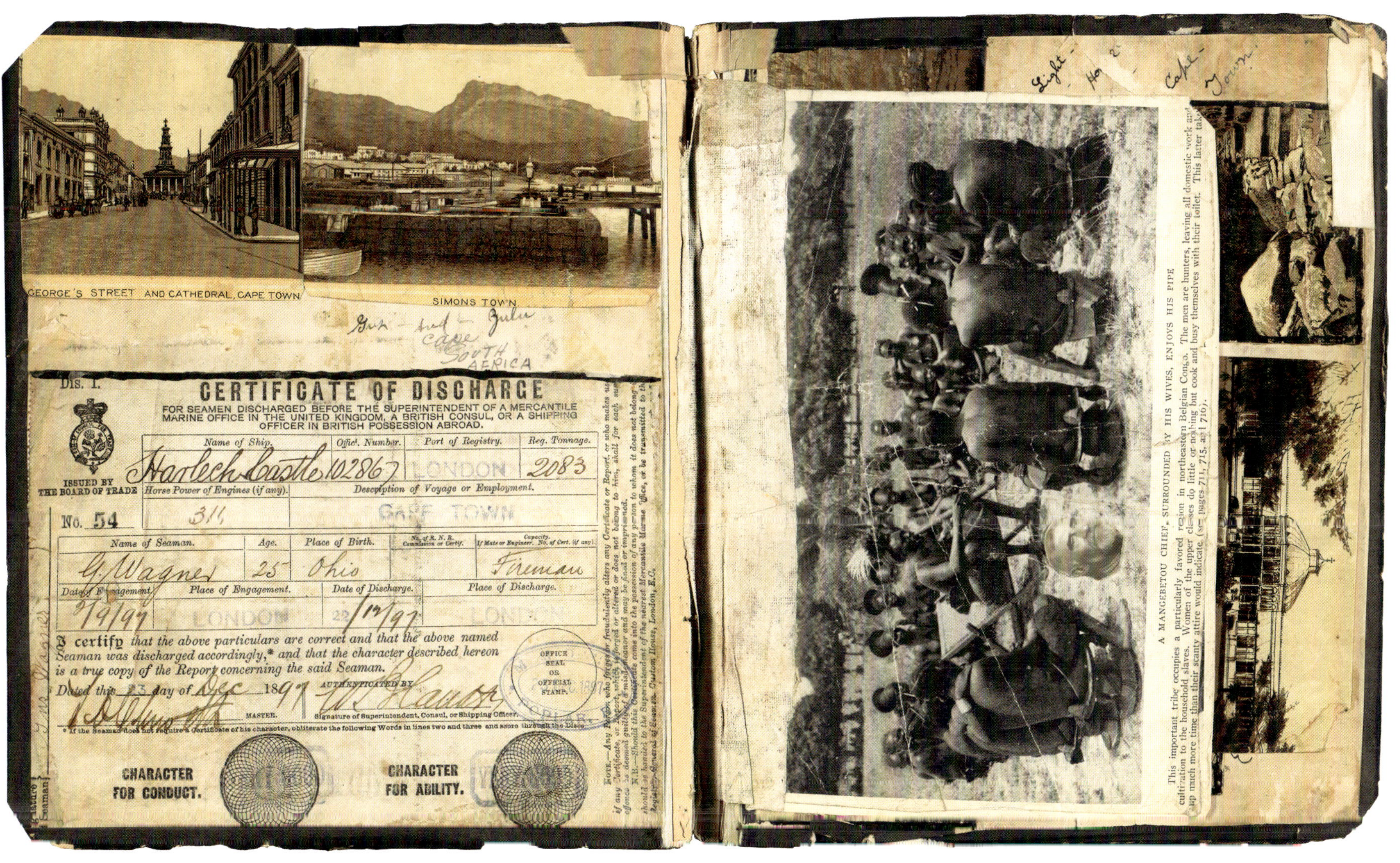

Dis. 1.

CERTIFICATE OF DISCHARGE

FOR SEAMEN DISCHARGED BEFORE THE SUPERINTENDENT OF A MERCANTILE MARINE OFFICE IN THE UNITED KINGDOM, A BRITISH CONSUL, OR A SHIPPING OFFICER IN BRITISH POSSESSION ABROAD.

ISSUED BY THE BOARD OF TRADE

No. 54

Name of Ship.	Offic¹. Number.	Port of Registry.	Reg. Tonnage.
Harlech Castle	102867	LONDON	2083

Horse Power of Engines (if any).	Description of Voyage or Employment.
311	CAPE TOWN

Name of Seaman.	Age.	Place of Birth.	No. of R. N. R. Commission or Certif.	Capacity. If Mate or Engineer. No. of Cert. (if any).
G. Wagner	25	Ohio		Fireman

Date of Engagement.	Place of Engagement.	Date of Discharge.	Place of Discharge.
7/9/97	LONDON	22/12/97	LONDON

I certify that the above particulars are correct and that the above named Seaman was discharged accordingly,* and that the character described hereon is a true copy of the Report concerning the said Seaman.

Dated this 23 day of Dec 1897 AUTHENTICATED BY

MASTER. Signature of Superintendent, Consul, or Shipping Officer.

OFFICE SEAL OR OFFICIAL STAMP.

* If the Seaman does not require a Certificate of his character, obliterate the following Words in lines two and three and score through the Discs

CHARACTER FOR CONDUCT.

CHARACTER FOR ABILITY.

NOTE.—Any Person who forges or fraudulently alters any Certificate or Report, or who makes use of any Certificate, or Report, which is forged or altered or does not belong to him, shall for each such offence be deemed guilty of a misdemeanor and may be fined or imprisoned.

N.B.—Should this Certificate come into the possession of any person to whom it does not belong, it should be handed to the Superintendent of the nearest Mercantile Marine Office, or be transmitted to the Registrar-General of Seamen, Custom House, London, E.C.

A MANGEBETOU CHIEF, SURROUNDED BY HIS WIVES, ENJOYS HIS PIPE

This important tribe occupies a particularly favored region in northeastern Belgian Congo. The men are hunters, leaving all domestic work and cultivation to the household slaves. Women of the upper classes do little or nothing but cook and busy themselves with their toilet. This latter takes up much more time than their scanty attire would indicate (see pages 711, 715, and 716).

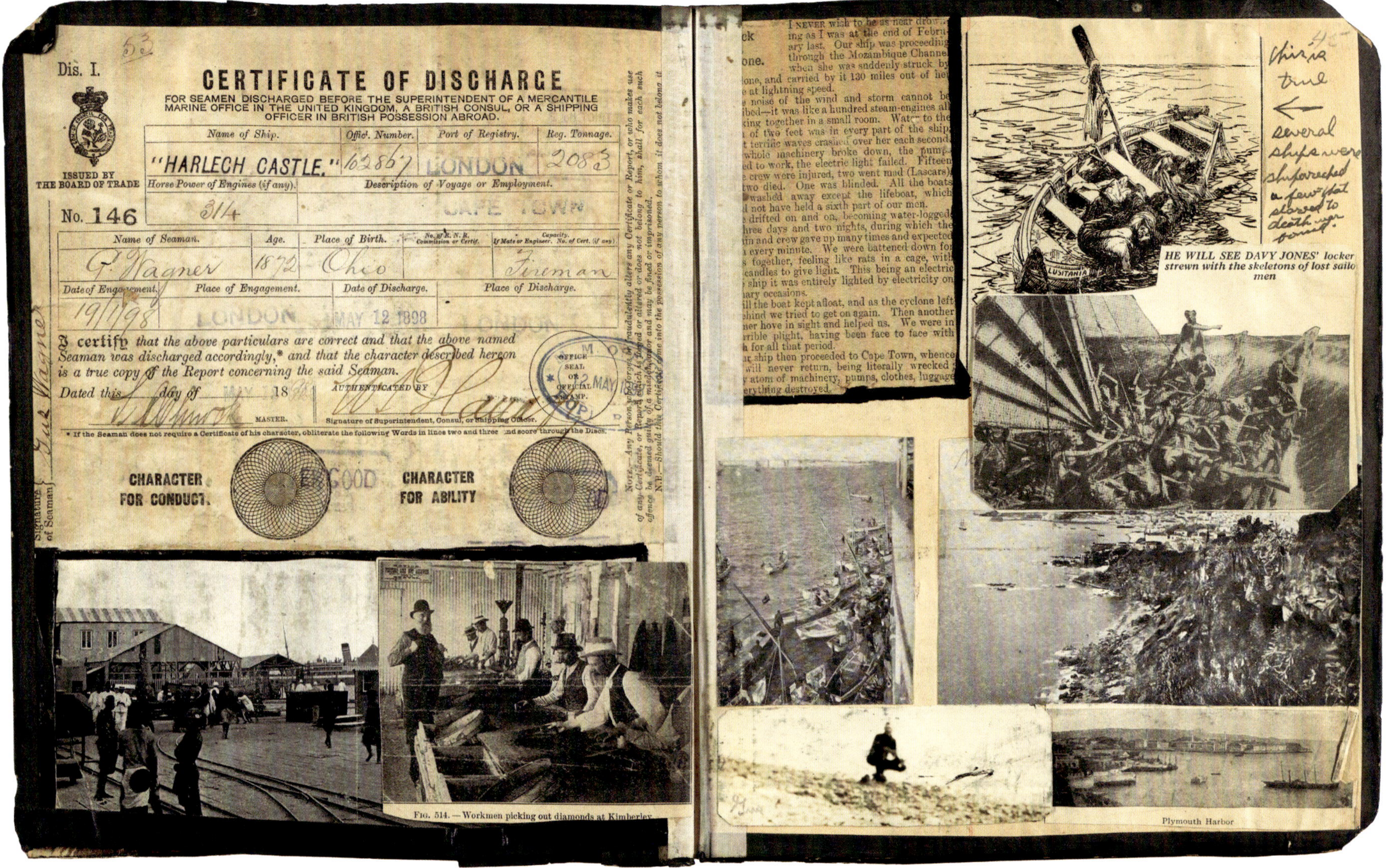

Dis. I.

53

CERTIFICATE OF DISCHARGE

FOR SEAMEN DISCHARGED BEFORE THE SUPERINTENDENT OF A MERCANTILE MARINE OFFICE IN THE UNITED KINGDOM, A BRITISH CONSUL, OR A SHIPPING OFFICER IN BRITISH POSSESSION ABROAD.

ISSUED BY THE BOARD OF TRADE

No. 146

Name of Ship.	Offic¹. Number.	Port of Registry.	Reg. Tonnage.
"HARLECH CASTLE."	102867	LONDON	2083

Horse Power of Engines (if any).	Description of Voyage or Employment.
314	CAPE TOWN

Name of Seaman.	Age.	Place of Birth.	No. of R. N. R. Commission or Certif.	If Mate or Engineer. No. of Cert. (if any) Capacity.
G. Wagner	1872	Ohio		Fireman

Date of Engagement.	Place of Engagement.	Date of Discharge.	Place of Discharge.
19/1/98	LONDON	MAY 12 1898	LONDON

I certify that the above particulars are correct and that the above named Seaman was discharged accordingly,* and that the character described hereon is a true copy of the Report concerning the said Seaman.

Dated this ... day of MAY 18 98 — AUTHENTICATED BY

MASTER. — Signature of Superintendent, Consul, or Shipping Officer.

OFFICIAL SEAL OR OFFICIAL STAMP. — M. O. — 12 MAY 1898

* If the Seaman does not require a Certificate of his character, obliterate the following Words in lines two and three and score through the Discs.

CHARACTER FOR CONDUCT. — GOOD — CHARACTER FOR ABILITY

NOTE.—Any Person who forges or fraudulently alters any Certificate or Report, or who makes use of any Certificate, or Report which is forged or altered or does not belong to him, shall for each such offence be deemed guilty of a misdemeanor and may be fined or imprisoned.

N.B.—Should this Certificate come into the possession of any person to whom it does not belong it

Signature of Seaman — Gus Wagner

Fig. 514.—Workmen picking out diamonds at Kimberley.

...ck
...one.

I never wish to be as near drown-
ing as I was at the end of Febru-
ary last. Our ship was proceeding
through the Mozambique Channel
when she was suddenly struck by
...one, and carried by it 130 miles out of her
...e at lightning speed.
...e noise of the wind and storm cannot be
...ibed—it was like a hundred steam-engines all
...king together in a small room. Water to the
... of two feet was in every part of the ship;
...t terrific waves crashed over her each second.
...whole machinery broke down, the pumps
...ed to work, the electric light failed. Fifteen
...e crew were injured, two went mad (Lascars),
...two died. One was blinded. All the boats
...washed away except the lifeboat, which
...l not have held a sixth part of our men.
...e drifted on and on, becoming water-logged
...hree days and two nights, during which the
...tin and crew gave up many times and expected
...every minute. We were battened down for
...s together, feeling like rats in a cage, with
...candles to give light. This being an electric
... ship it was entirely lighted by electricity on
...nary occasions.
...ill the boat kept afloat, and as the cyclone left
...ehind we tried to get on again. Then another
...ner hove in sight and helped us. We were in
...rrible plight, having been face to face with
...h for all that period.
...ur ship then proceeded to Cape Town, whence
... will never return, being literally wrecked;
...y atom of machinery, pumps, clothes, luggage
...erything destroyed.

this is true ← several ships were shipwrecked a few that starved to death were found.

LUSITANIA

HE WILL SEE DAVY JONES' locker strewn with the skeletons of lost sailo... men

Gus

Plymouth Harbor

Pages from Gus Wagner's scrapbook

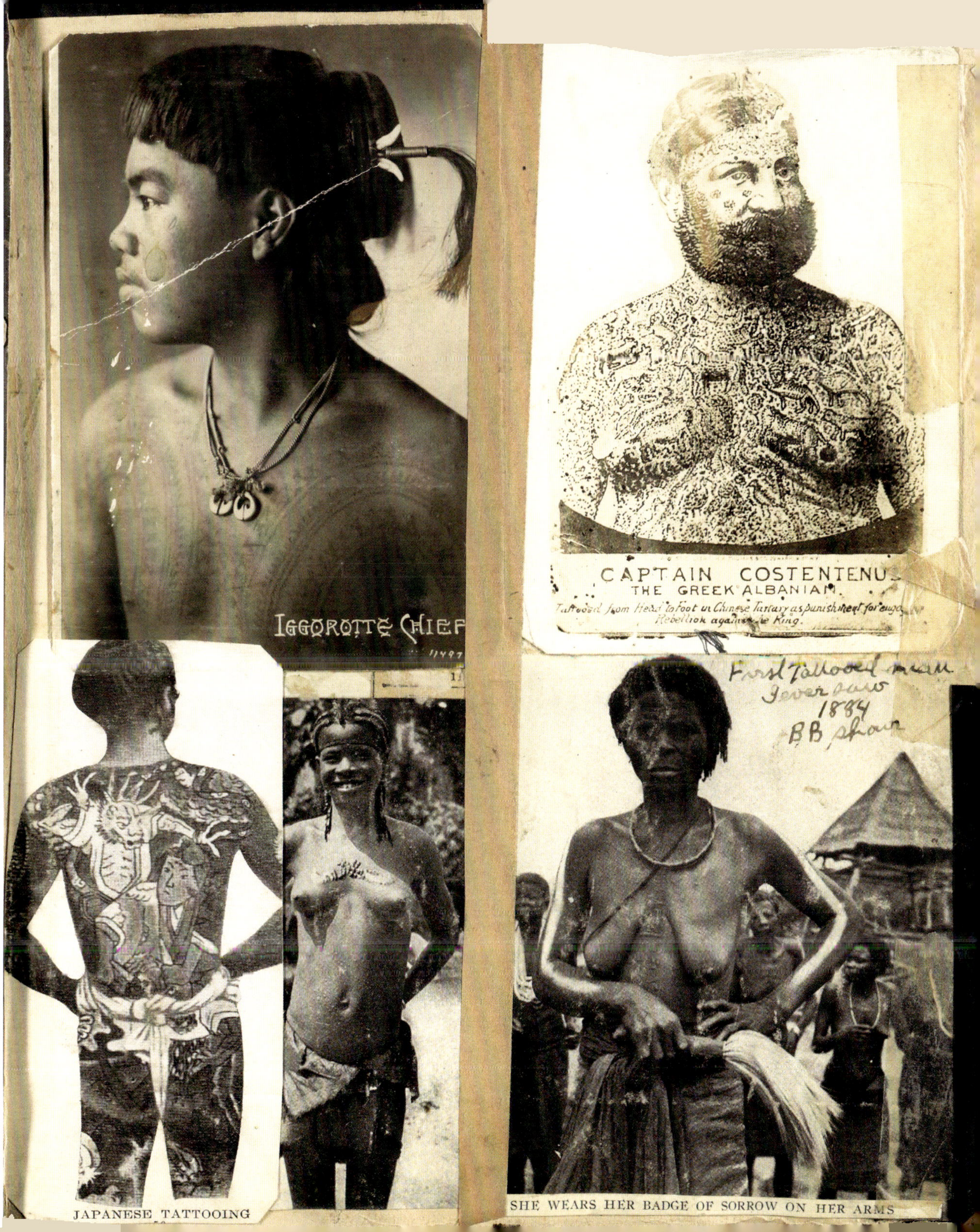

IGGOROTTE CHIEF

CAPTAIN COSTENTENUS

THE GREEK ALBANIAN

JAPANESE TATTOOING

SHE WEARS HER BADGE OF SORROW ON HER ARMS

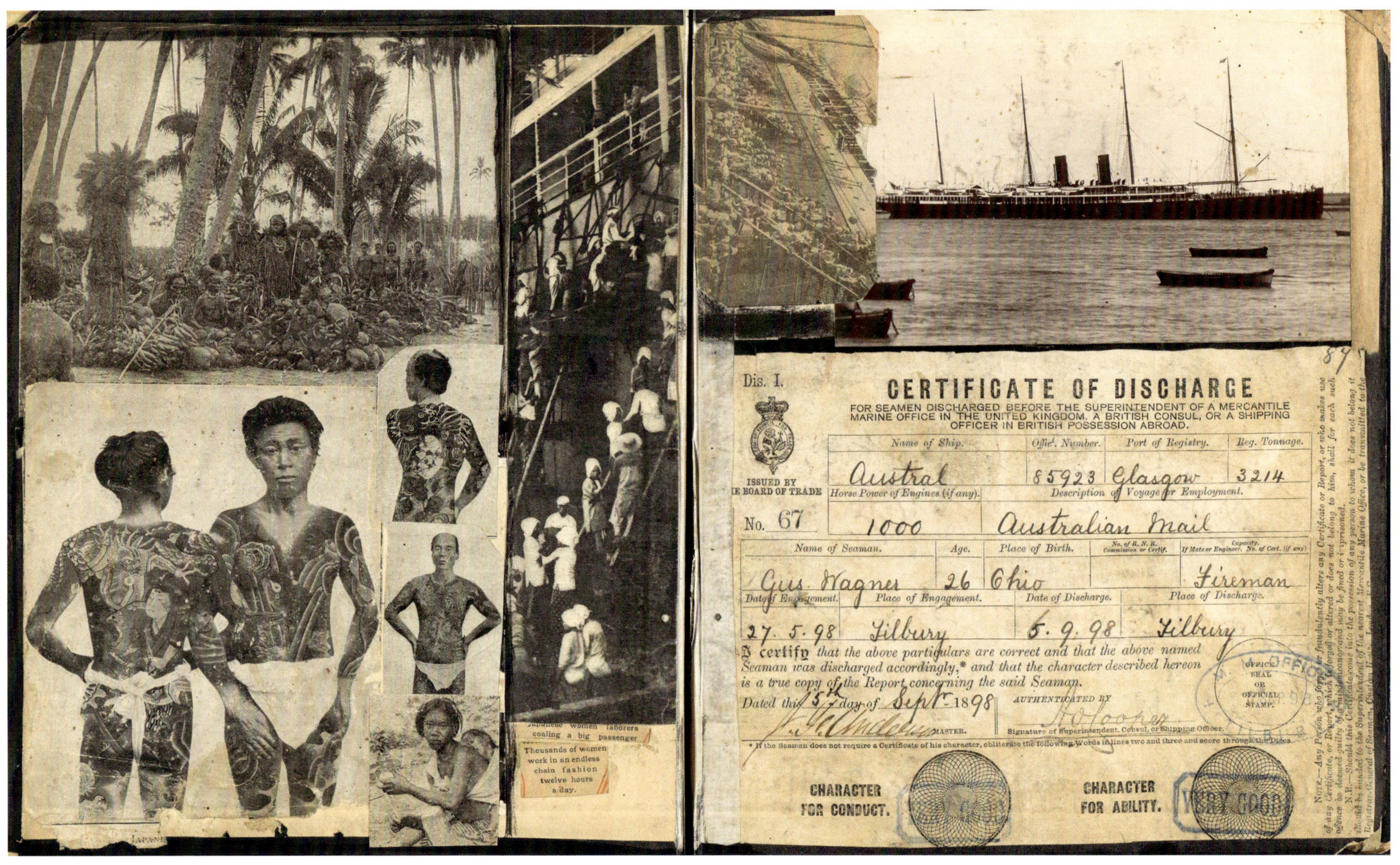

Dis. I.

CERTIFICATE OF DISCHARGE

FOR SEAMEN DISCHARGED BEFORE THE SUPERINTENDENT OF A MERCANTILE MARINE OFFICE IN THE UNITED KINGDOM, A BRITISH CONSUL, OR A SHIPPING OFFICER IN BRITISH POSSESSION ABROAD.

ISSUED BY THE BOARD OF TRADE

No. 67

Name of Ship.	Offic. Number.	Port of Registry.	Reg. Tonnage.
Austral	85923	Glasgow	3214

Horse Power of Engines (if any).	Description of Voyage or Employment.
1000	Australian Mail

Name of Seaman.	Age.	Place of Birth.	No. of R. N. R. Commission or Certif.	Capacity. If Mate or Engineer. No. of Cert. (if any)
Gus Wagner	26	Ohio		Fireman

Date of Engagement.	Place of Engagement.	Date of Discharge.	Place of Discharge.
27. 5. 98	Tilbury	5. 9. 98	Tilbury

I certify that the above particulars are correct and that the above named Seaman was discharged accordingly,* and that the character described hereon is a true copy of the Report concerning the said Seaman.

Dated this 5th day of Sept. 1898

MASTER.

AUTHENTICATED BY

Signature of Superintendent, Consul, or Shipping Officer.

OFFICIAL SEAL OR OFFICIAL STAMP.

* If the Seaman does not require a Certificate of his character, obliterate the following Words in lines two and three and score through the Discs.

CHARACTER FOR CONDUCT.

CHARACTER FOR ABILITY. VERY GOOD

Pages from Gus Wagner's scrapbook

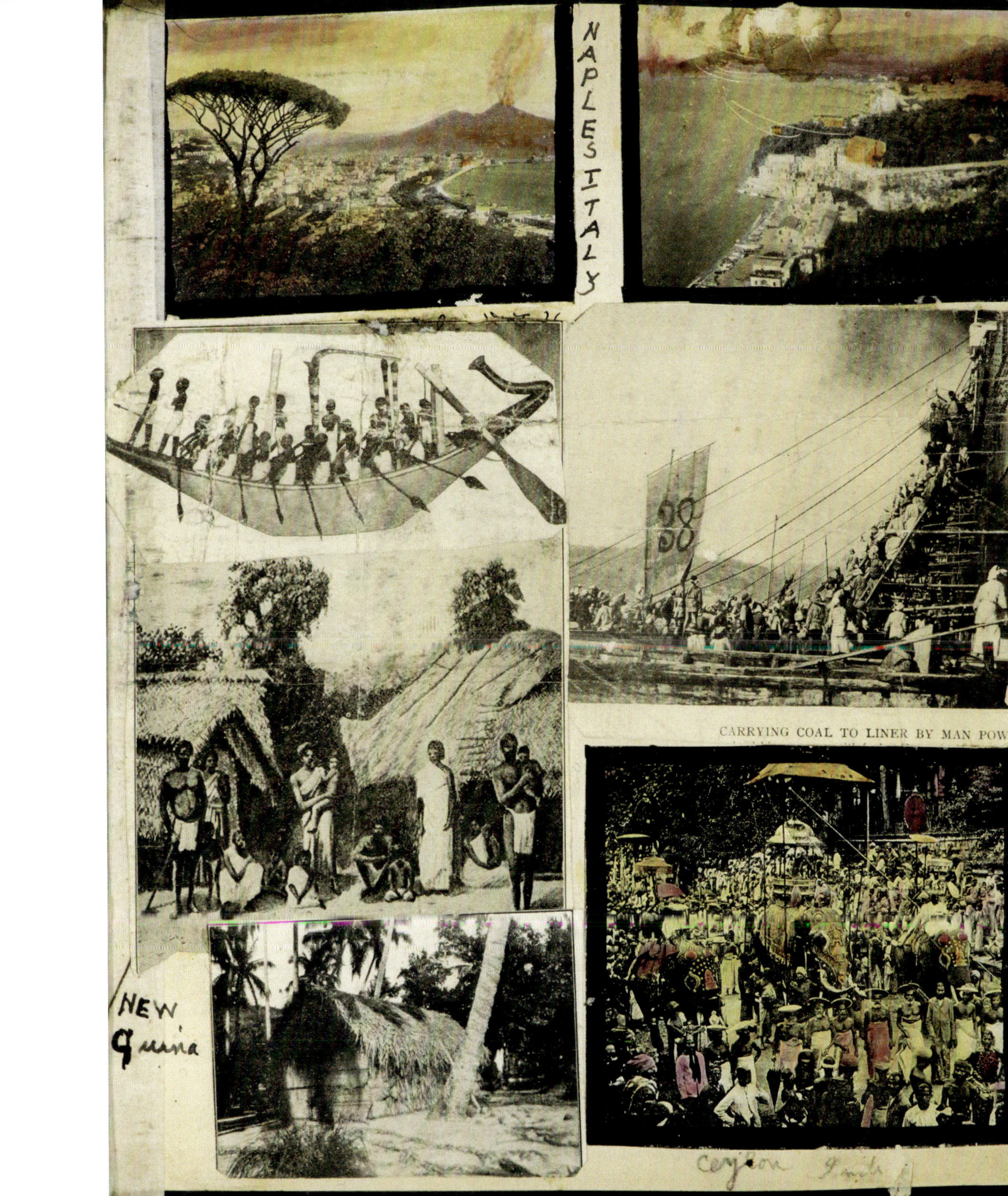

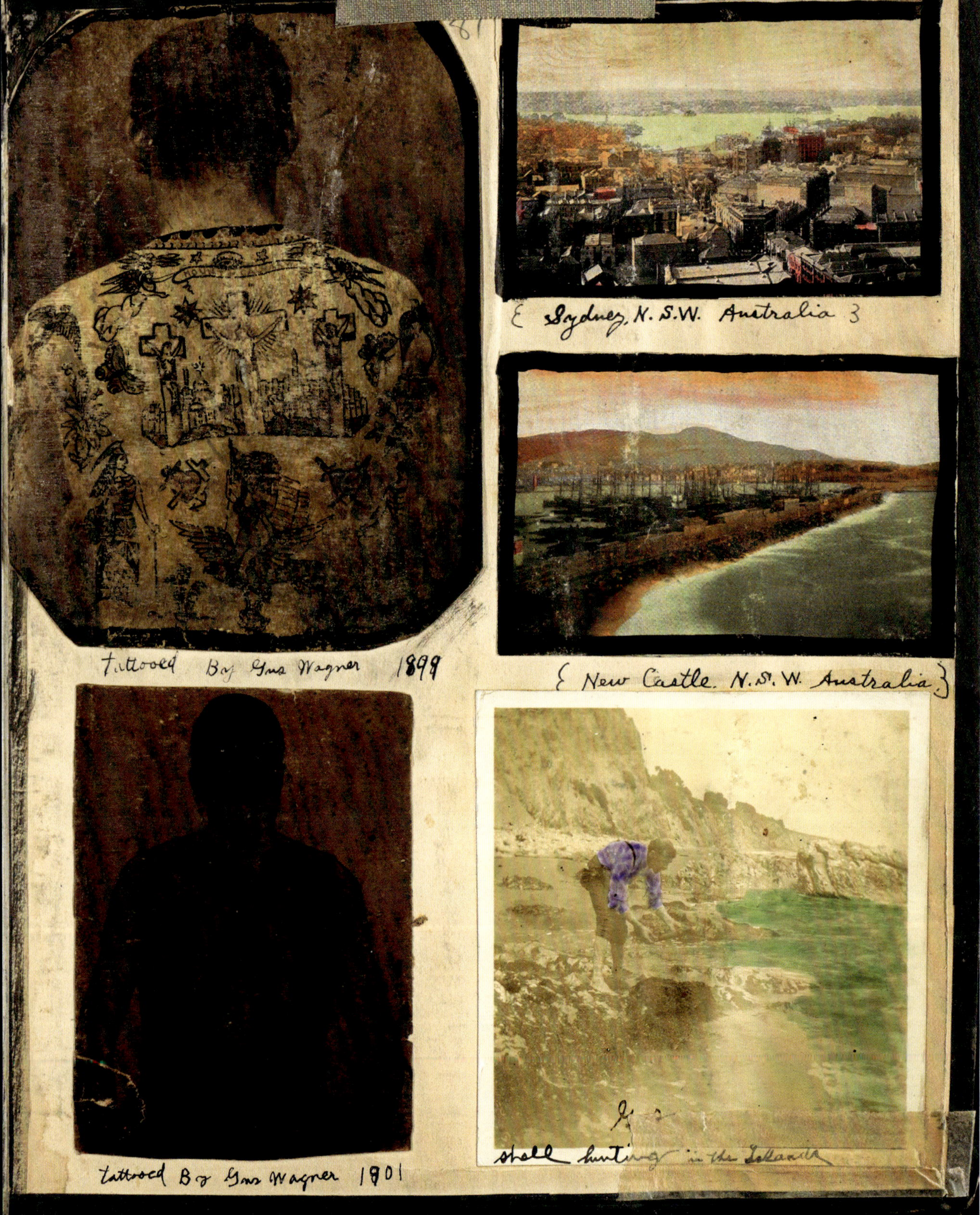

Pages from Gus Wagner's scrapbook

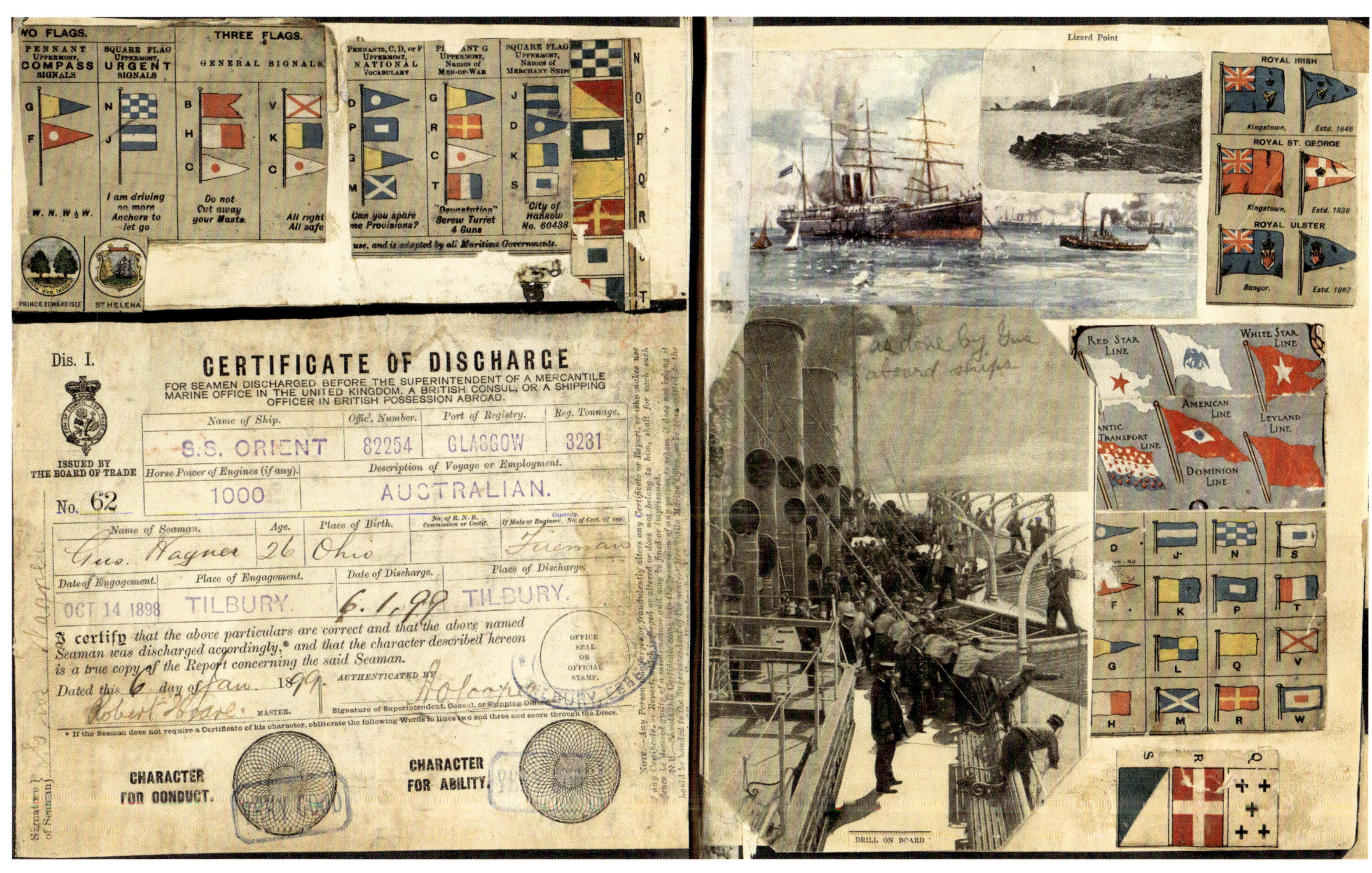

Dis. I.

CERTIFICATE OF DISCHARGE

FOR SEAMEN DISCHARGED BEFORE THE SUPERINTENDENT OF A MERCANTILE MARINE OFFICE IN THE UNITED KINGDOM, A BRITISH CONSUL, OR A SHIPPING OFFICER IN BRITISH POSSESSION ABROAD.

ISSUED BY THE BOARD OF TRADE

No. 62

Name of Ship.	Offic¹. Number.	Port of Registry.	Reg. Tonnage.
S.S. ORIENT	82254	GLASGOW	3231

Horse Power of Engines (if any).	Description of Voyage or Employment.
1000	AUSTRALIAN.

Name of Seaman.	Age.	Place of Birth.	No. of R. N. R. Commission or Certif.	Capacity. If Mate or Engineer, No. of Cert. (if any).
Gus. Wagner	26	Ohio		Fireman

Date of Engagement.	Place of Engagement.	Date of Discharge.	Place of Discharge.
OCT 14 1898	TILBURY.	6.1.99	TILBURY.

I certify that the above particulars are correct and that the above named Seaman was discharged accordingly,* and that the character described hereon is a true copy of the Report concerning the said Seaman.

Dated this 6 day of Jan. 1899. AUTHENTICATED BY

Robert Hoare. MASTER. Signature of Superintendent, Consul, or Shipping Officer.

OFFICE SEAL OR OFFICIAL STAMP.

* If the Seaman does not require a Certificate of his character, obliterate the following Words in lines two and three and score through the Discs.

CHARACTER FOR CONDUCT.

CHARACTER FOR ABILITY.

Signature of Seaman

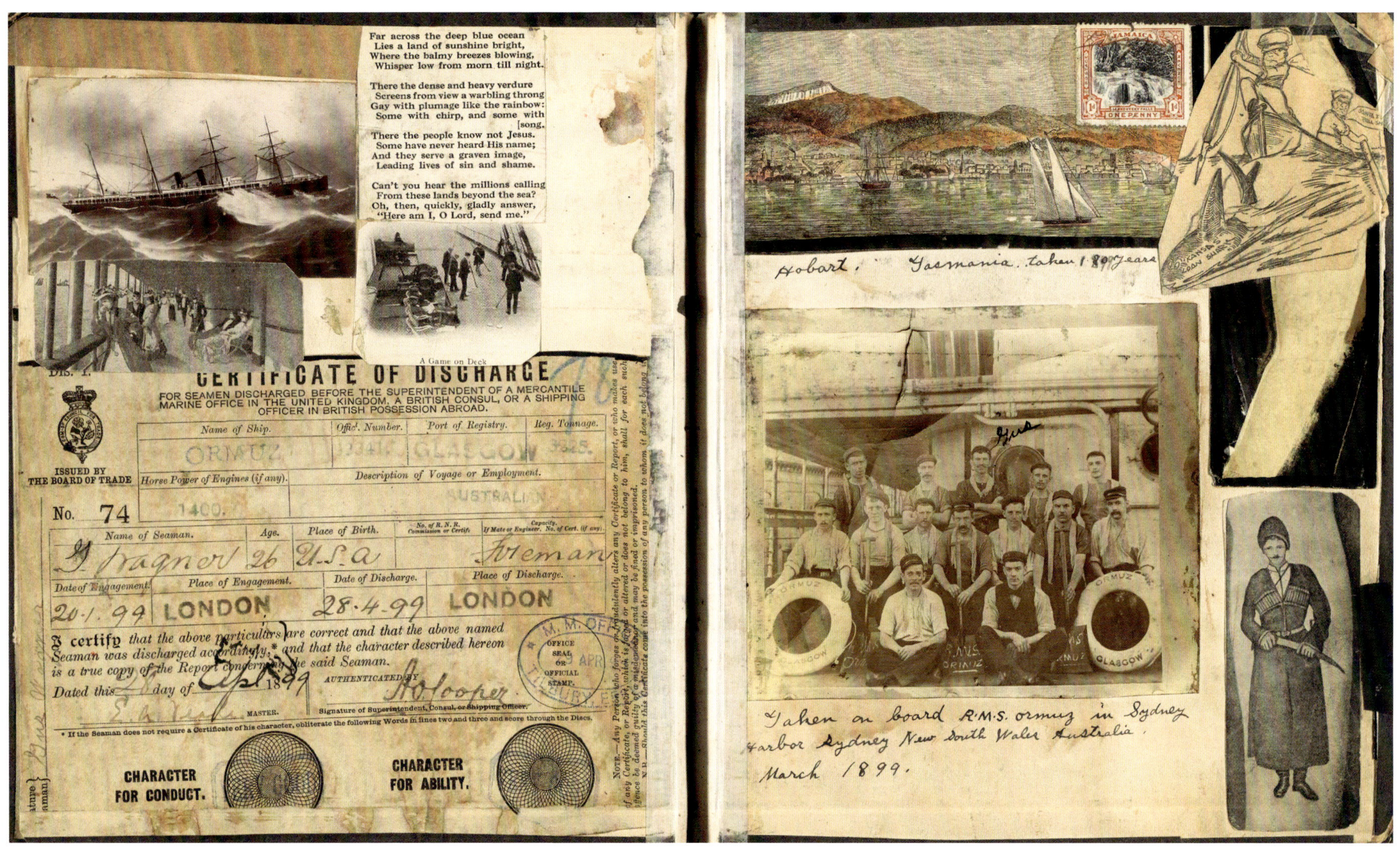
Far across the deep blue ocean
Lies a land of sunshine bright,
Where the balmy breezes blowing,
Whisper low from morn till night.
There the dense and heavy verdure
Screens from view a warbling throng
Gay with plumage like the rainbow:
Some with chirp, and some with [song.
There the people know not Jesus.
Some have never heard His name;
And they serve a graven image,
Leading lives of sin and shame.
Can't you hear the millions calling
From these lands beyond the sea?
Oh, then, quickly, gladly answer,
"Here am I, O Lord, send me."
A Game on Deck
CERTIFICATE OF DISCHARGE
FOR SEAMEN DISCHARGED BEFORE THE SUPERINTENDENT OF A MERCANTILE MARINE OFFICE IN THE UNITED KINGDOM, A BRITISH CONSUL, OR A SHIPPING OFFICER IN BRITISH POSSESSION ABROAD.
ISSUED BY THE BOARD OF TRADE
No. 74
Name of Ship. ORMUZ
Port of Registry. GLASGOW
Horse Power of Engines (if any). 1400.
Description of Voyage or Employment. AUSTRALIAN
Name of Seaman. G. Wagner
Age. 26
Place of Birth. U.S.A
Fireman
Date of Engagement. 20.1.99
Place of Engagement. LONDON
Date of Discharge. 28.4.99
Place of Discharge. LONDON
I certify that the above particulars are correct and that the above named Seaman was discharged accordingly,* and that the character described hereon is a true copy of the Report concerning the said Seaman.
Dated this 28 day of April 1899
AUTHENTICATED BY
MASTER.
Signature of Superintendent, Consul, or Shipping Officer.
* If the Seaman does not require a Certificate of his character, obliterate the following Words in lines two and three and score through the Discs.
CHARACTER FOR CONDUCT.
CHARACTER FOR ABILITY.
JAMAICA
ONE PENNY
Hobart, Tasmania. taken 1899 years
Gus
ORMUZ
GLASGOW
Taken on board R.M.S. ormuz in Sydney Harbor Sydney New South Wales Australia.
March 1899.

Street scene in Calcutta Indi City. Capital of India & Bengal, on the River Hugli

"Oilette"

6b

S.S. CLUMBERHALL

Gus

Taken on board the S.S. Clumberhall at the wharfe at Philadelphia P.A. March 1900.

Pages from Gus Wagner's scrapbook

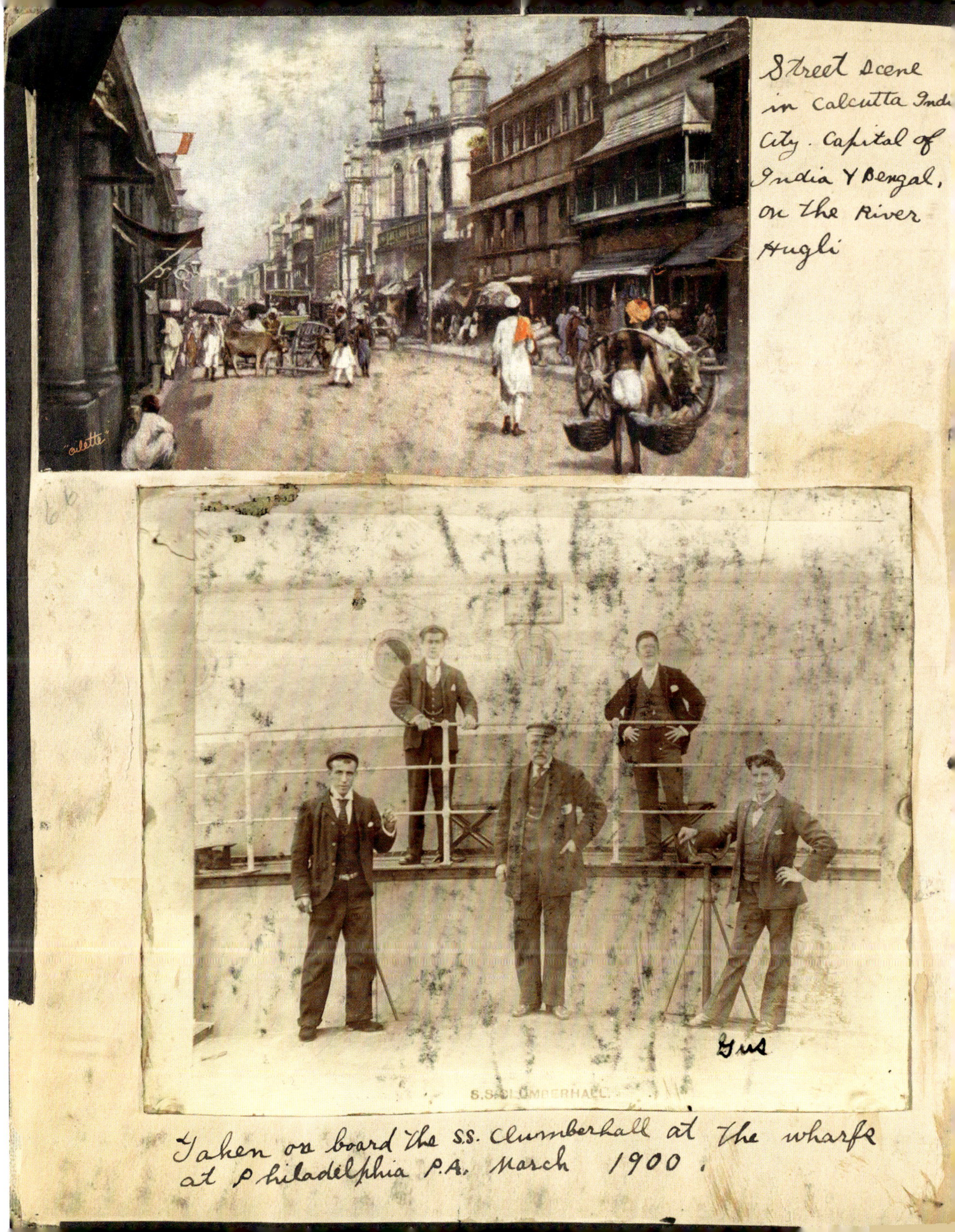

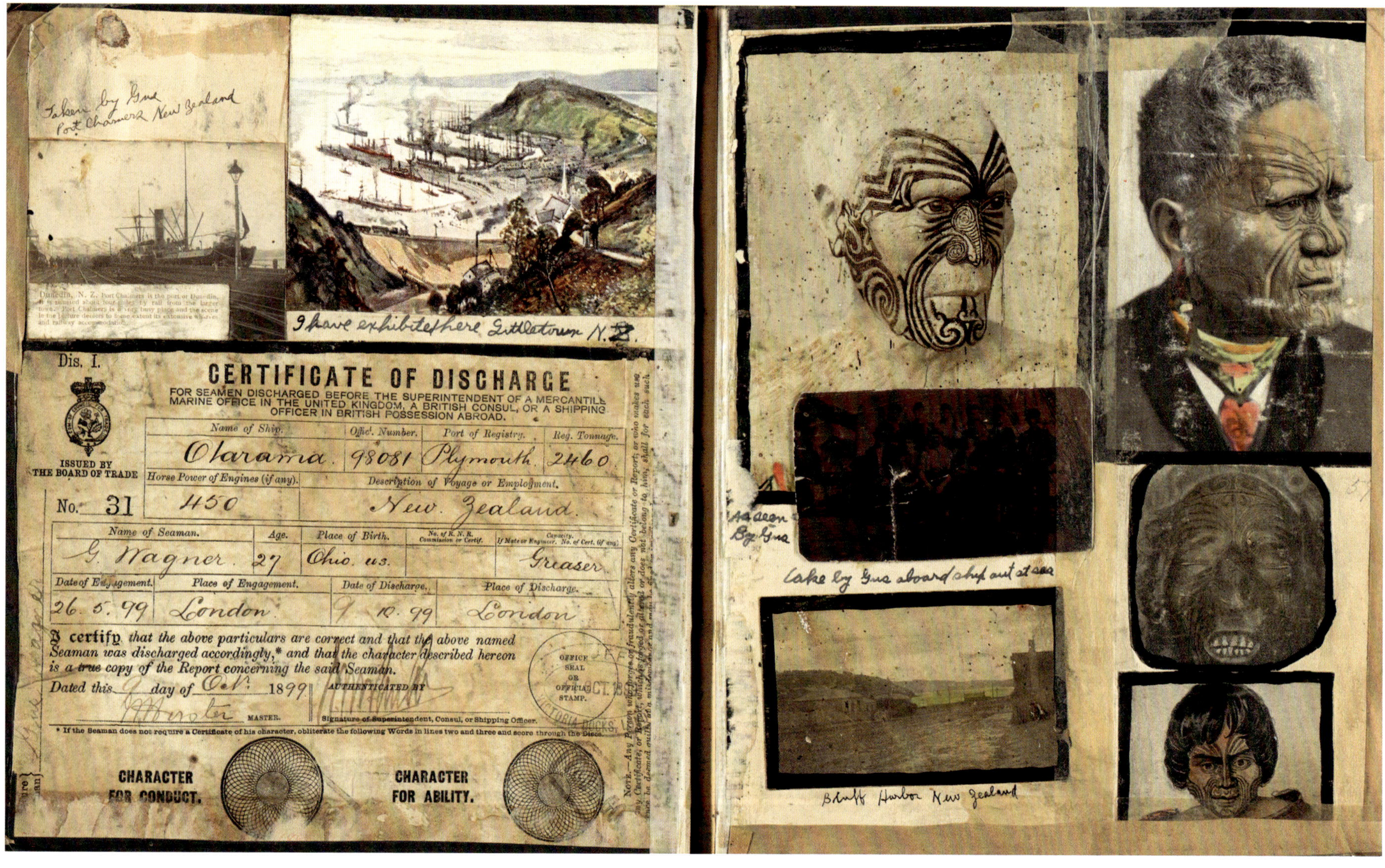
Taken by Gus
Port Chalmers New Zealand
I have exhibited here Lyttleton N.Z.
Dis. I.
CERTIFICATE OF DISCHARGE
FOR SEAMEN DISCHARGED BEFORE THE SUPERINTENDENT OF A MERCANTILE MARINE OFFICE IN THE UNITED KINGDOM, A BRITISH CONSUL, OR A SHIPPING OFFICER IN BRITISH POSSESSION ABROAD.
ISSUED BY THE BOARD OF TRADE
No. 31
Name of Ship. Olarama
Offic'. Number. 98081
Port of Registry. Plymouth
Reg. Tonnage. 2460
Horse Power of Engines (if any). 450
Description of Voyage or Employment. New Zealand
Name of Seaman. G. Wagner
Age. 27
Place of Birth. Ohio. us.
Capacity. Greaser
Date of Engagement. 26. 5. 99
Place of Engagement. London
Date of Discharge. 9. 10. 99
Place of Discharge. London
I certify that the above particulars are correct and that the above named Seaman was discharged accordingly,* and that the character described hereon is a true copy of the Report concerning the said Seaman.
Dated this 9 day of Oct. 1899
AUTHENTICATED BY
MASTER.
Signature of Superintendent, Consul, or Shipping Officer.
* If the Seaman does not require a Certificate of his character, obliterate the following Words in lines two and three and score through the Discs.
CHARACTER FOR CONDUCT.
CHARACTER FOR ABILITY.
OFFICE SEAL OR OFFICIAL STAMP.
Taken by Gus
Take by Gus aboard ship out at sea
Bluff Harbor New Zealand

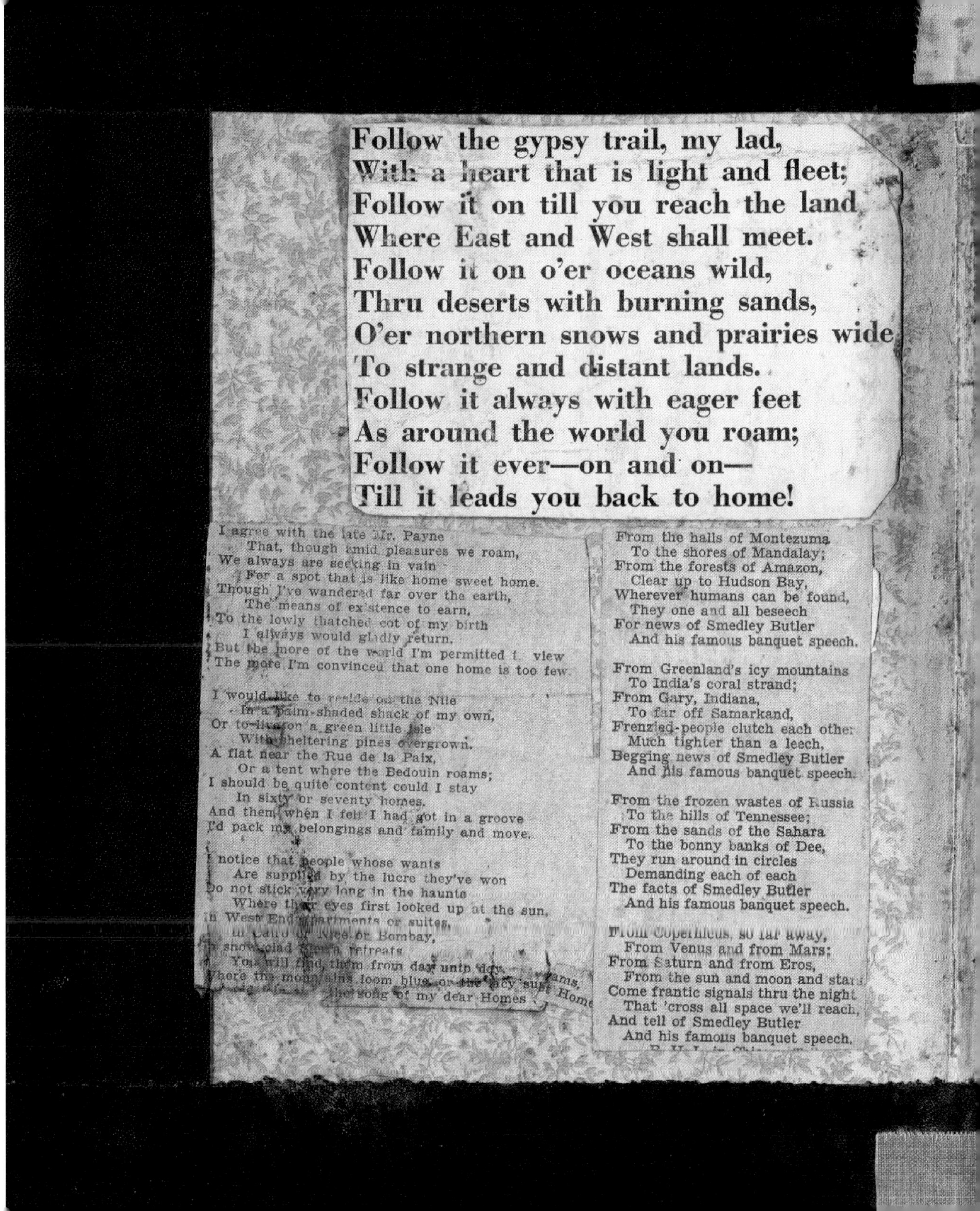

Follow the gypsy trail, my lad,
With a heart that is light and fleet;
Follow it on till you reach the land
Where East and West shall meet.
Follow it on o'er oceans wild,
Thru deserts with burning sands,
O'er northern snows and prairies wide
To strange and distant lands.
Follow it always with eager feet
As around the world you roam;
Follow it ever—on and on—
Till it leads you back to home!

I agree with the late Mr. Payne
That, though amid pleasures we roam,
We always are seeking in vain
For a spot that is like home sweet home.
Though I've wandered far over the earth,
The means of existence to earn,
To the lowly thatched cot of my birth
I always would gladly return.
But the more of the world I'm permitted to view
The more I'm convinced that one home is too few.

I would like to reside on the Nile
In a palm-shaded shack of my own,
Or to live on a green little isle
With sheltering pines overgrown.
A flat near the Rue de la Paix,
Or a tent where the Bedouin roams;
I should be quite content could I stay
In sixty or seventy homes.
And then, when I felt I had got in a groove
I'd pack my belongings and family and move.

I notice that people whose wants
Are supplied by the lucre they've won
Do not stick very long in the haunts
Where their eyes first looked up at the sun.
In West End apartments or suites,
In Cairo or Nice or Bombay,
In snow-clad [illegible] retreats
You will find them from day unto day,
Where the mountains loom blue or the [illegible] ...ams,
[illegible] the song of my dear Homes [illegible] Home

From the halls of Montezuma
To the shores of Mandalay;
From the forests of Amazon,
Clear up to Hudson Bay,
Wherever humans can be found,
They one and all beseech
For news of Smedley Butler
And his famous banquet speech.

From Greenland's icy mountains
To India's coral strand;
From Gary, Indiana,
To far off Samarkand,
Frenzied people clutch each other
Much tighter than a leech,
Begging news of Smedley Butler
And his famous banquet speech.

From the frozen wastes of Russia
To the hills of Tennessee;
From the sands of the Sahara
To the bonny banks of Dee,
They run around in circles
Demanding each of each
The facts of Smedley Butler
And his famous banquet speech.

From Copernicus, so far away,
From Venus and from Mars;
From Saturn and from Eros,
From the sun and moon and stars
Come frantic signals thru the night
That 'cross all space we'll reach,
And tell of Smedley Butler
And his famous banquet speech.

Pages from Gus Wagner's scrapbook

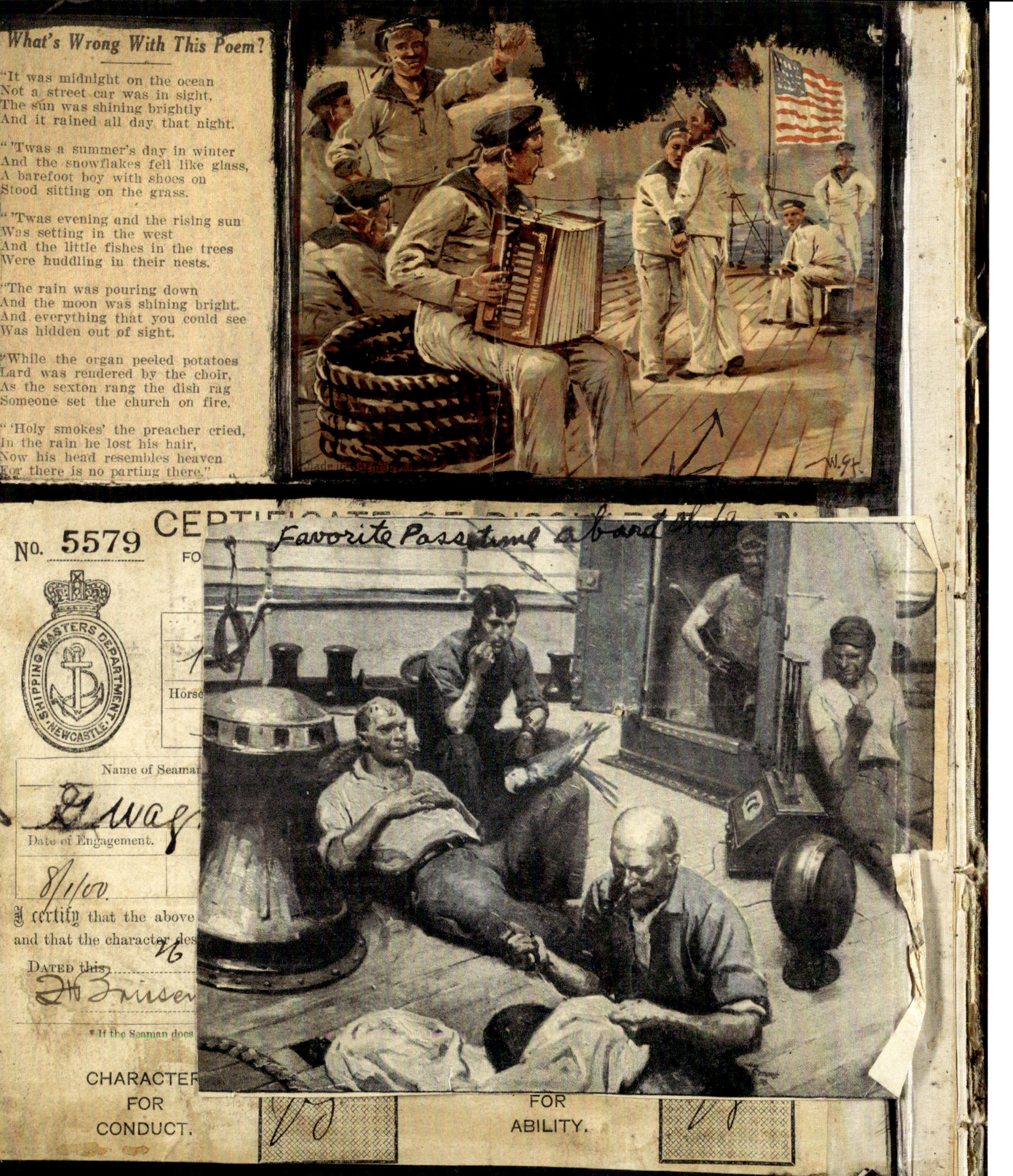

What's Wrong With This Poem?

"It was midnight on the ocean
Not a street car was in sight,
The sun was shining brightly
And it rained all day that night.

"'Twas a summer's day in winter
And the snowflakes fell like glass,
A barefoot boy with shoes on
Stood sitting on the grass.

"'Twas evening and the rising sun
Was setting in the west
And the little fishes in the trees
Were huddling in their nests.

"The rain was pouring down
And the moon was shining bright.
And everything that you could see
Was hidden out of sight.

"While the organ peeled potatoes
Lard was rendered by the choir,
As the sexton rang the dish rag
Someone set the church on fire.

"'Holy smokes' the preacher cried,
In the rain he lost his hair,
Now his head resembles heaven
For there is no parting there."

Pages from Gus Wagner's scrapbook

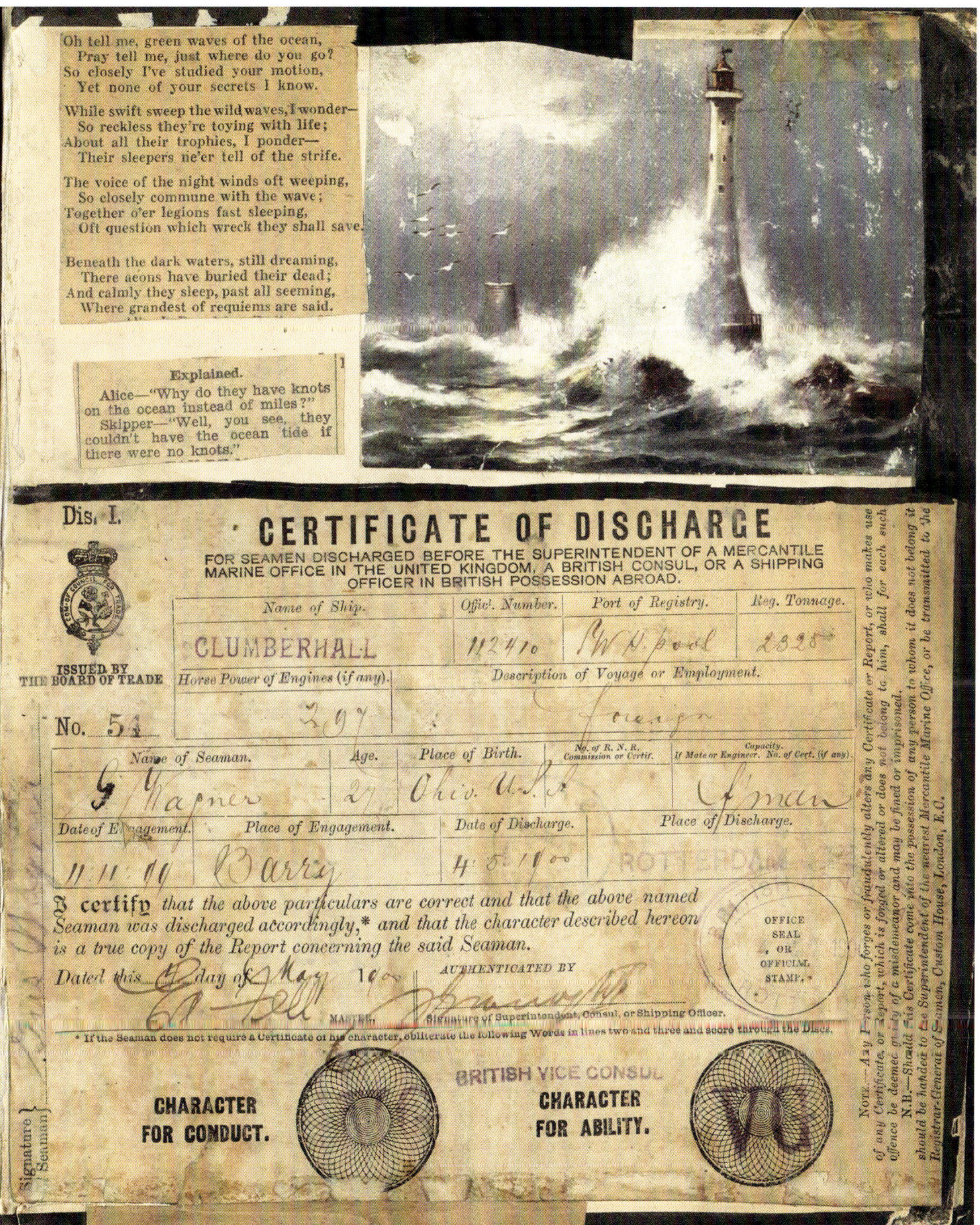

Oh tell me, green waves of the ocean,
Pray tell me, just where do you go?
So closely I've studied your motion,
Yet none of your secrets I know.

While swift sweep the wild waves, I wonder—
So reckless they're toying with life;
About all their trophies, I ponder—
Their sleepers ne'er tell of the strife.

The voice of the night winds oft weeping,
So closely commune with the wave;
Together o'er legions fast sleeping,
Oft question which wreck they shall save.

Beneath the dark waters, still dreaming,
There aeons have buried their dead;
And calmly they sleep, past all seeming,
Where grandest of requiems are said.

Explained.

Alice—"Why do they have knots on the ocean instead of miles?"
Skipper—"Well, you see, they couldn't have the ocean tide if there were no knots."

Dis. 1.

CERTIFICATE OF DISCHARGE

FOR SEAMEN DISCHARGED BEFORE THE SUPERINTENDENT OF A MERCANTILE MARINE OFFICE IN THE UNITED KINGDOM, A BRITISH CONSUL, OR A SHIPPING OFFICER IN BRITISH POSSESSION ABROAD.

ISSUED BY THE BOARD OF TRADE

No. 54

Name of Ship.	Offic'. Number.	Port of Registry.	Reg. Tonnage.
CLUMBERHALL	112410	L'pool	2325

Horse Power of Engines (if any).	Description of Voyage or Employment.
297	Foreign

Name of Seaman.	Age.	Place of Birth.	No. of R. N. R. Commission or Certif.	Capacity. If Mate or Engineer. No. of Cert. (if any).
G Wagner	27	Ohio U.S.		F'man

Date of Engagement.	Place of Engagement.	Date of Discharge.	Place of Discharge.
11.11.99	Barry	4.5.1900	ROTTERDAM

I certify that the above particulars are correct and that the above named Seaman was discharged accordingly,* and that the character described hereon is a true copy of the Report concerning the said Seaman.

Dated this 4 day of May 1900

AUTHENTICATED BY

MASTER. Signature of Superintendent, Consul, or Shipping Officer.

OFFICE SEAL OR OFFICIAL STAMP.

* If the Seaman does not require a Certificate of his character, obliterate the following Words in lines two and three and score through the Discs.

BRITISH VICE CONSUL

CHARACTER FOR CONDUCT.

CHARACTER FOR ABILITY.

Signature of Seaman

NOTE.—Any Person who forges or fraudulently alters any Certificate or Report, or who makes use of any Certificate, or Report, which is forged or altered or does not belong to him, shall for each such offence be deemed guilty of a misdemeanor and may be fined or imprisoned.

N.B.—Should this Certificate come into the possession of any person to whom it does not belong it should be handed to the Superintendent of the nearest Mercantile Marine Office, or be transmitted to the Registrar-General of Seamen, Custom House, London, E.C.

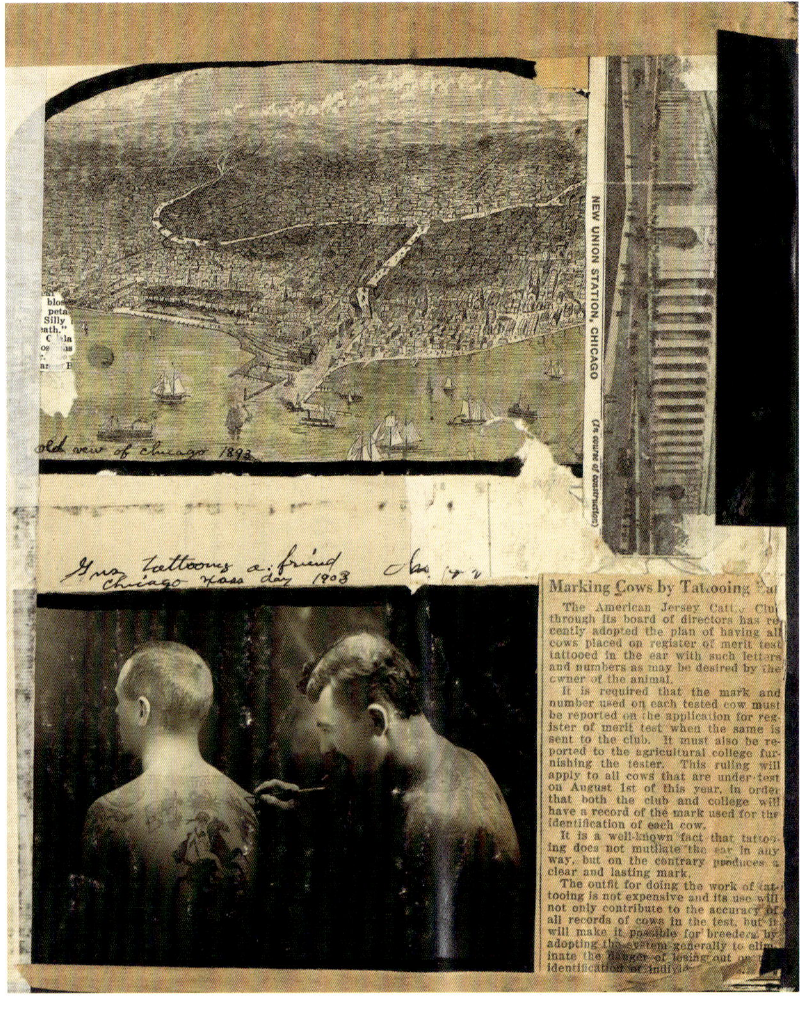

Marking Cows by Tattooing

The American Jersey Cattle Club through its board of directors has recently adopted the plan of having all cows placed on register of merit test tattooed in the ear with such letters and numbers as may be desired by the owner of the animal.

It is required that the mark and number used on each tested cow must be reported on the application for register of merit test when the same is sent to the club. It must also be reported to the agricultural college furnishing the tester. This ruling will apply to all cows that are under test on August 1st of this year, in order that both the club and college will have a record of the mark used for the identification of each cow.

It is a well-known fact that tattooing does not mutilate the ear in any way, but on the contrary produces a clear and lasting mark.

The outfit for doing the work of tattooing is not expensive and its use will not only contribute to the accuracy of all records of cows in the test, but it will make it possible for breeders by adopting the system generally to eliminate the danger of losing out on the identification of indiv

Page from Gus Wagner's scrapbook

It doesn't hurt. That's the first question people ask; they seem to think it's something like vaccination—it's got to hurt before it will "take." But it doesn't. In St. Louis this summer I have put dragons and birds and portraits and lodge seals on more than 1,900 people, and in all that number I have had just four sore arms—sore for a day or two, and that was the end of it.

It's a paying business, all right, if you know how to go at it. First, you've got to know the business—how to handle the needles, how to apply them without going too deep, and, above all, how to use pigments that are pure and that will not cause irritations. Then you've got to be able to deliver the goods—that is, do what you say you are going to do, do it quick, and have it over with.[1]

It isn't so with portraits. A young man comes in with a good arm and a picture of a girl—O, it would be a peach done in blue and yellow with a touch of brown and green here and there. He asks me what I will charge to put it on him; I tell him. He's willing. But he seems to think of something.

"If I get it on, can I ever get it off?" says he.

"No," says I.

1. *St. Louis Dispatch,* December 8, 1904.

"But suppose she goes back on me?" says he, and blushed.

"You might get your arm cut off in a railroad accident," says I, not noticing his blush. "As long as there's life there's hope."

But he usually decided he won't have the picture put on; for if the girl didn't change, he might, and that would be as bad. So, he takes a lodge sign or his initials or a dragon.

Dragons are a mighty strong line. I do them all styles and colors. I believe I have the finest line of dragons of any tattooer in the country—all shapes, sizes, and colors. Peacocks are good too; I've got a big line of them, and they are in steady demand. Heroes—sailors and soldiers and firemen and policemen—sometimes—they are popular; it's worked into a lot of designs. The American eagle is a good line; I've got him in all sorts of shapes; the one with the green beak seems to go best.

When tattooing gets dull, I got with a show as a tattooed man. I can show them on that, you know, and as I can double as a contortionist and can also pick up a few dollars now and then tattooing the country boys and girls, I'm not in much danger of starving.

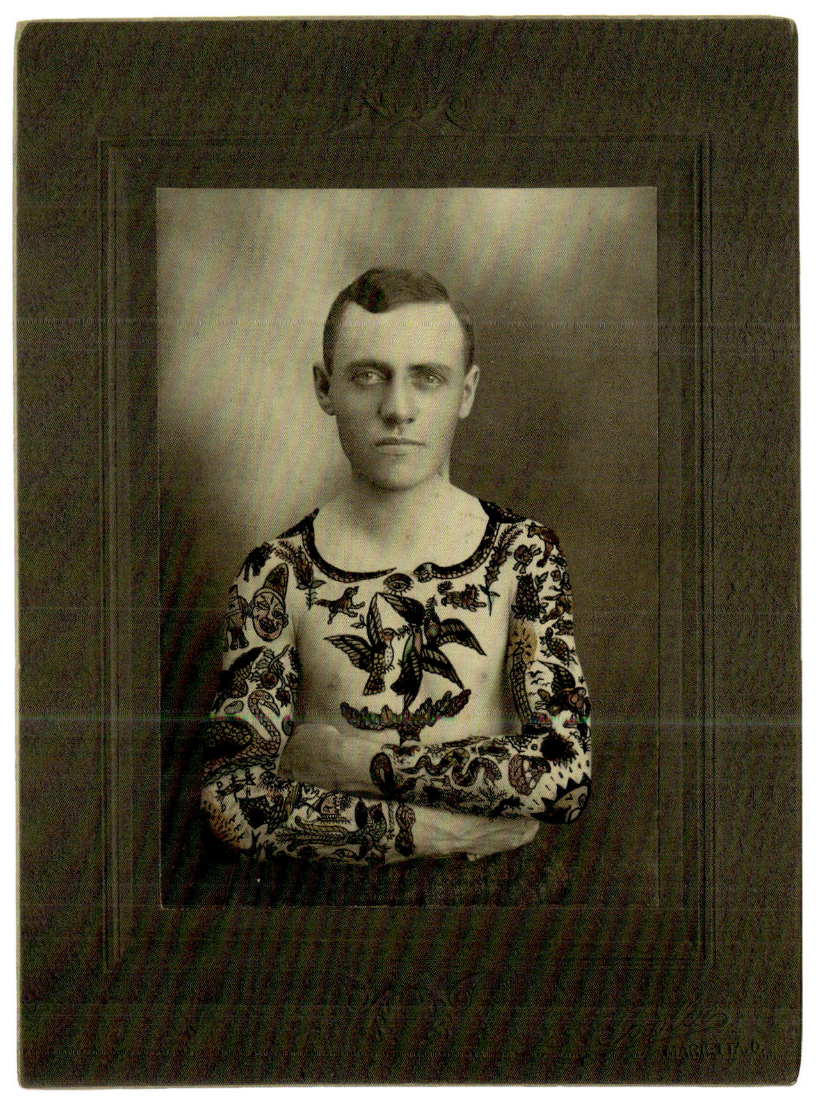

Man tattooed by Gus Wagner

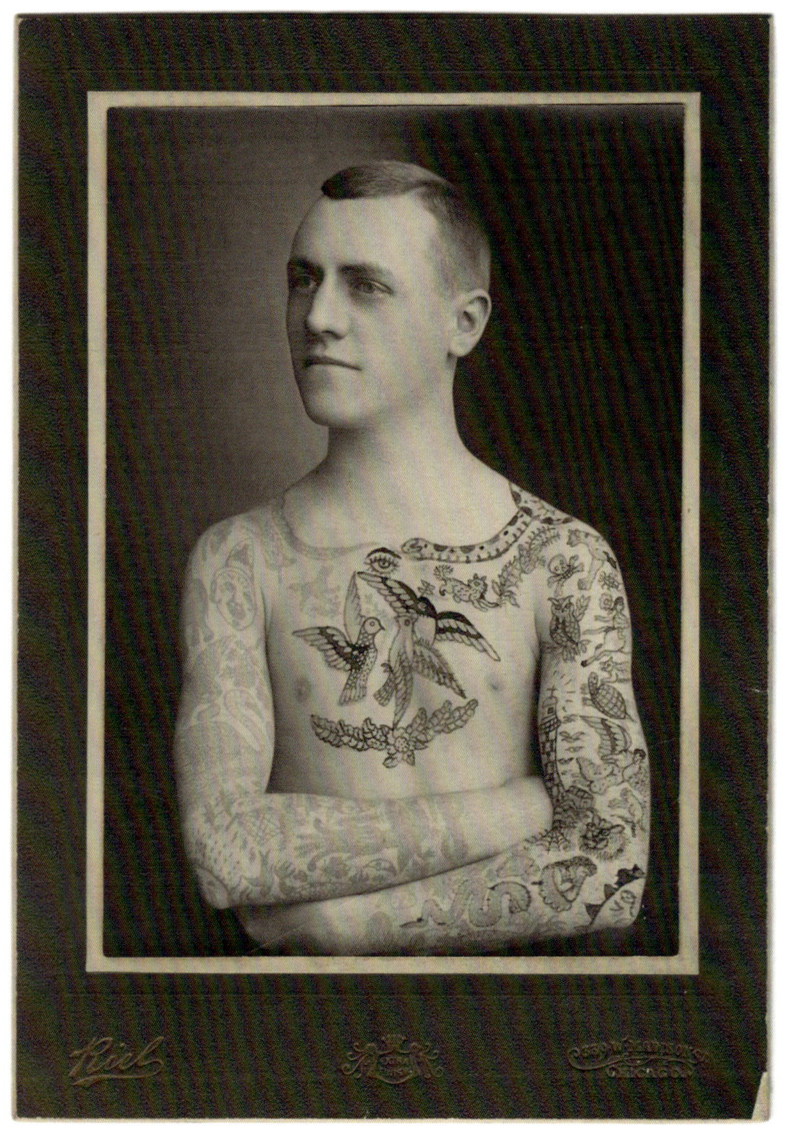

Man tattooed by Gus Wagner

There's one thing I can't do, and that is remove tattooing. It can't be done safely; they've told me in Japan and Java, and what the tattooers of those two countries don't know about tattooing is not discovered as yet. I've tried it, myself; I've gone over the tattoo marks carefully, dot by dot, with erasing preparations, but was no good. One young man offered me $200 to remove from the back of his hand the pictures of a girl whom he didn't think as much of just then as he had thought. I would work pretty hard for $200 in a lump, but I couldn't get that girl off the back of his hand. Of course, it can be done with carbolic acid and ammonia, but that will leave an ugly scar, and scars are not in my line.[2]

There is something about tattooing which I cannot explain, and why so many people have it done I don't know. It may be in vain, but I find it fascinating and very useful in traveling. Every symbol and every design made up of symbols has a meaning. These on my body, for instance, are mementos featuring incidents of my life and travels. Then, too, in every country where tattooing is practiced, a tattooed person who is able to tattoo needs no further introduction to the natives, be they civilized or uncivilized, or even barbaric and cannibalistic. In this way one can win the hearts of the most-primitive peoples.

2. Gus Wagner: *Souvenirs of the Travels and Experiences of the Original Gus Wagner, Globe Trotter and Tattoo Artist* (unique scrapbook, ca. 1890–1930s), 97.

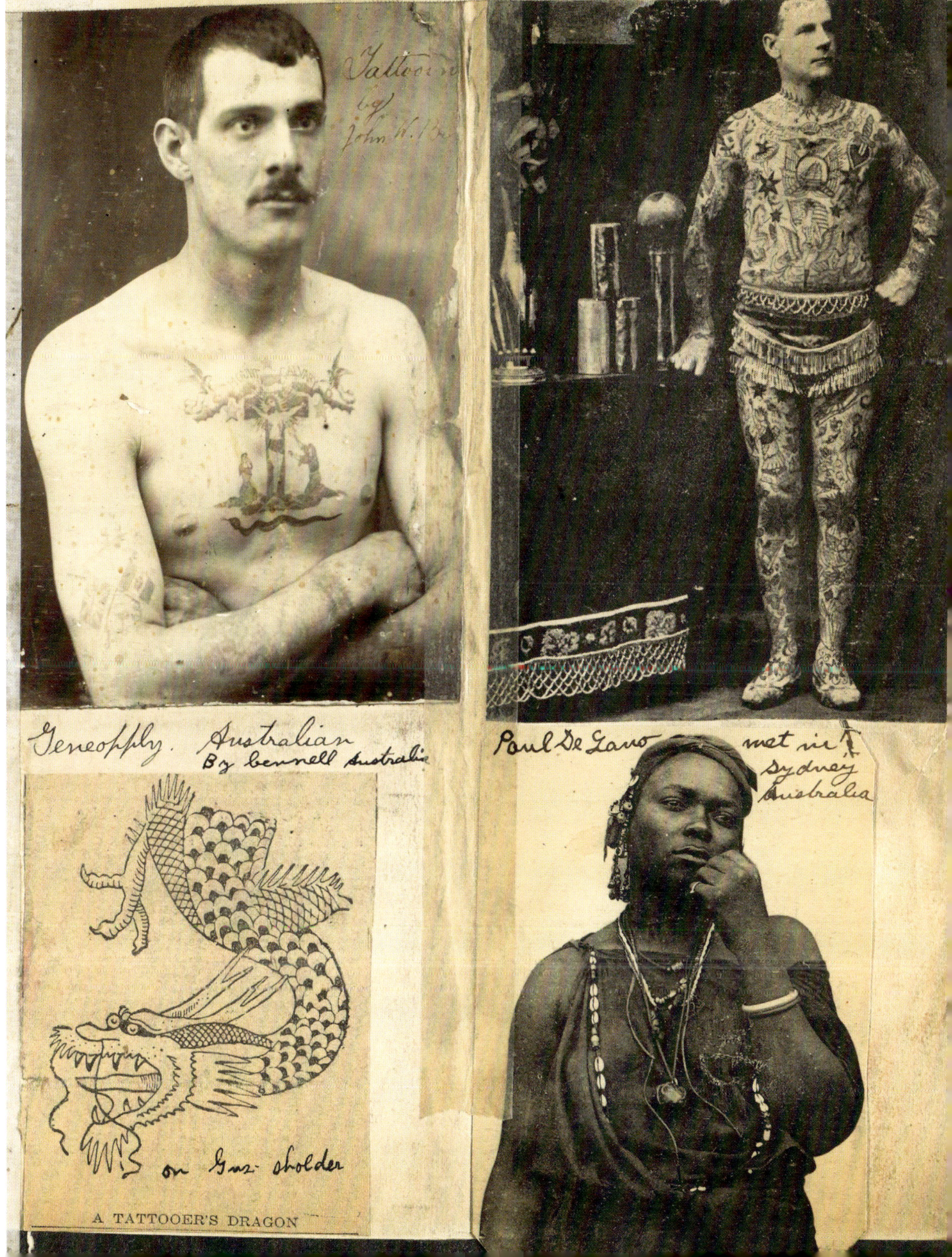

Page from Gus Wagner's scrapbook

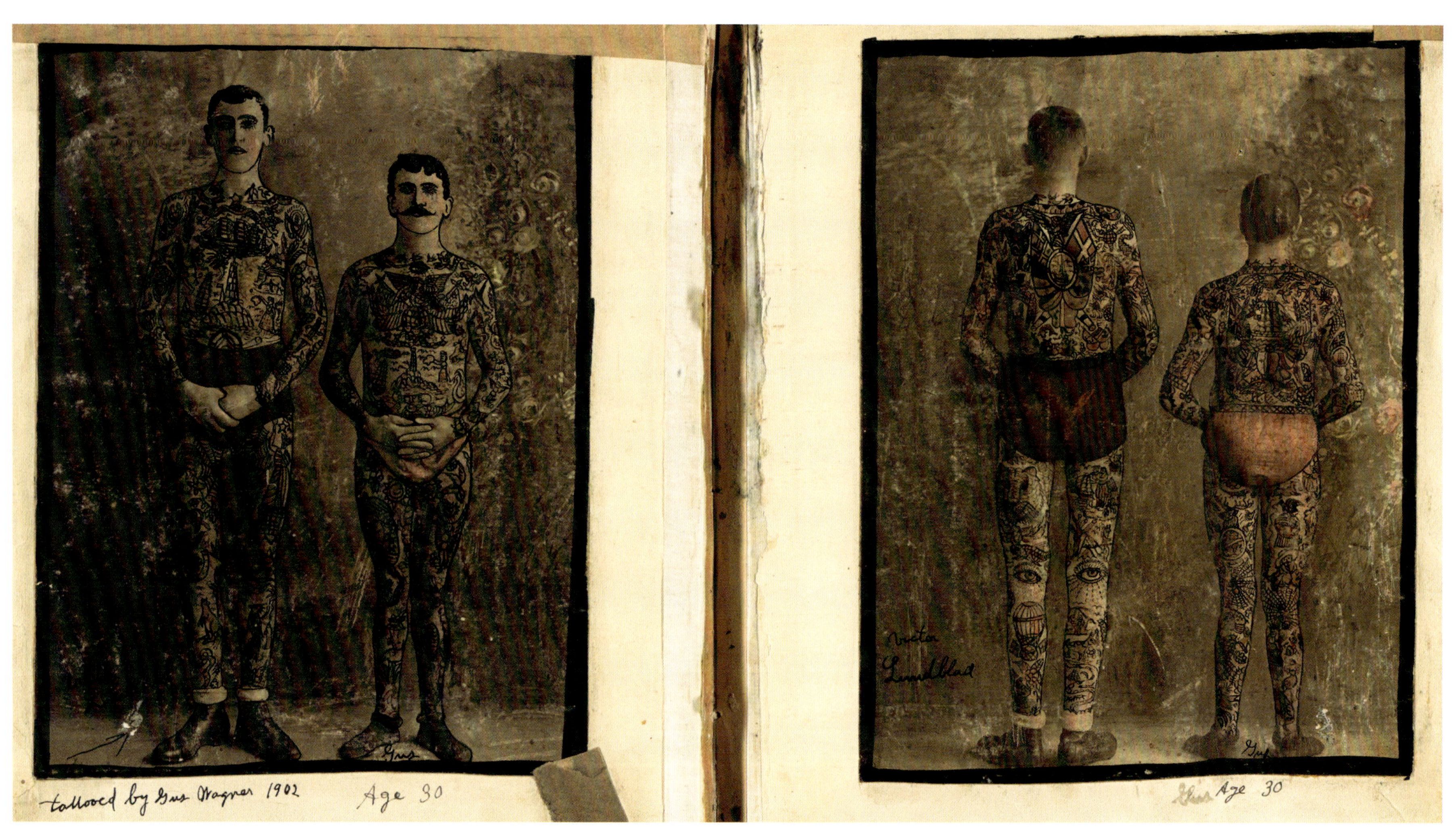

Details from Gus Wagner's scrapbook

No. 1.

RECORD OF SERVICE.

Name of Ship.	COMMENCEMENT OF SERVICE. Date of.	Rating.	TERMINATION OF SERVICE. Date of.	Ability.	Signature of Official or Stamp, and Date of Entry.
85 Bellona	8.2.97	Fmn	19.3.97	V.G.	[illegible]
" Indian Prince	2.4.97	"	28.7.97	"	
" Harlech Castle	3.9.97	"	22.12.97	"	N.F.
" do	19.1.98	"	12.5.98	"	N.F.
" Austral	27.5.98	"	5.9.98	"	
" "Orient"	14.10.98	Do.	6.1.99	"	
" "Ormuz"	20.1.99	Do.	28.4.99	"	
" "Otarama"	26.5.99	Greaser	9.10.99	"	S.F. 8 NOV. 99 BARRY DK.
" Clumberhall	11 11 99	Fman	4 5 1900	V.G.	
" Nuristan	12 5 1900	"	29 6 1900	V.G.	S.F. 7 JUL. 00 VICTORIA DK.
Whakatane	[illegible]		[illegible]		
" Karaweera	8.1 1901		26.4 1901	"	
" Mariposa	29.6 1901		23.7 1901	"	

THE SHIPPING FEDERATION L.TD THAMES DISTRICT No. 2 13 JUL 1899 TIDAL BASIN, VICTORIA DOCKS LONDON E.

FLASH BY GUS WAGNER

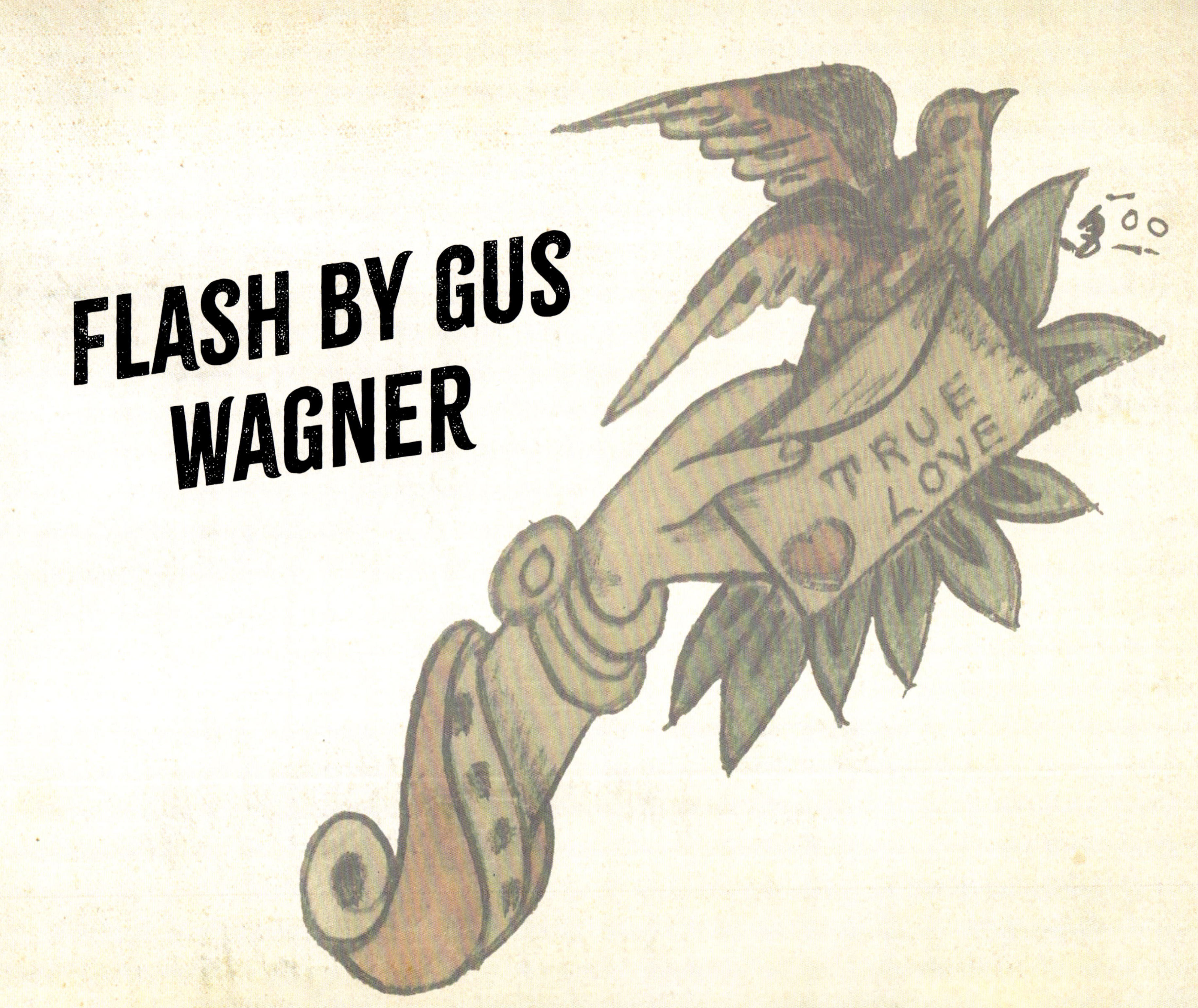

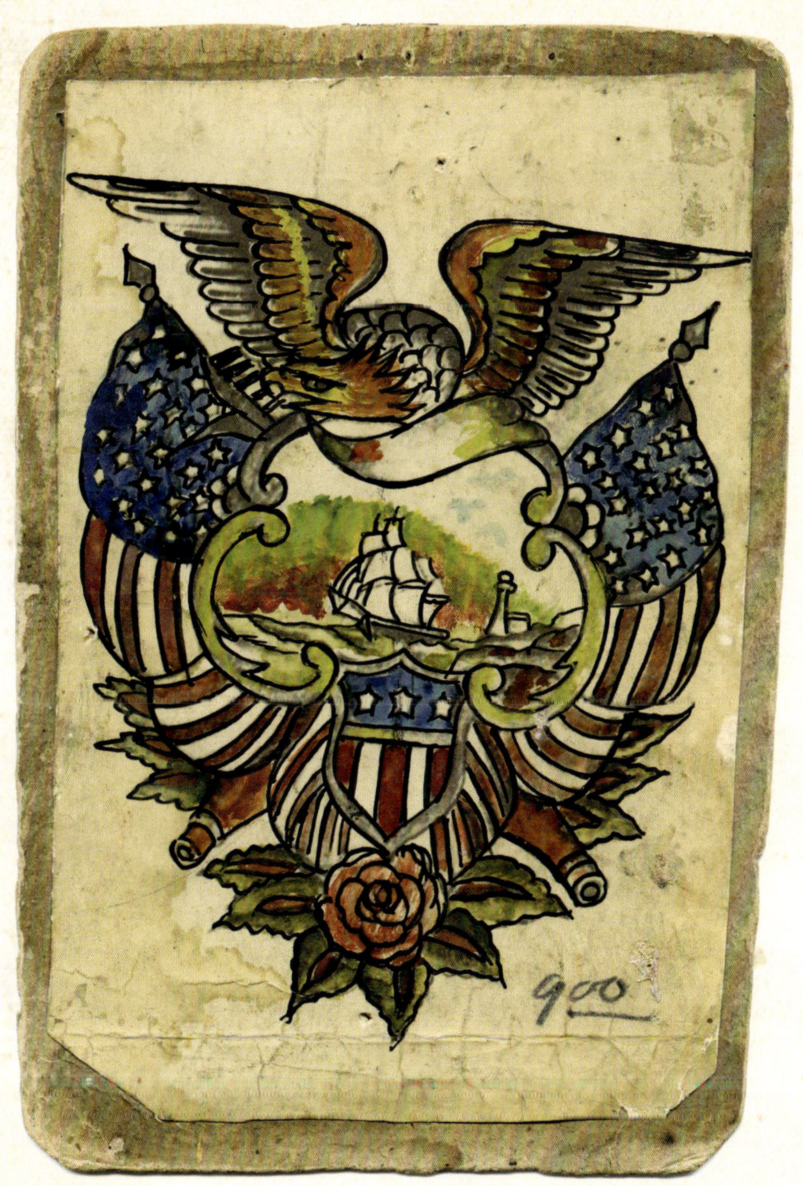
900

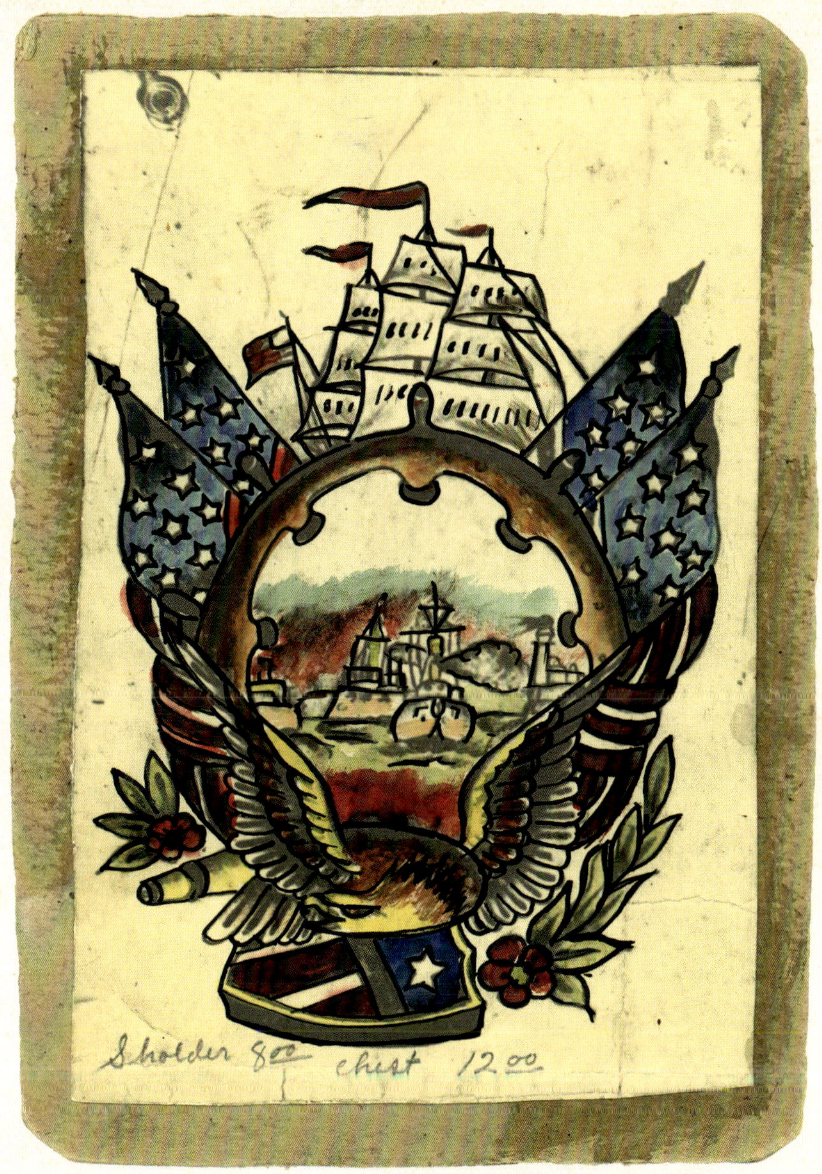
Sholder 800 chest 1200

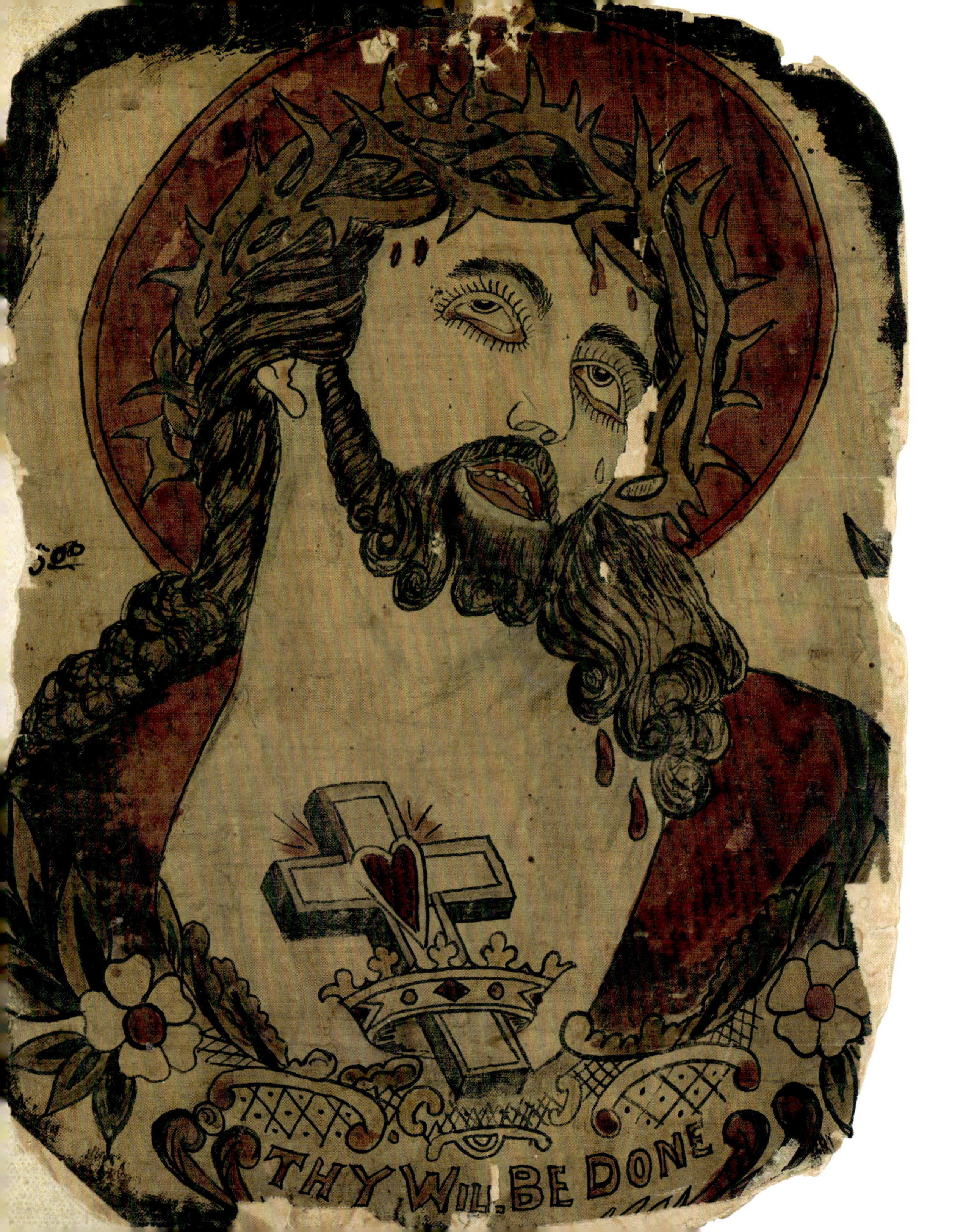
THY WILL BE DONE

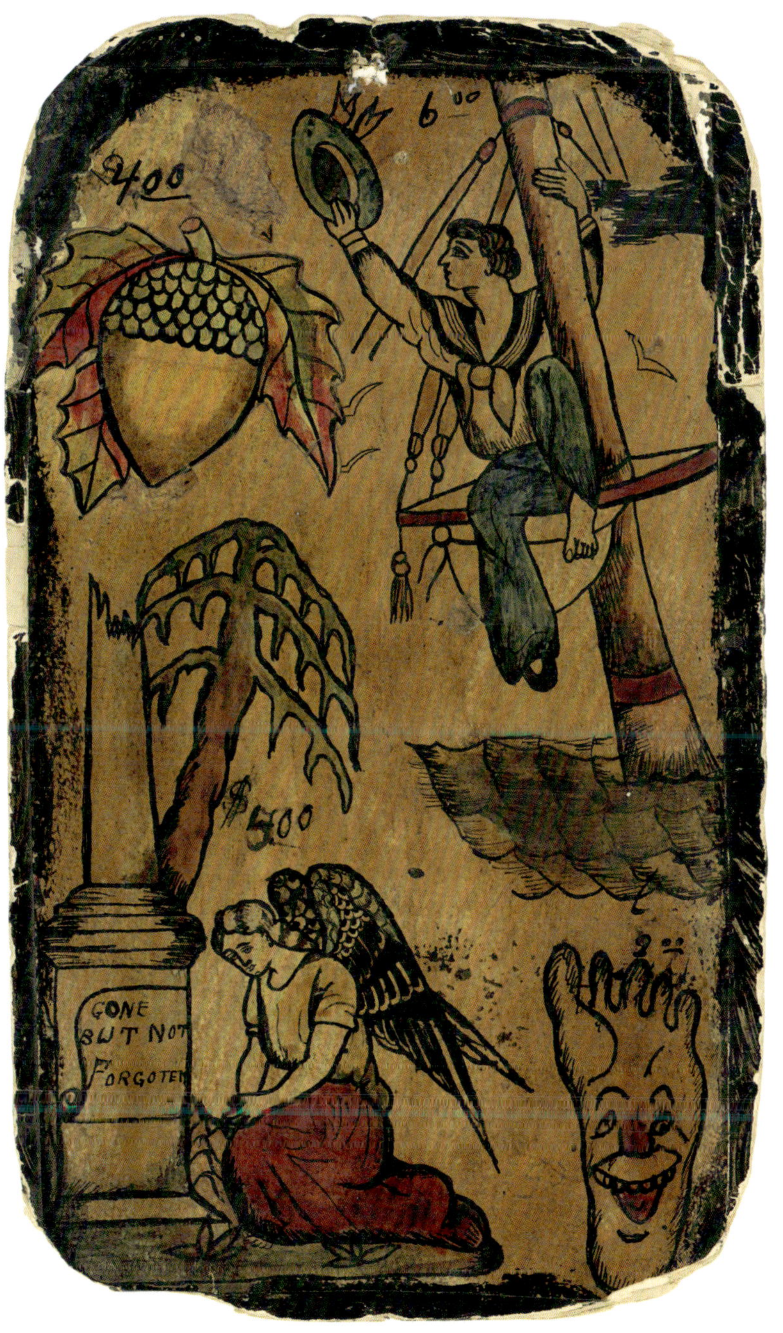

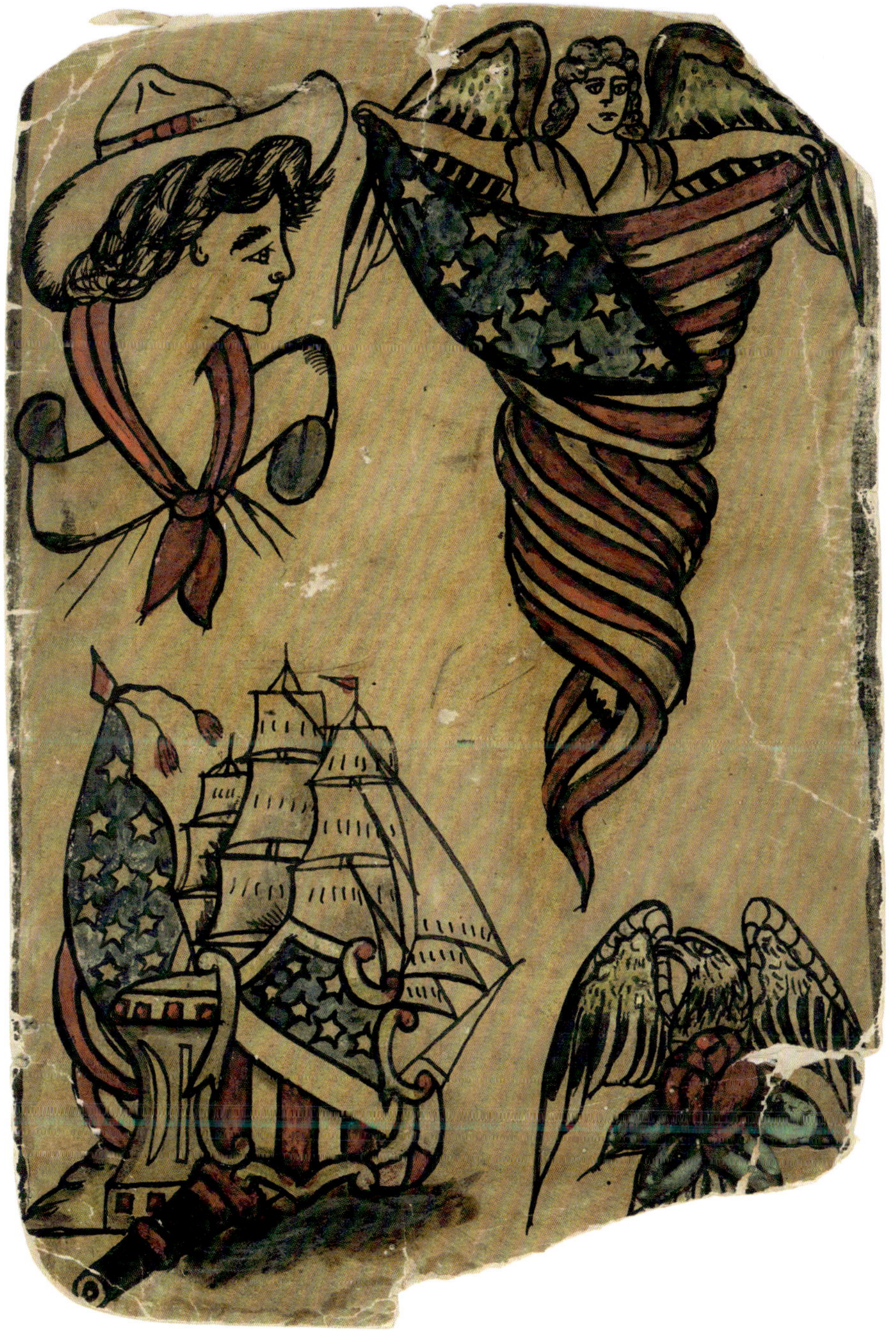

Flash by Gus Wagner

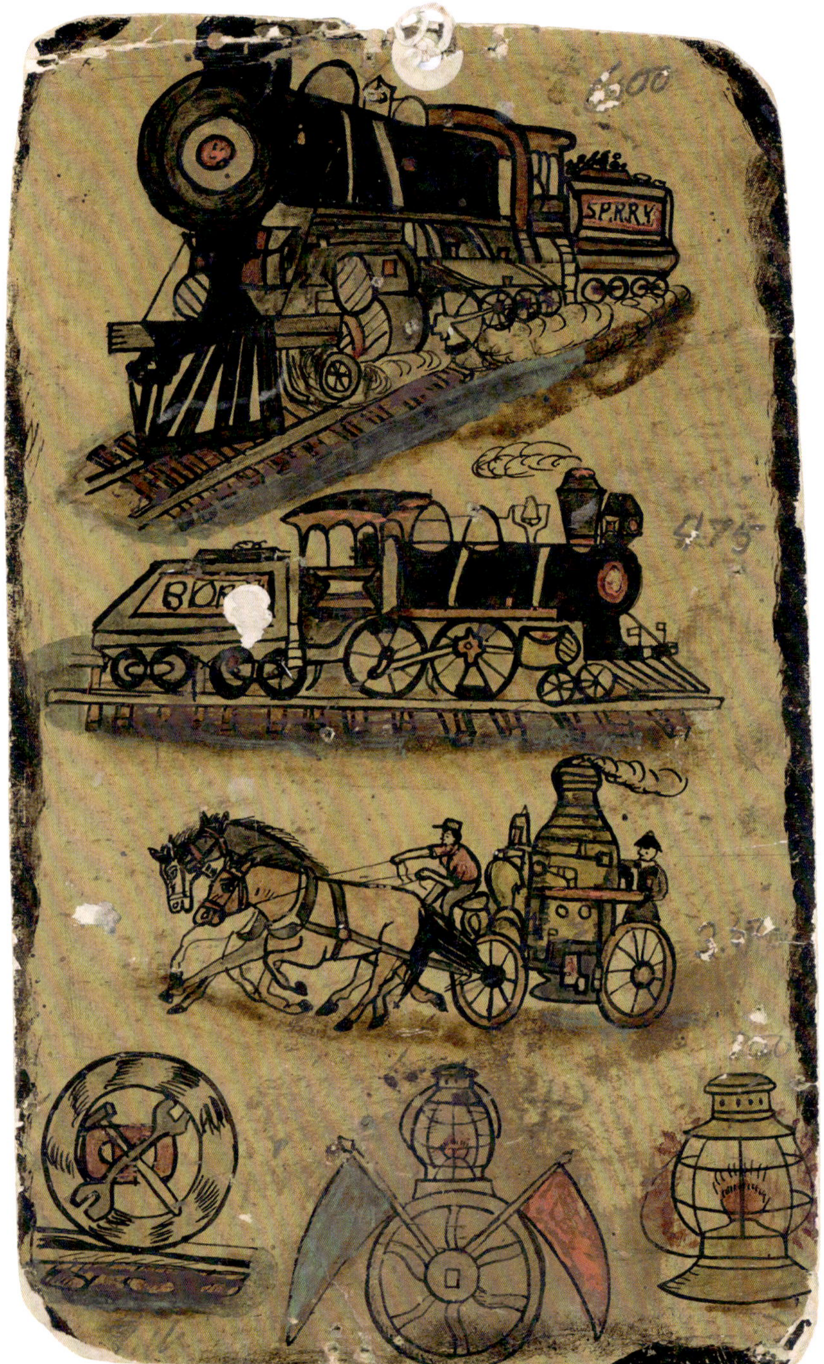

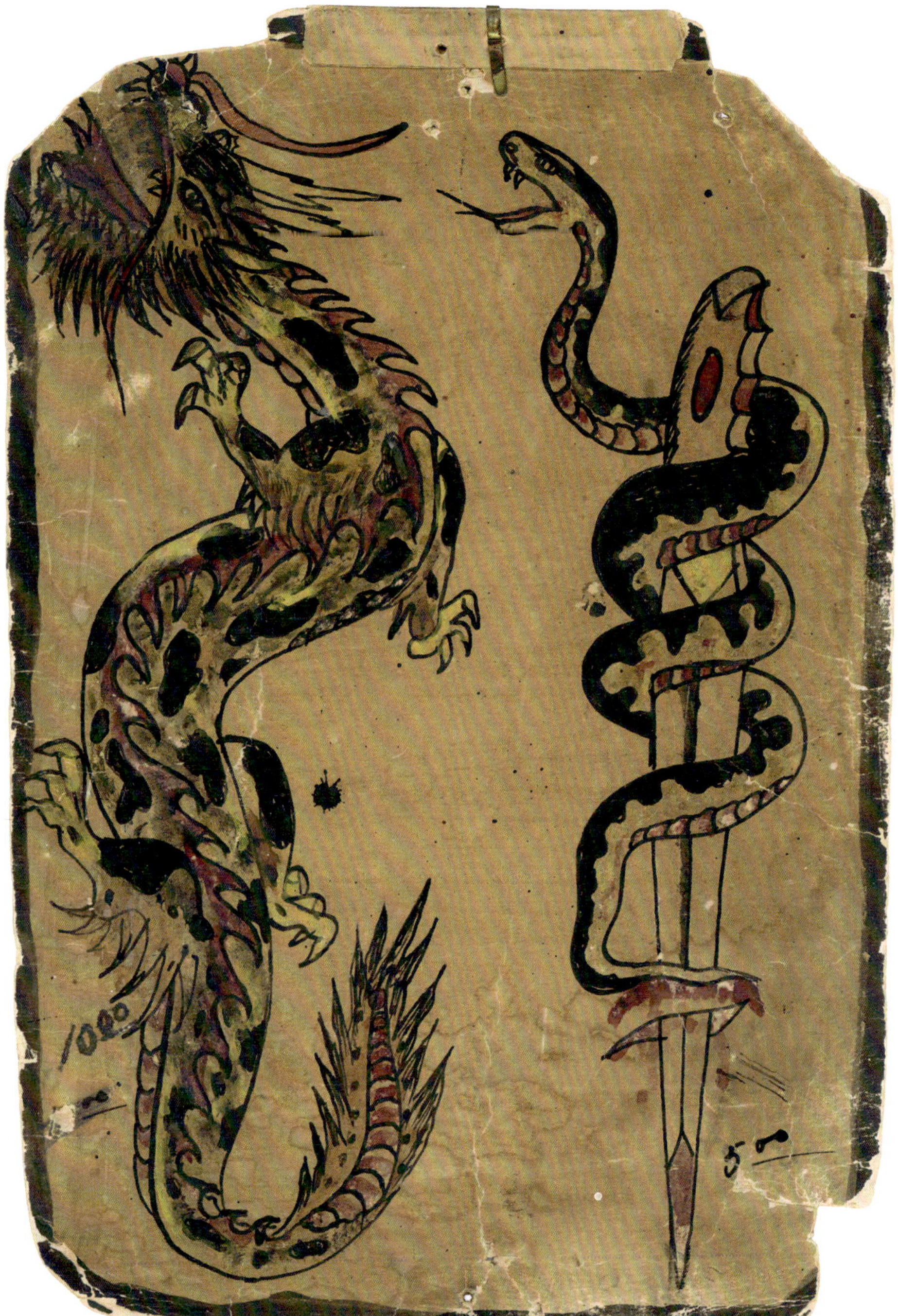

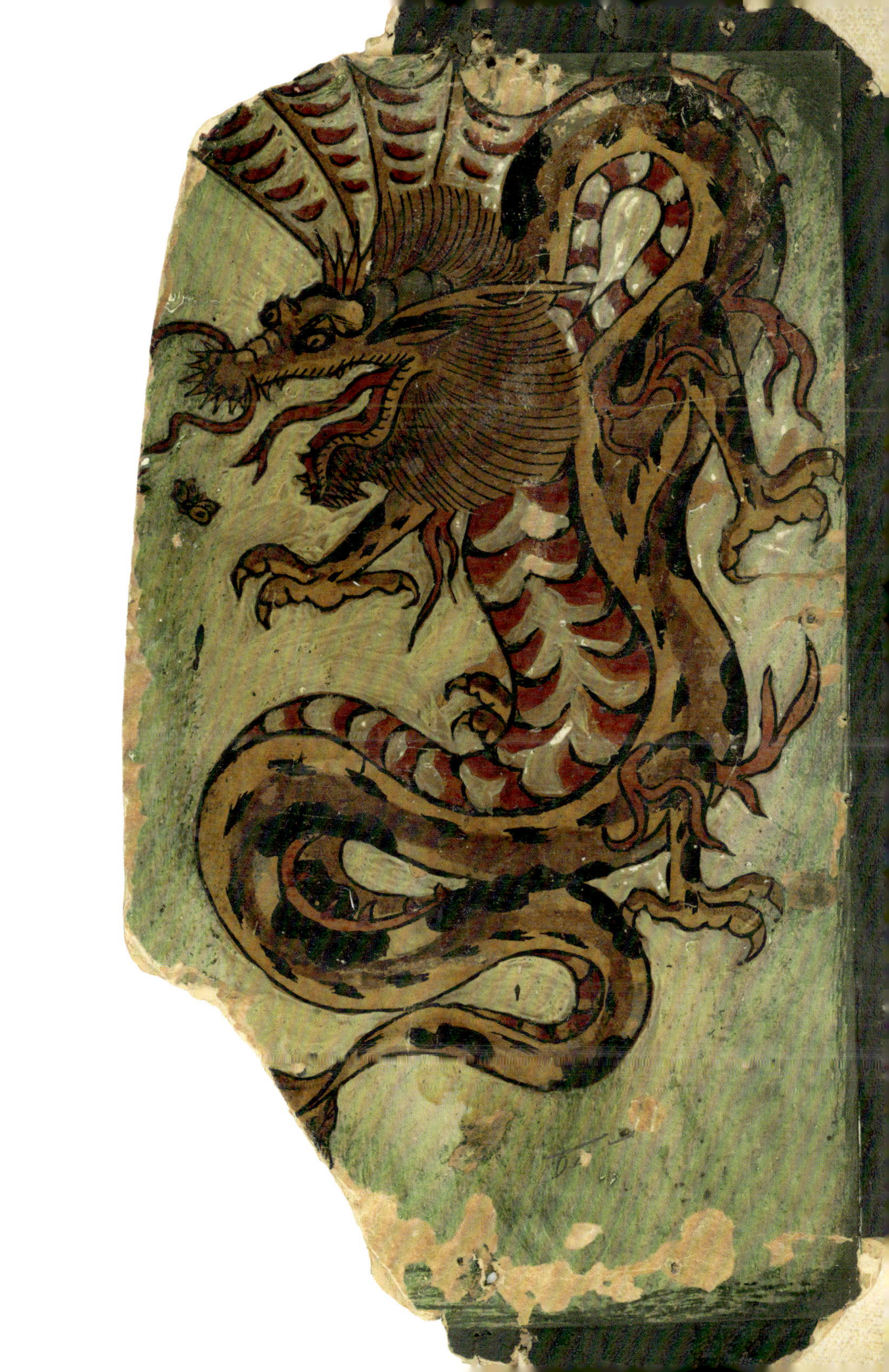

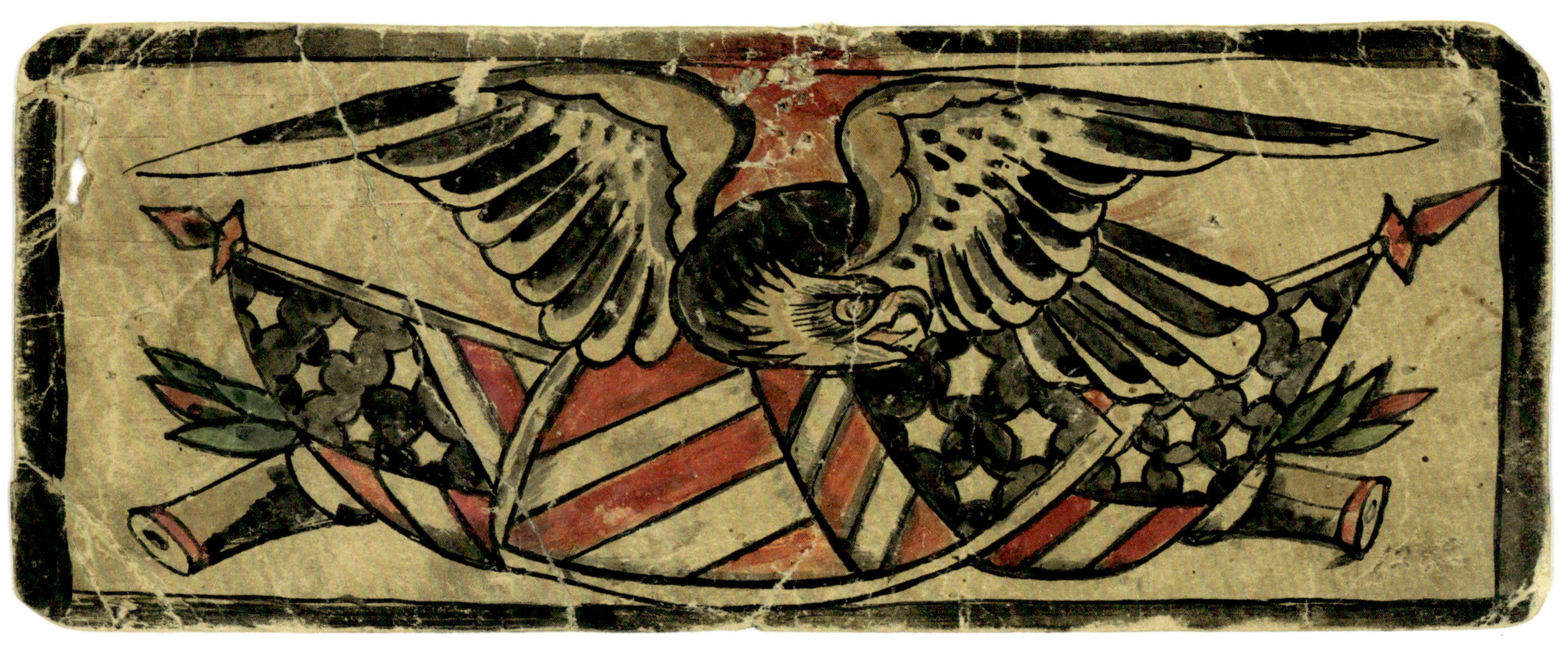

 Flash by Gus Wagner

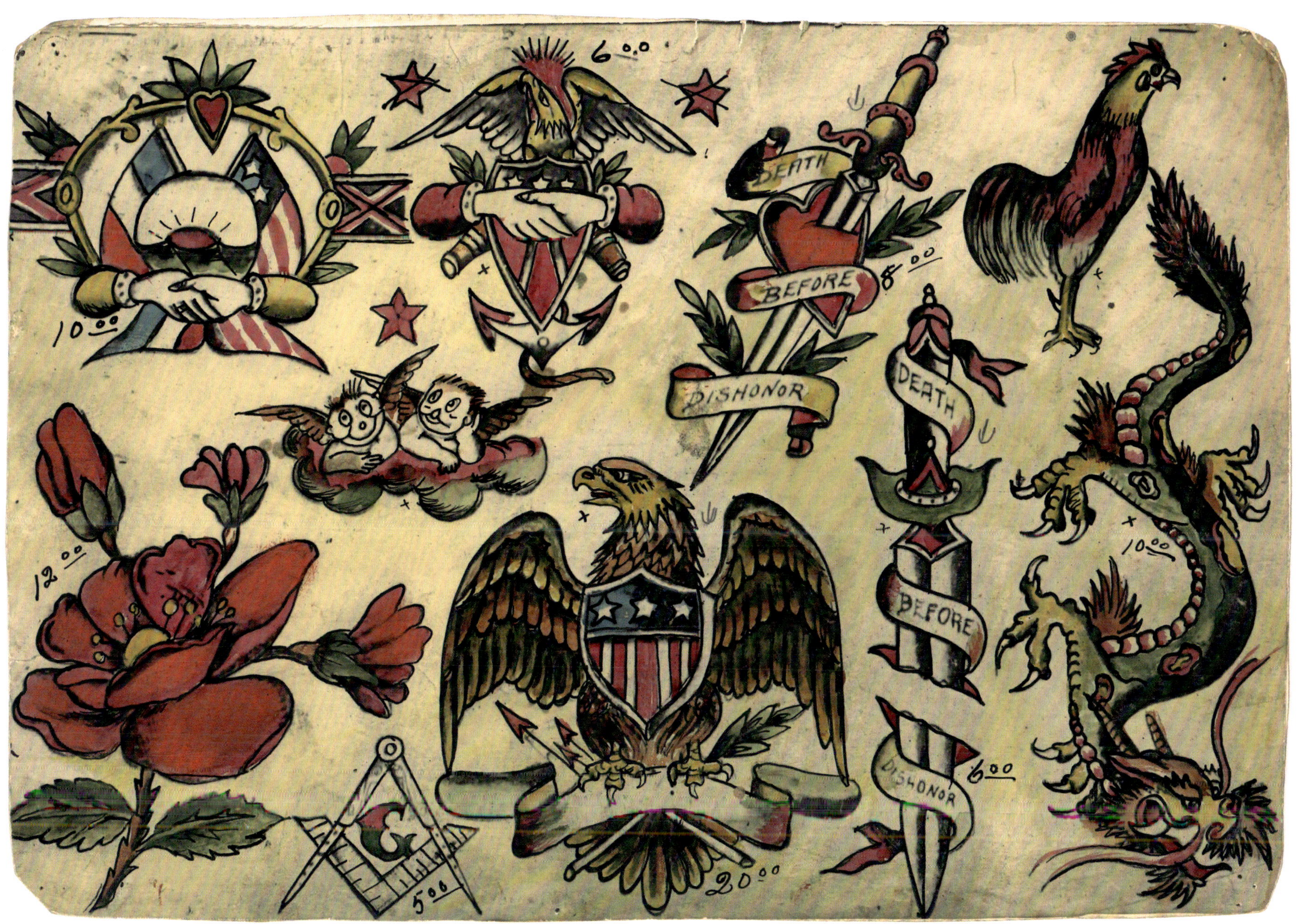
6.00
DEATH
BEFORE
DISHONOR
8.00
10.00
DEATH
BEFORE
DISHONOR
12.00
10.00
6.00
5.00
20.00

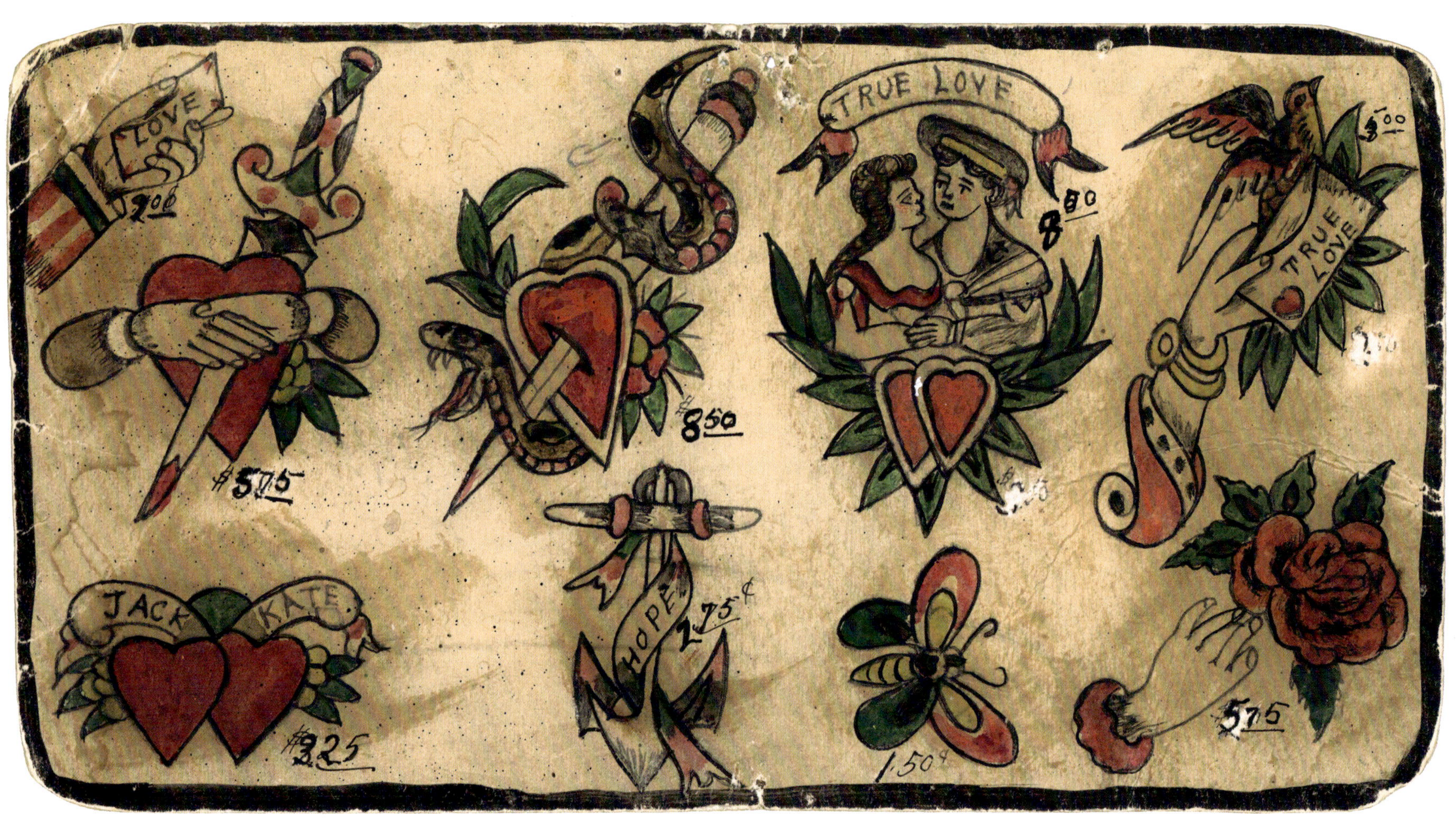

Flash by Gus Wagner

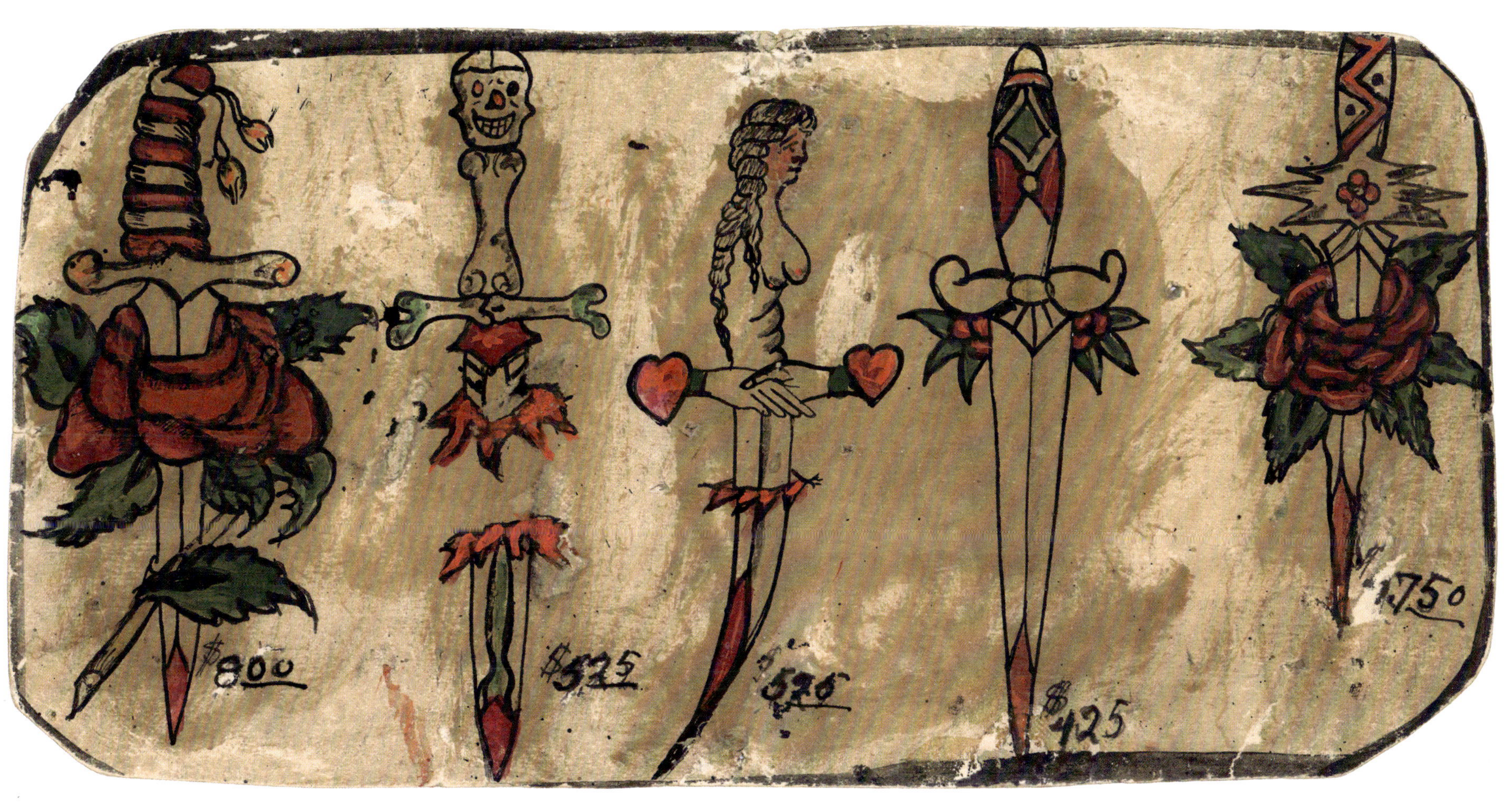

Flash by Gus Wagner

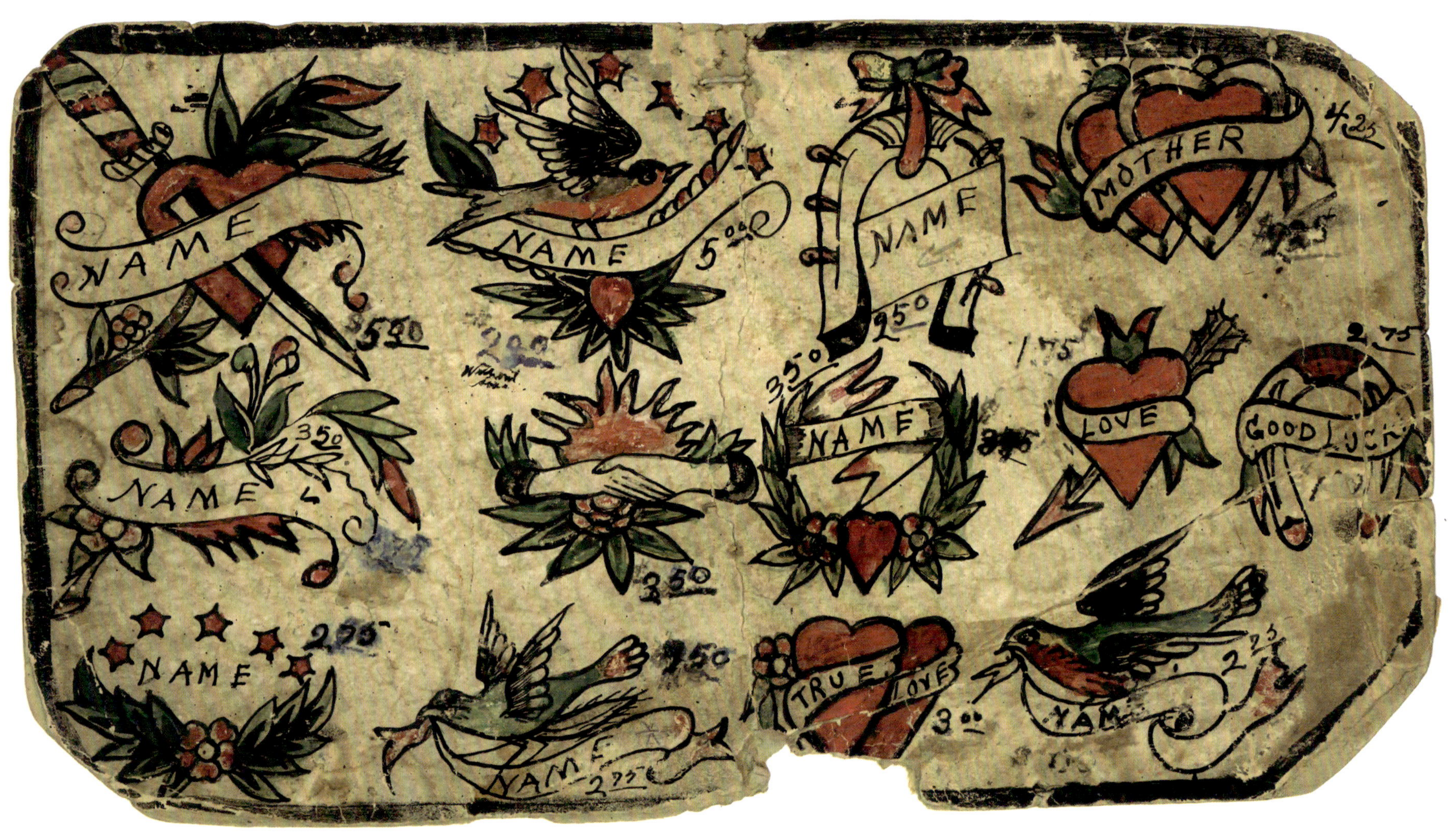

 Flash by Gus Wagner

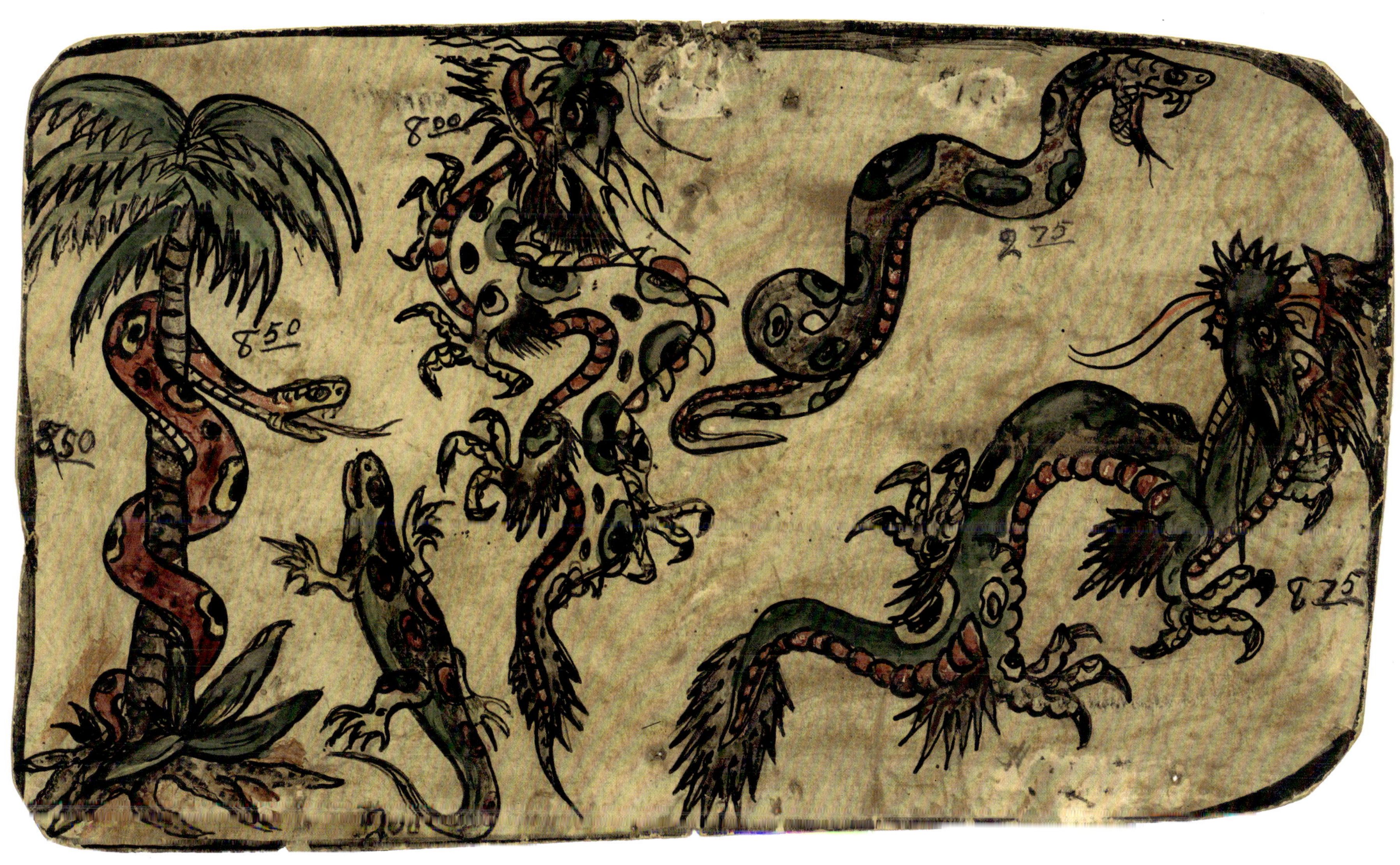

Flash by Gus Wagner

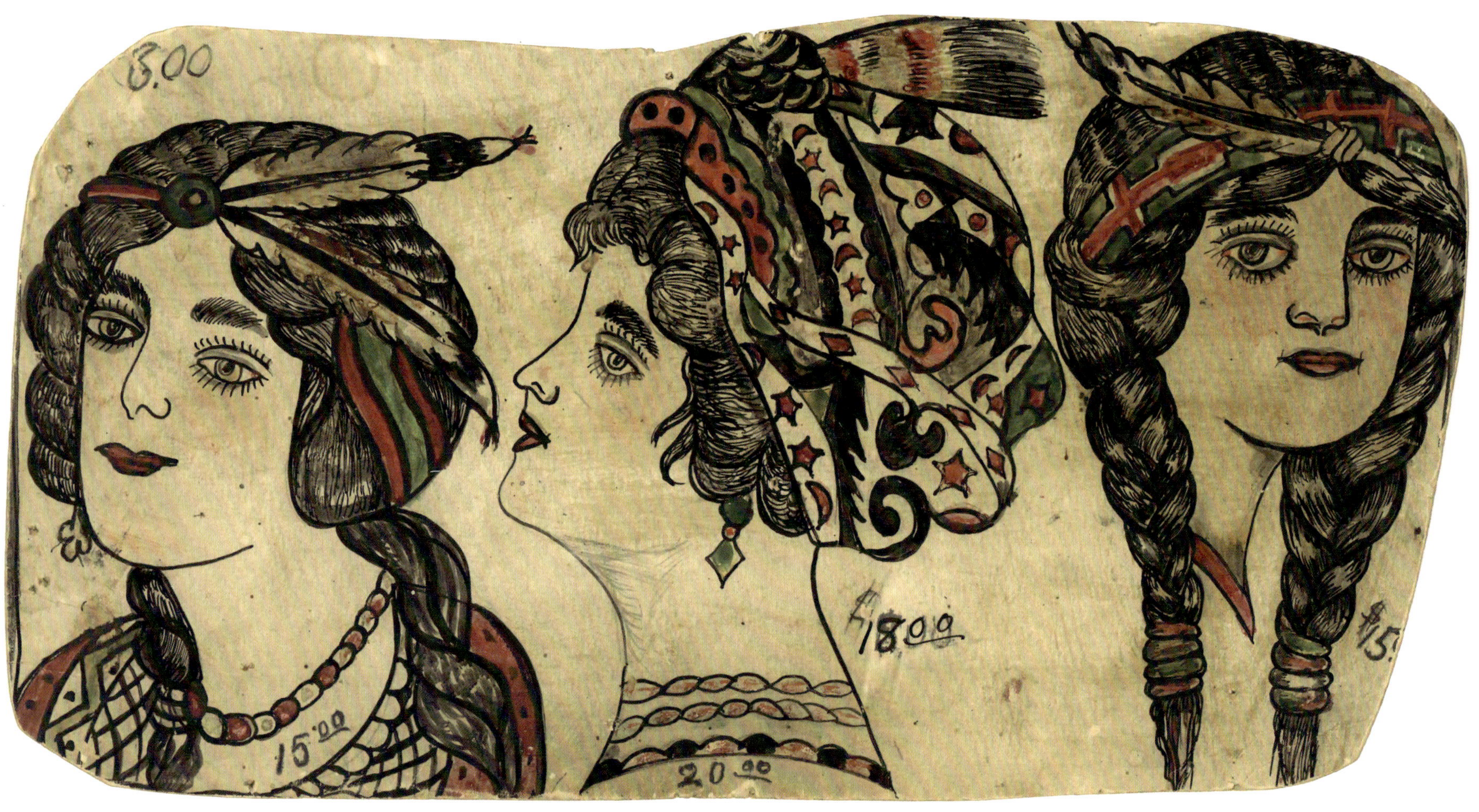

Flash by Gus Wagner

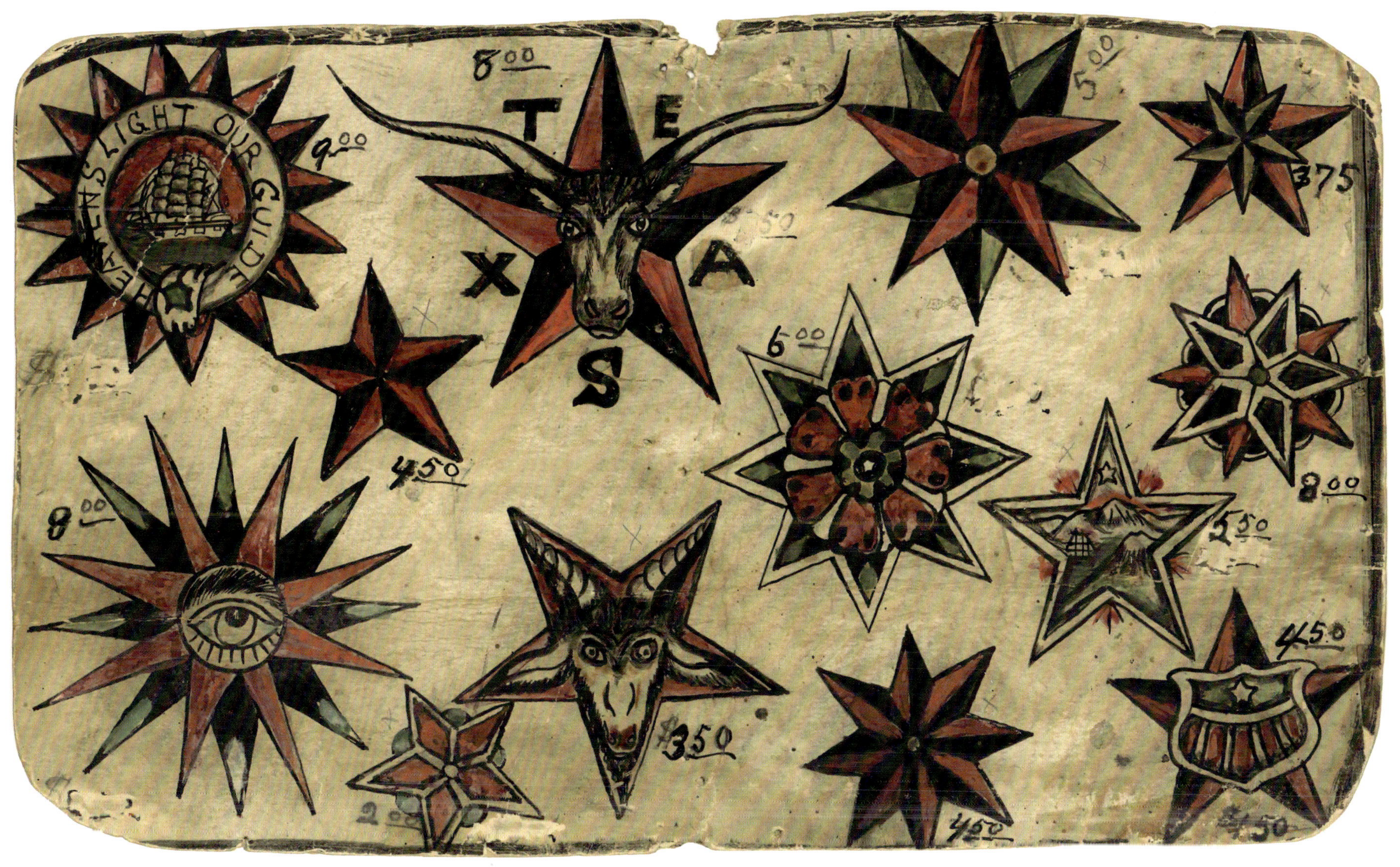
HEAVENS LIGHT OUR GUIDE
9.00
8.00
T E X A S
5.00
375
4.50
6.00
8.00
550
450
350
4.50

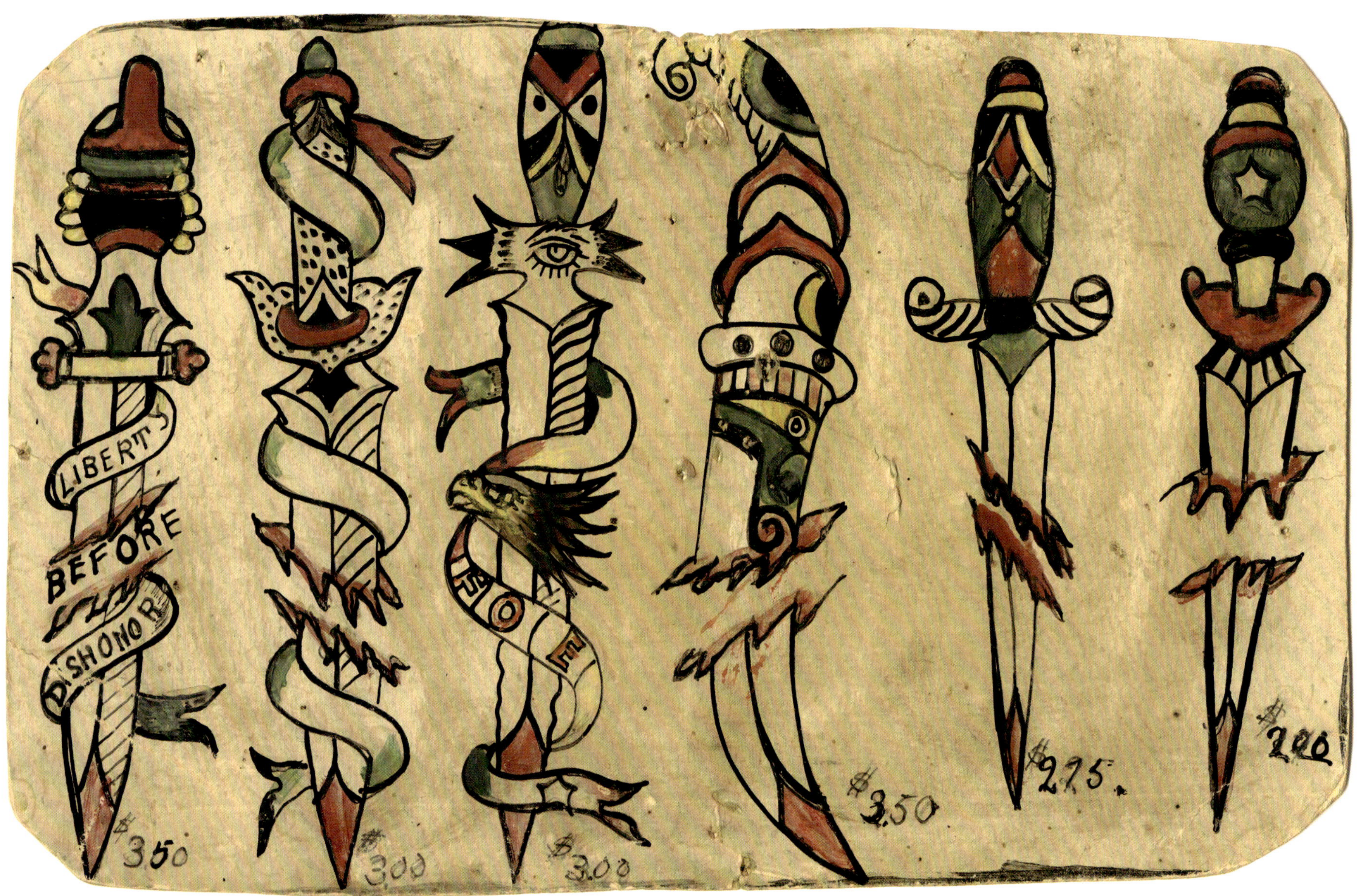

Flash by Gus Wagner

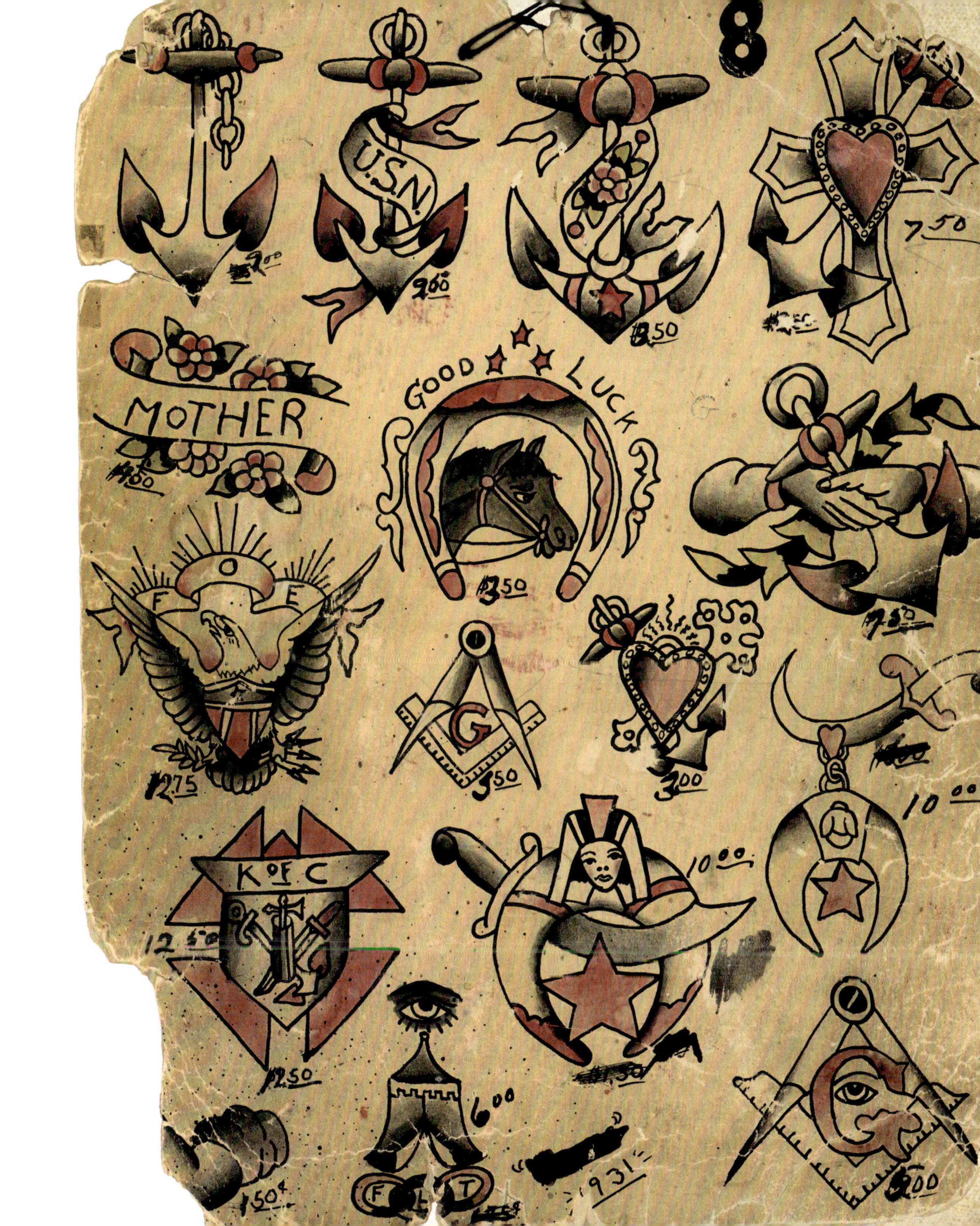
8
U.S.N.
MOTHER
GOOD LUCK
F O E
K of C
1931

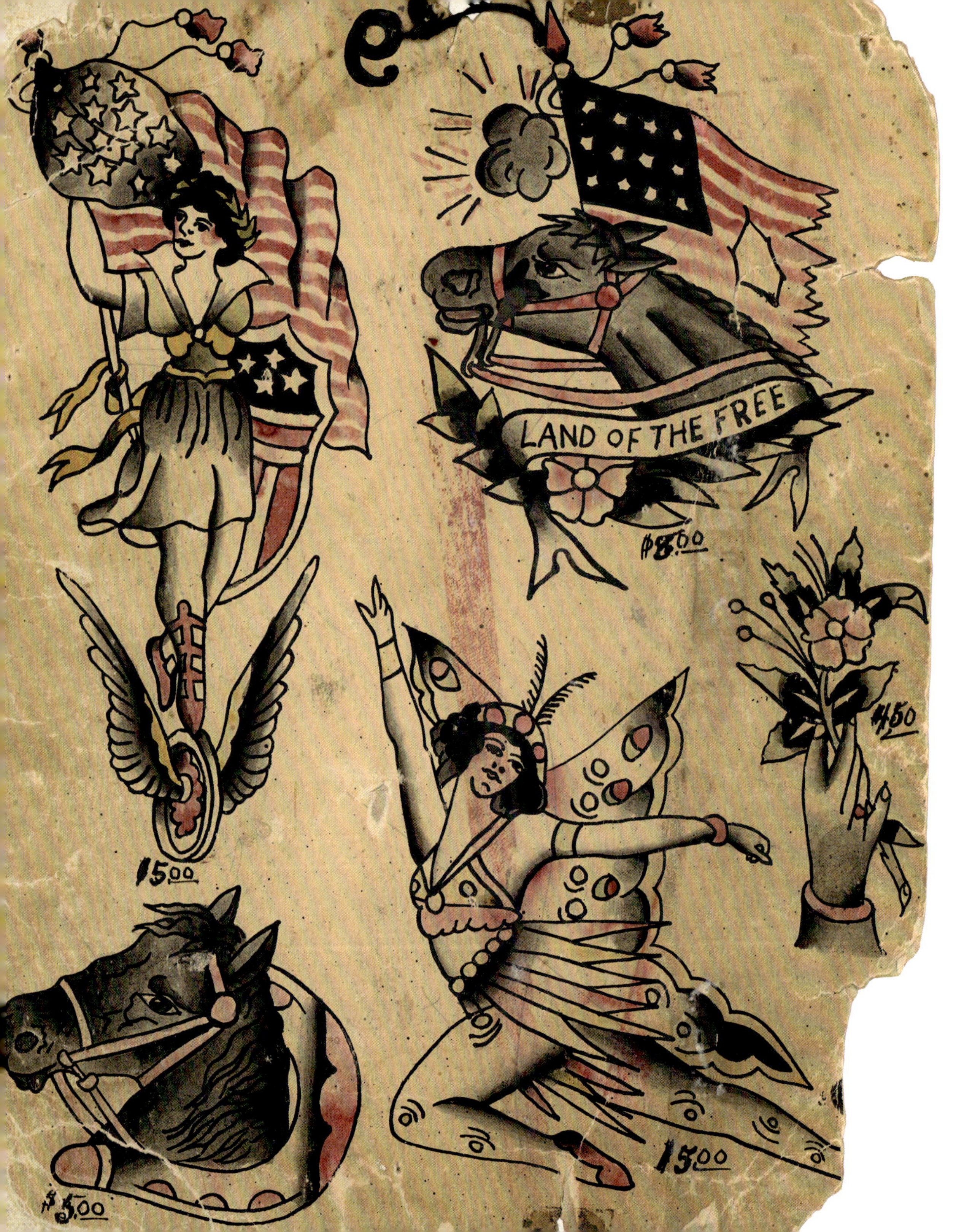
LAND OF THE FREE
15.00
$4.50
15.00

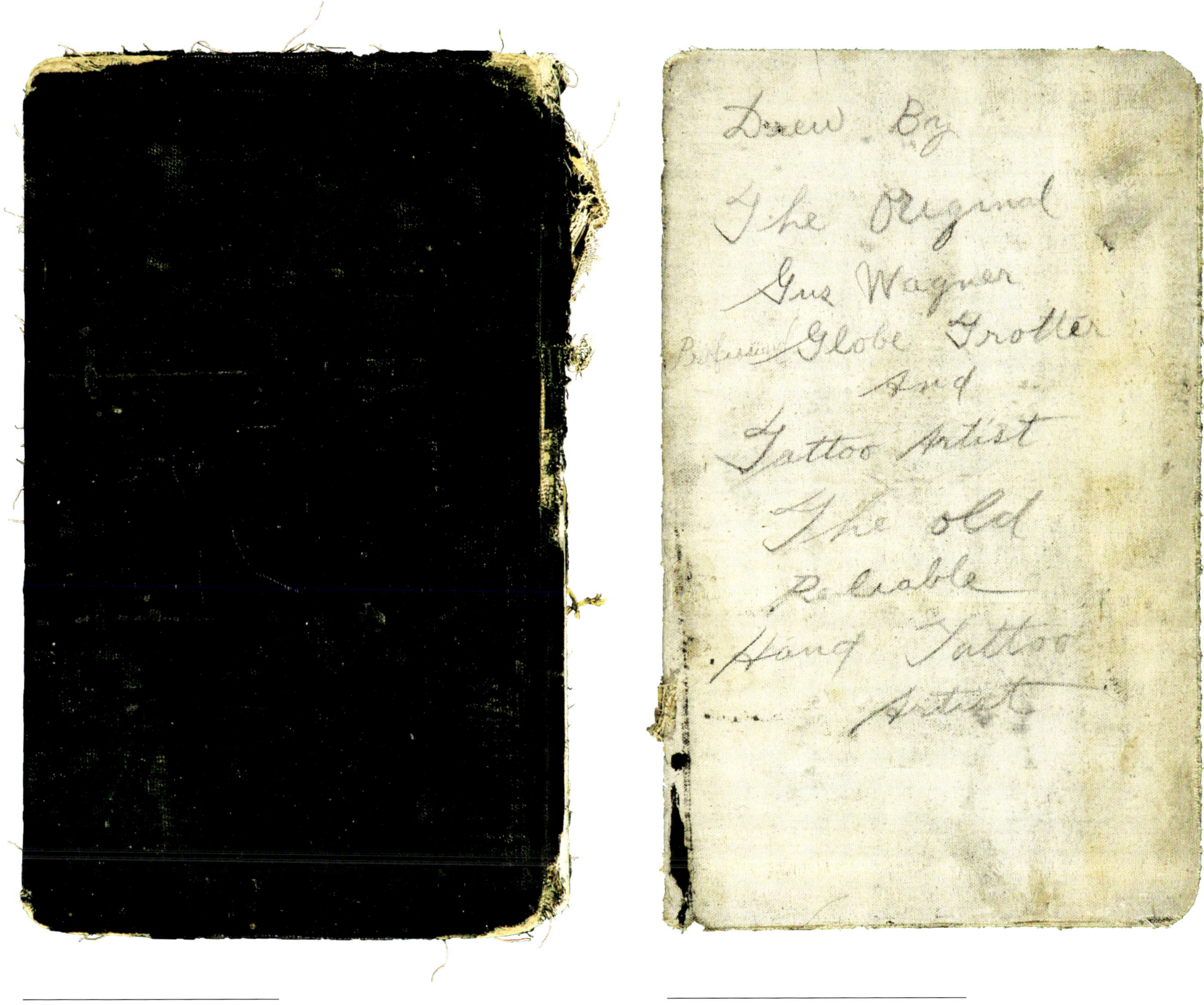

Gus Wagner flash book, cover

Gus Wagner flash book, inside page

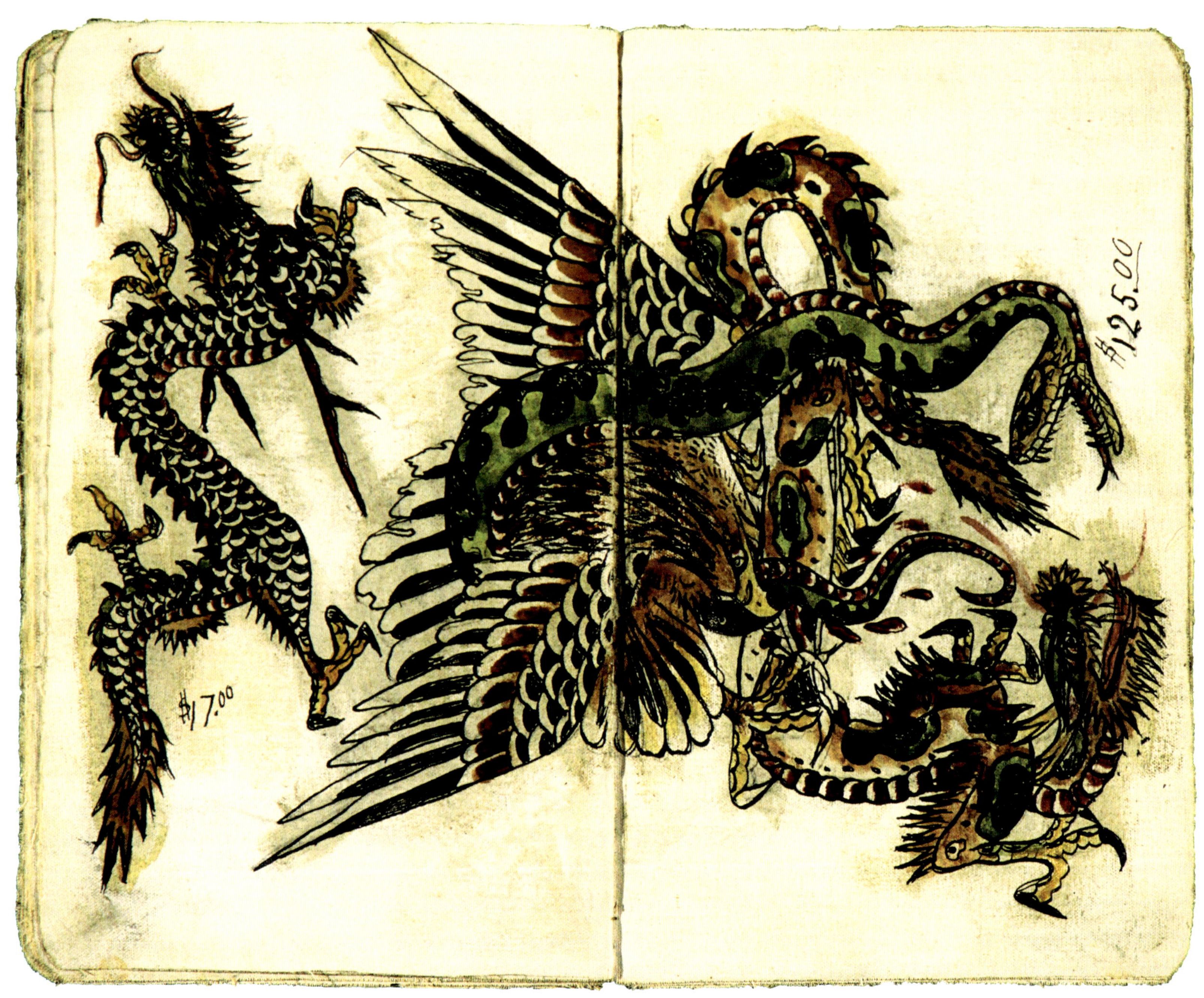

Gus Wagner flash book

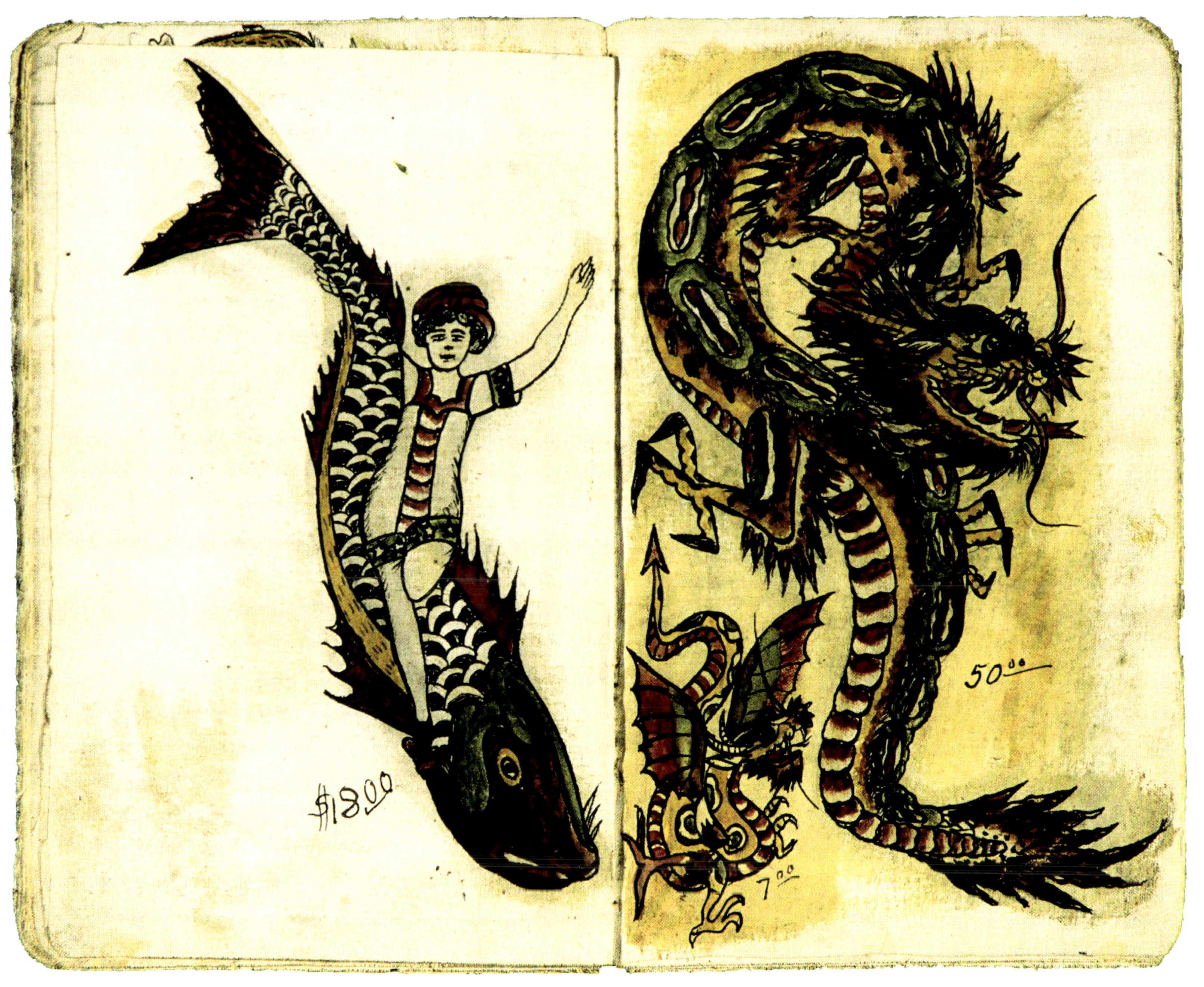
$18.00
50.00
7.00

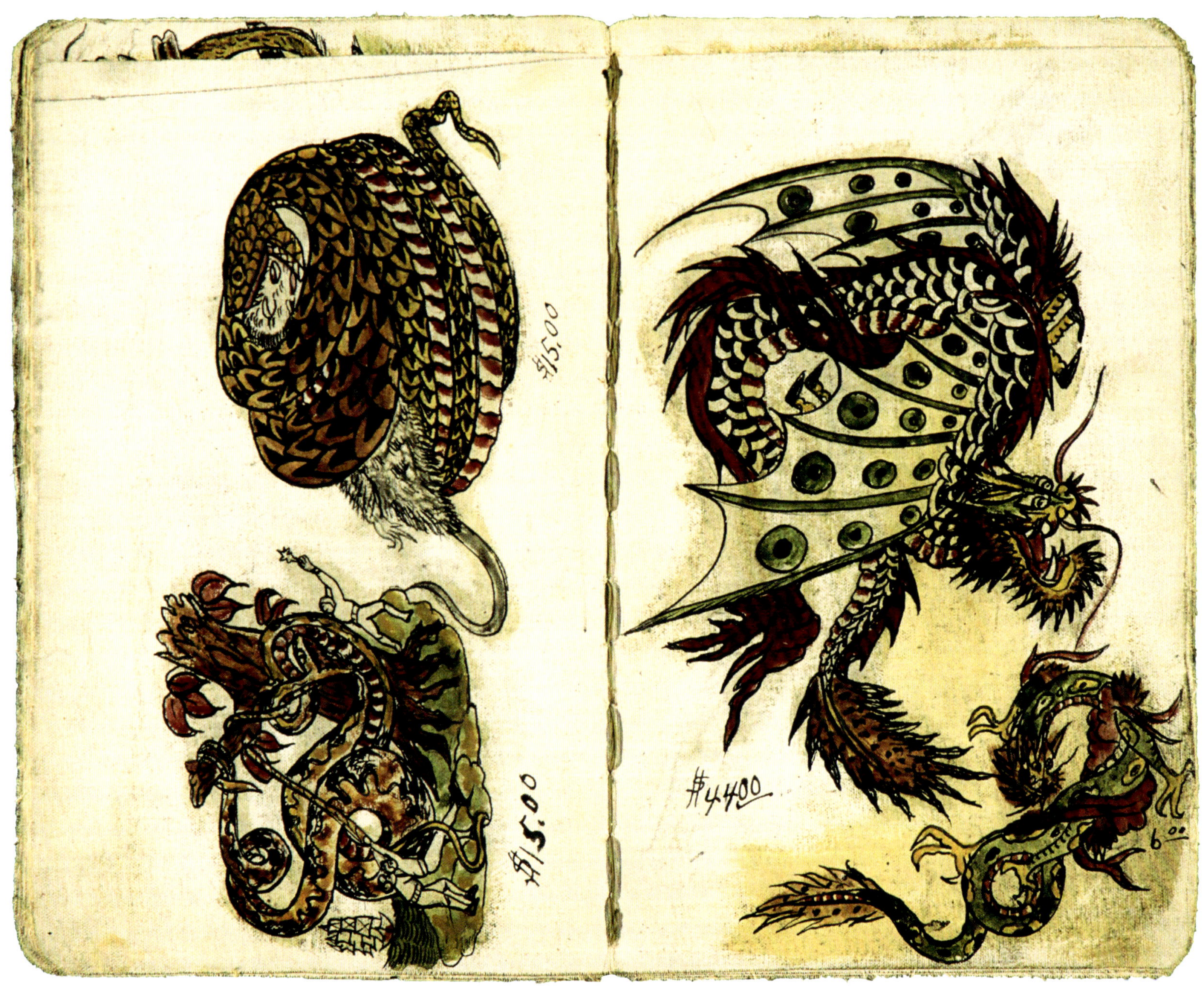

Gus Wagner flash book

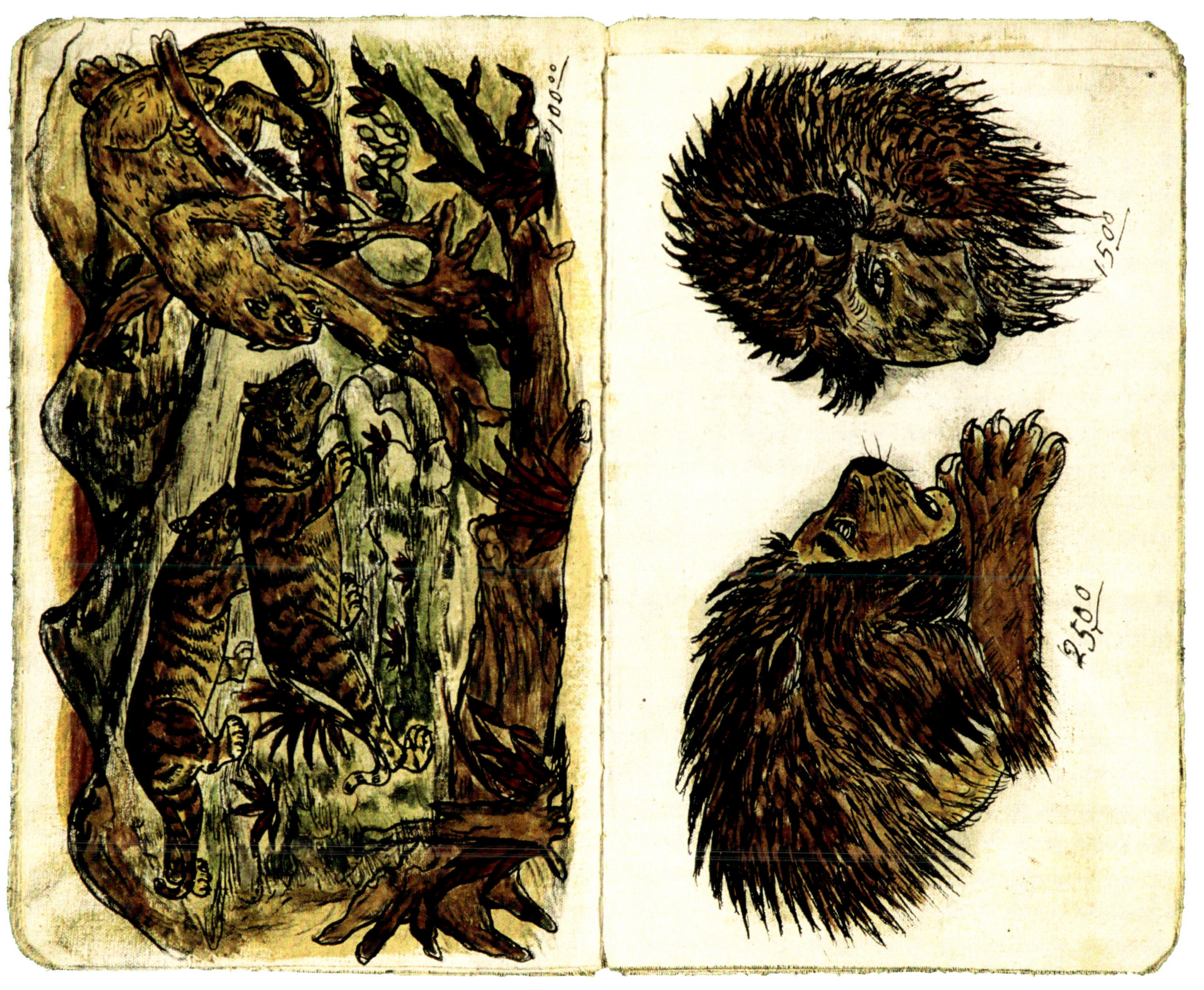
1500
2500

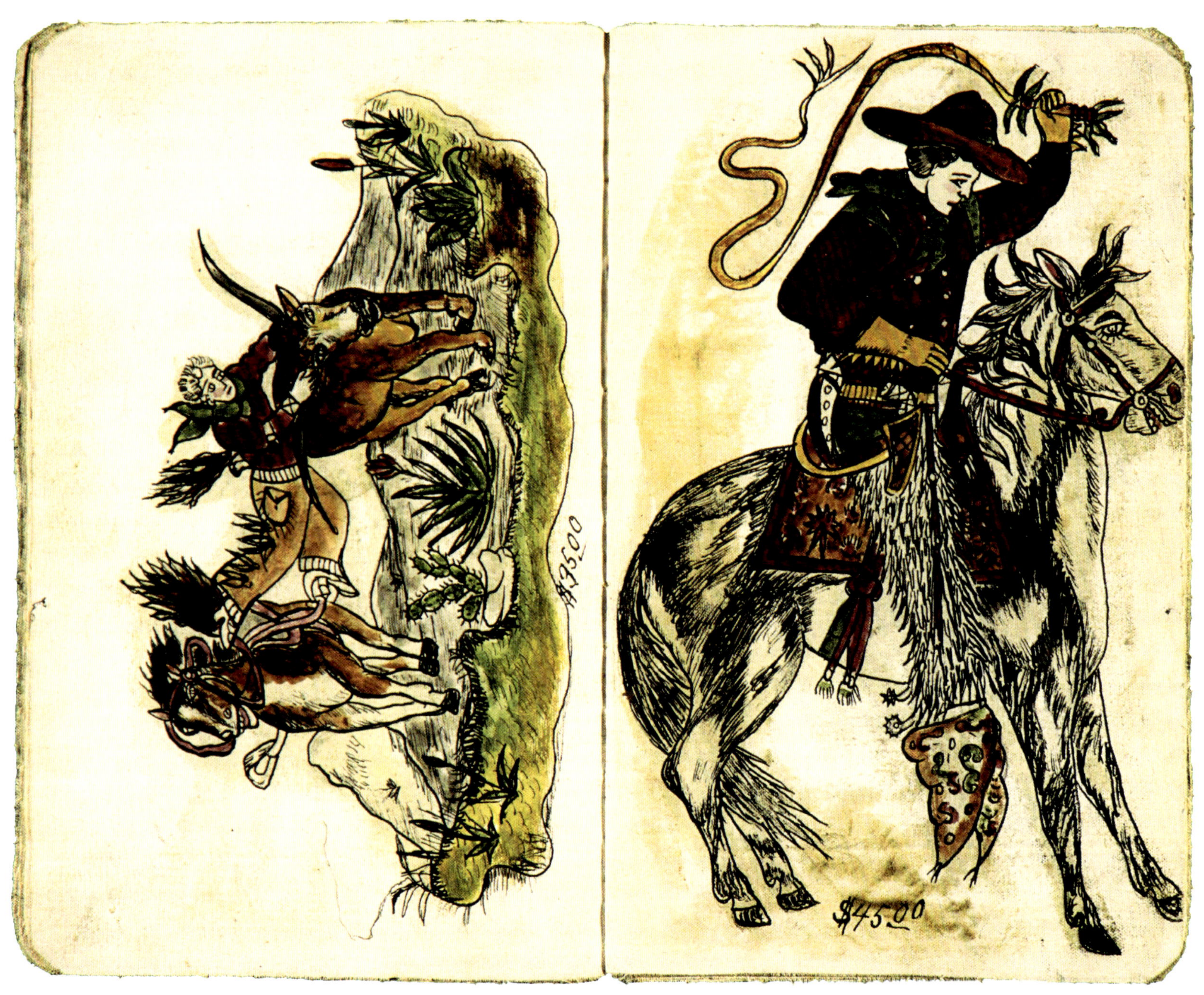

Gus Wagner flash book

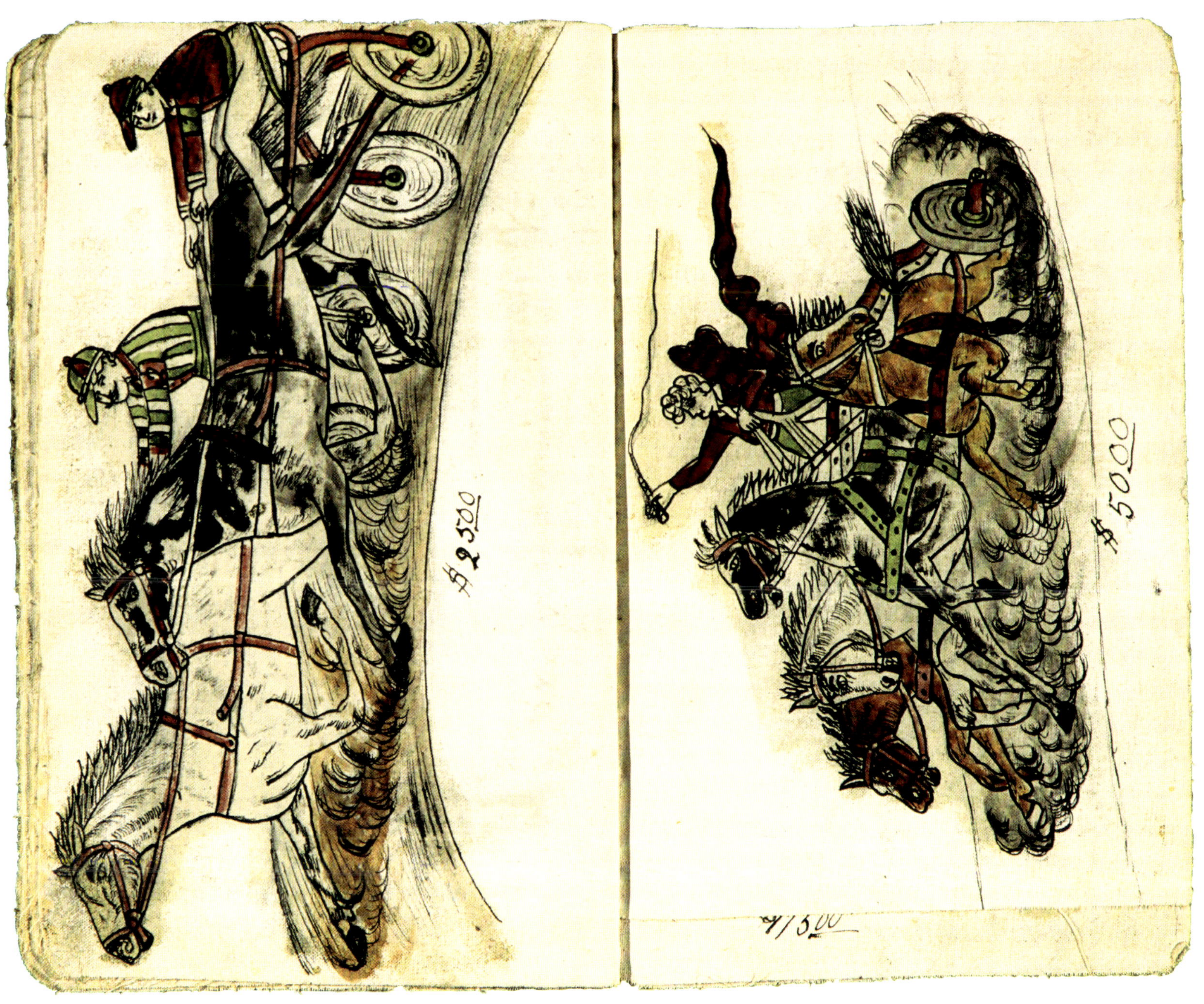
$25.00
$50.00
$75.00

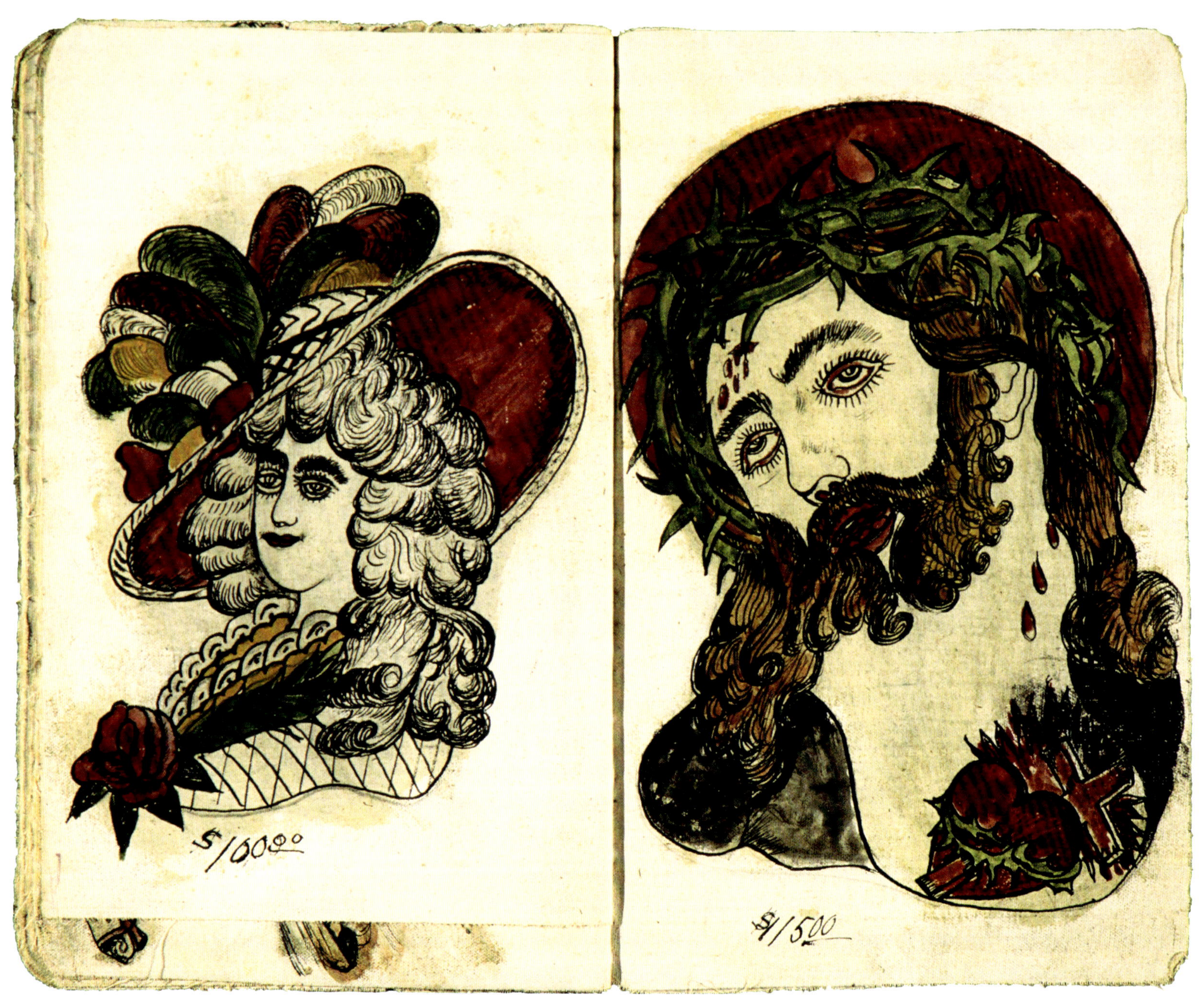

Gus Wagner flash book

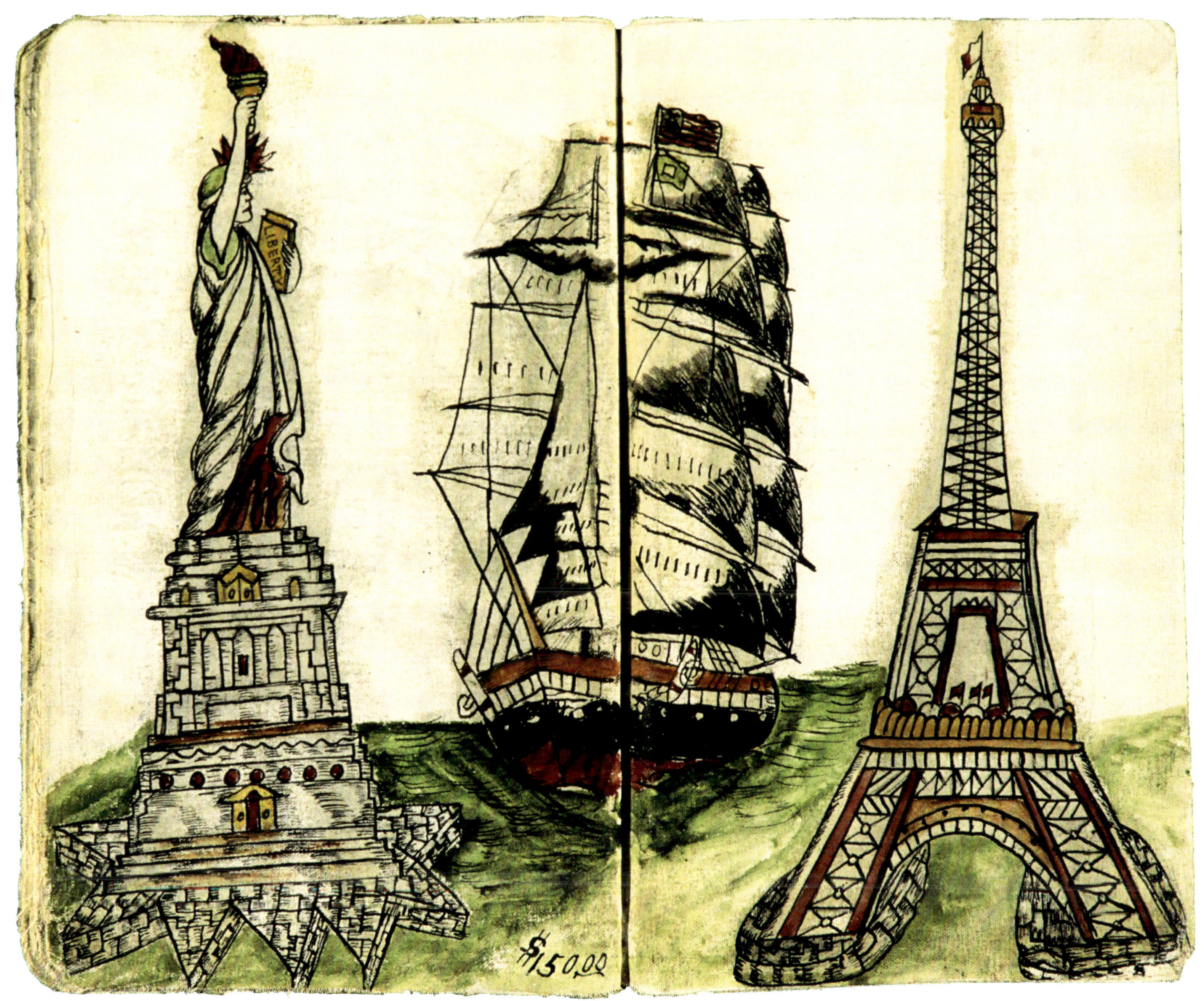

Flash by Gus Wagner

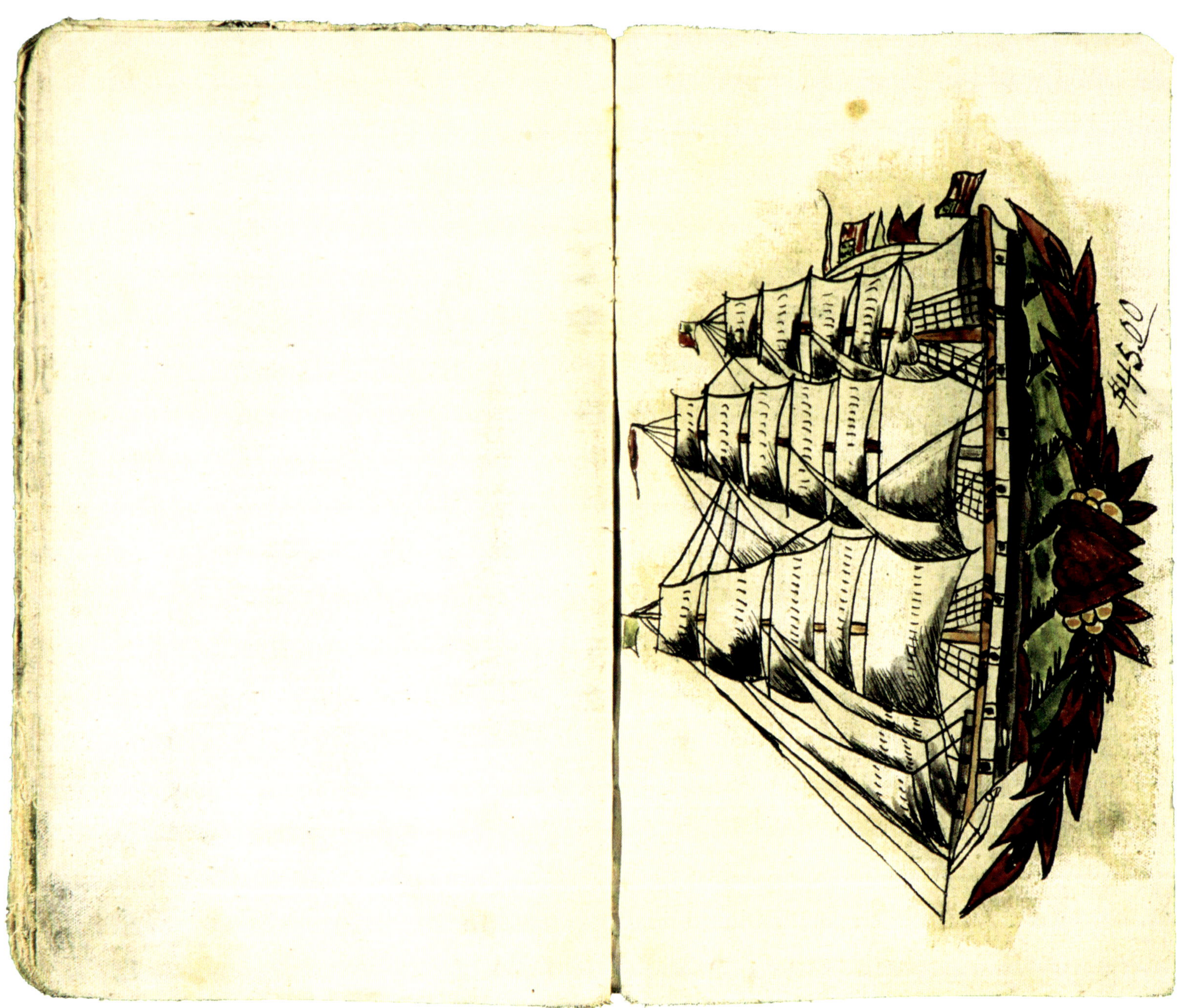

Gus Wagner flash book

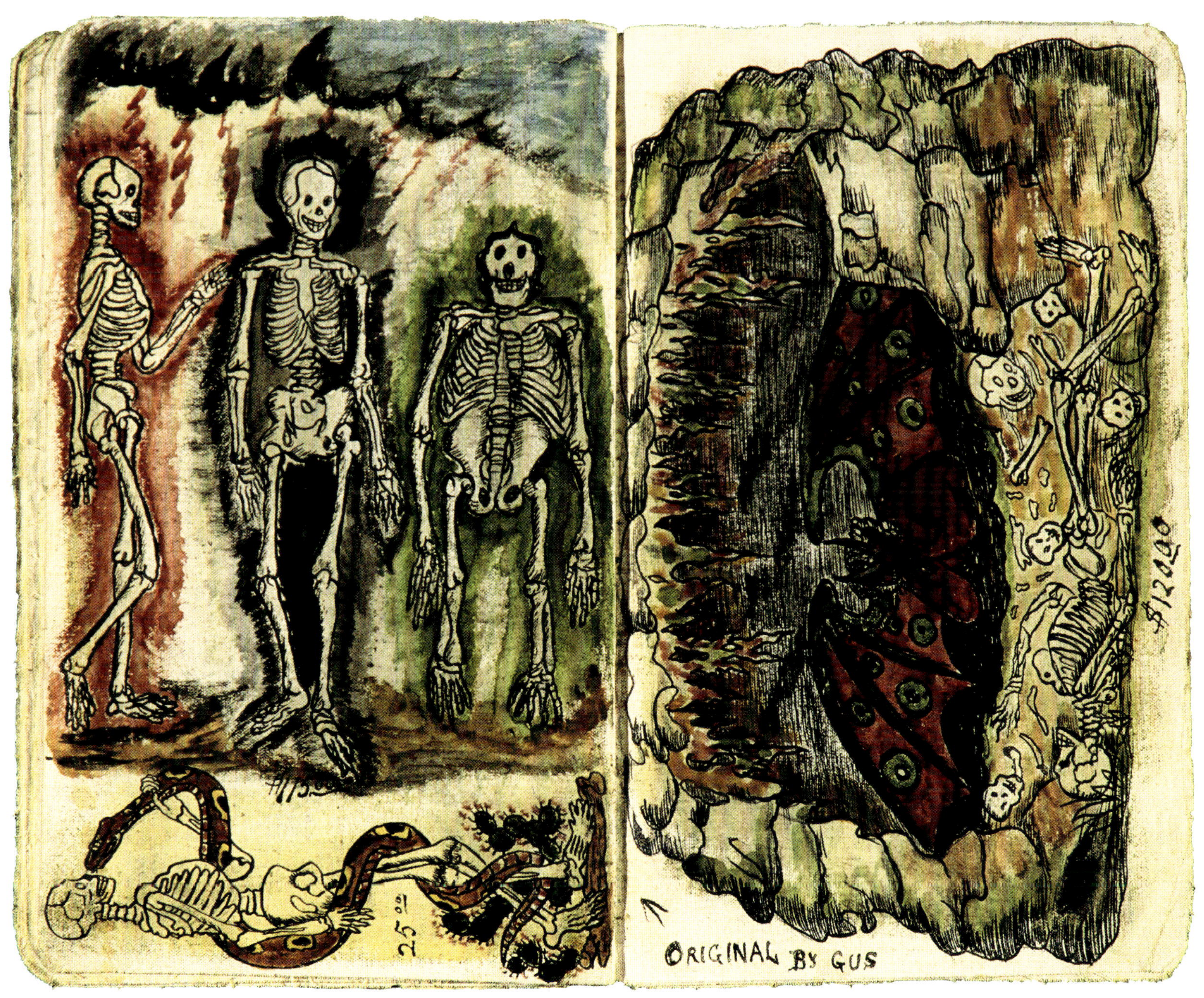
ORIGINAL BY GUS

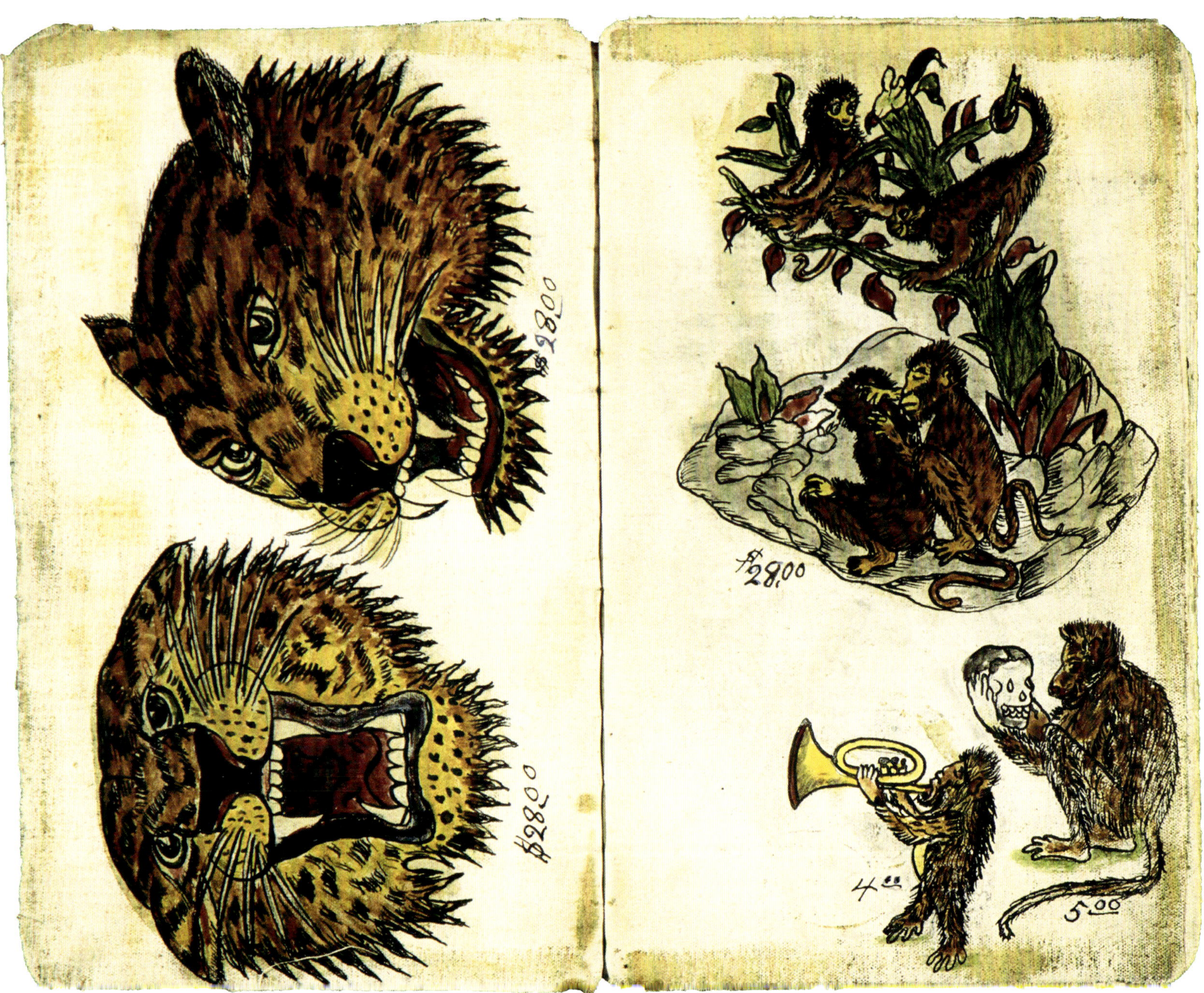

Gus Wagner flash book

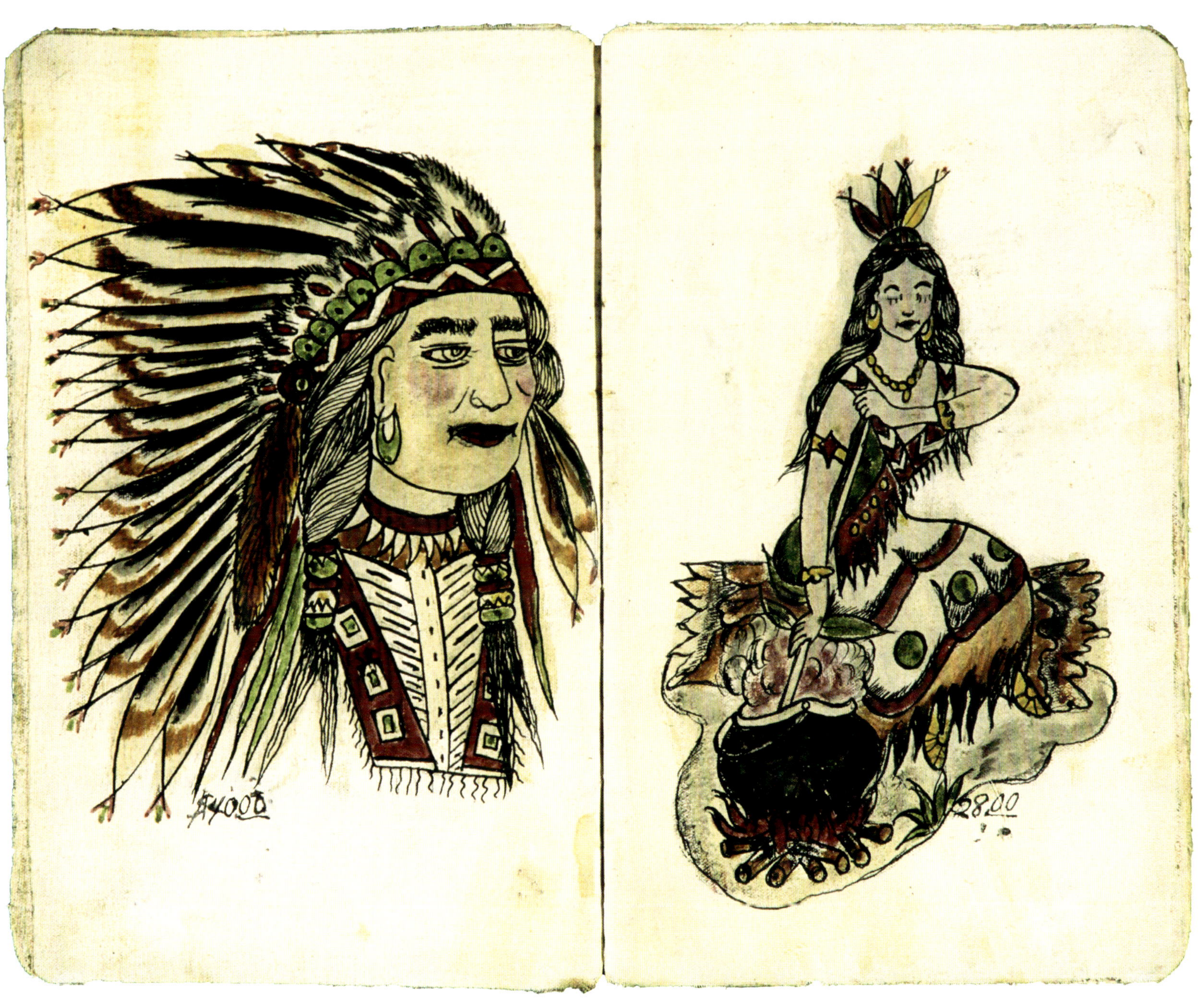
$40.00
28.00

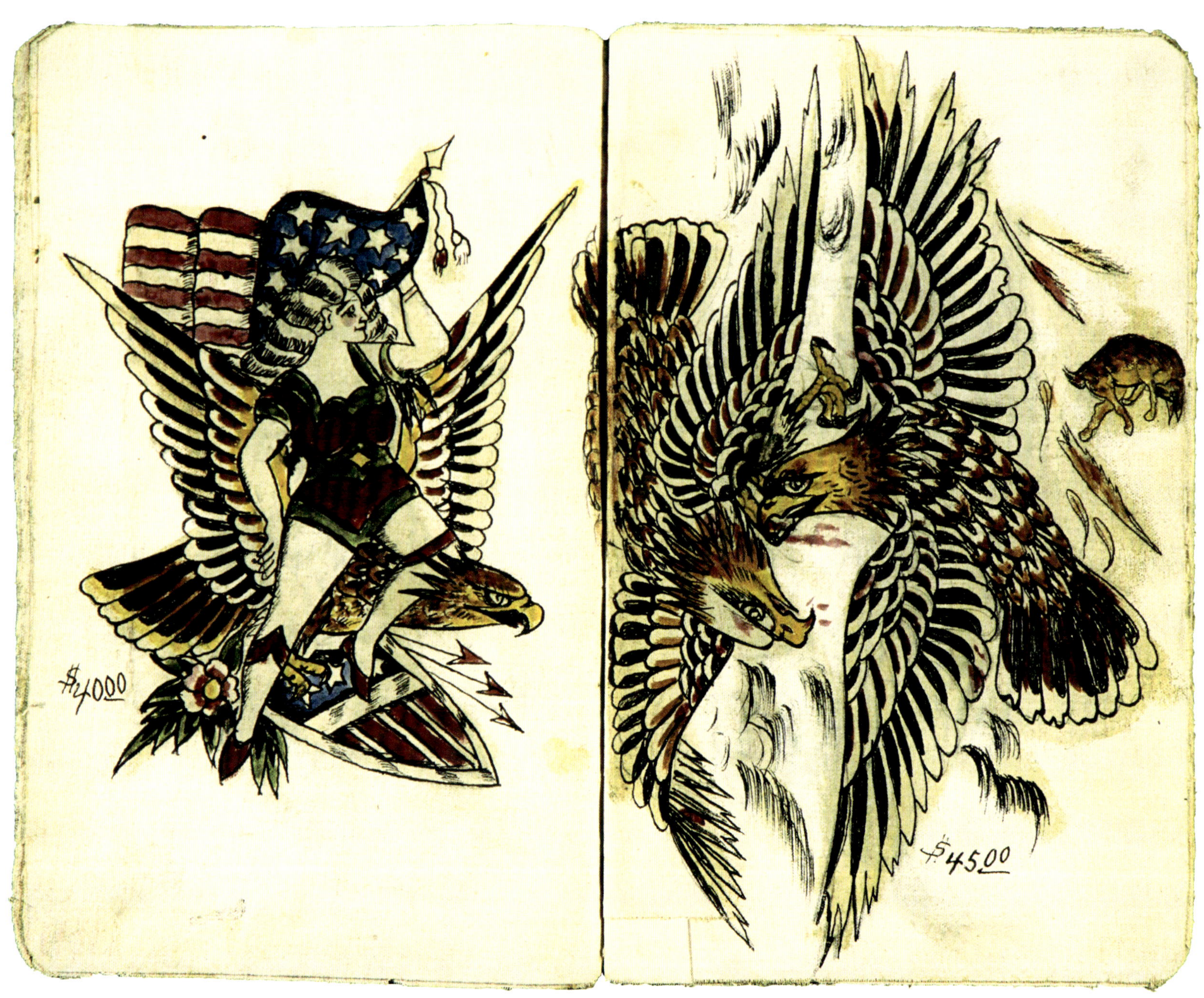

Gus Wagner flash book

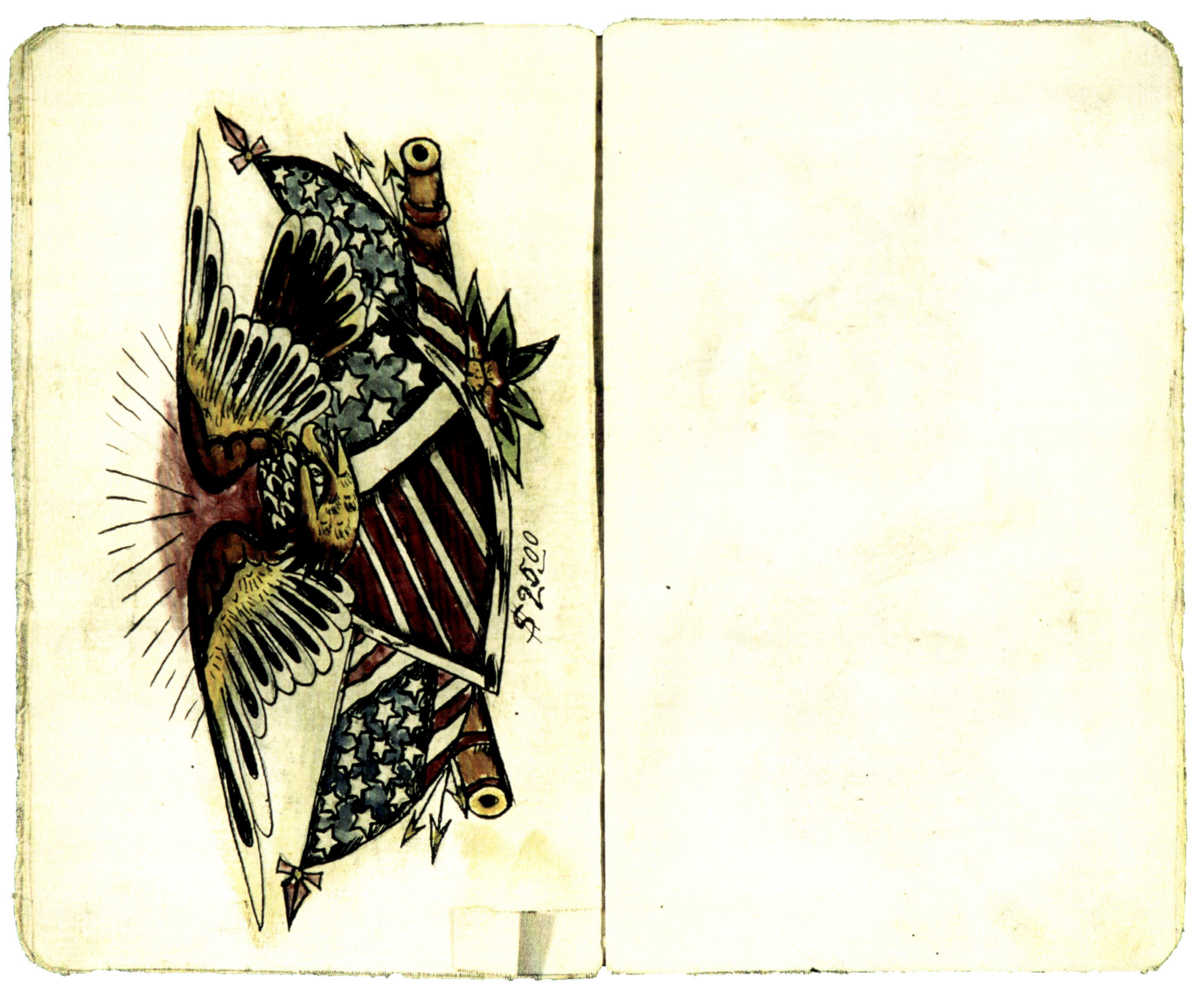
$25.00

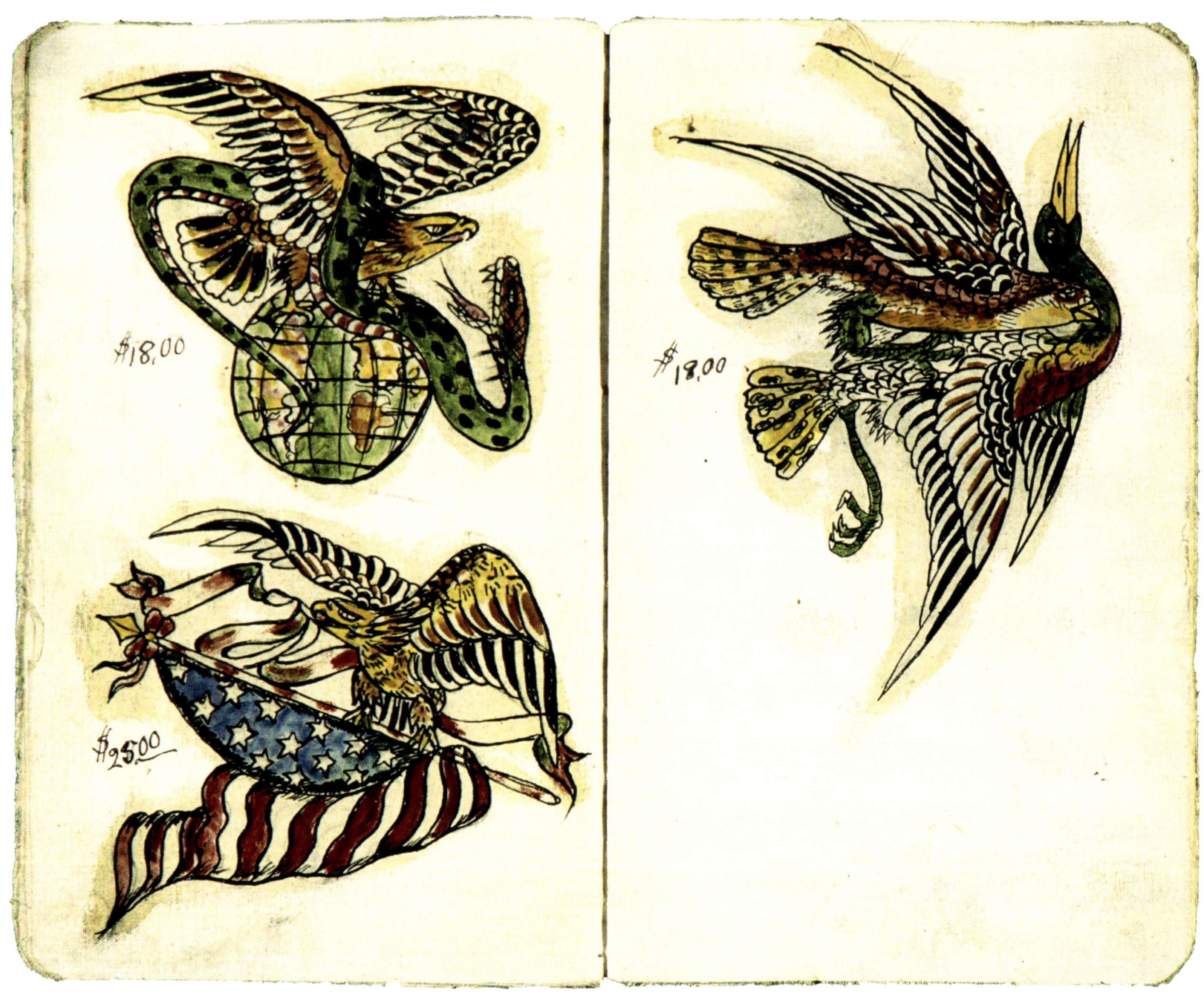

Gus Wagner flash book

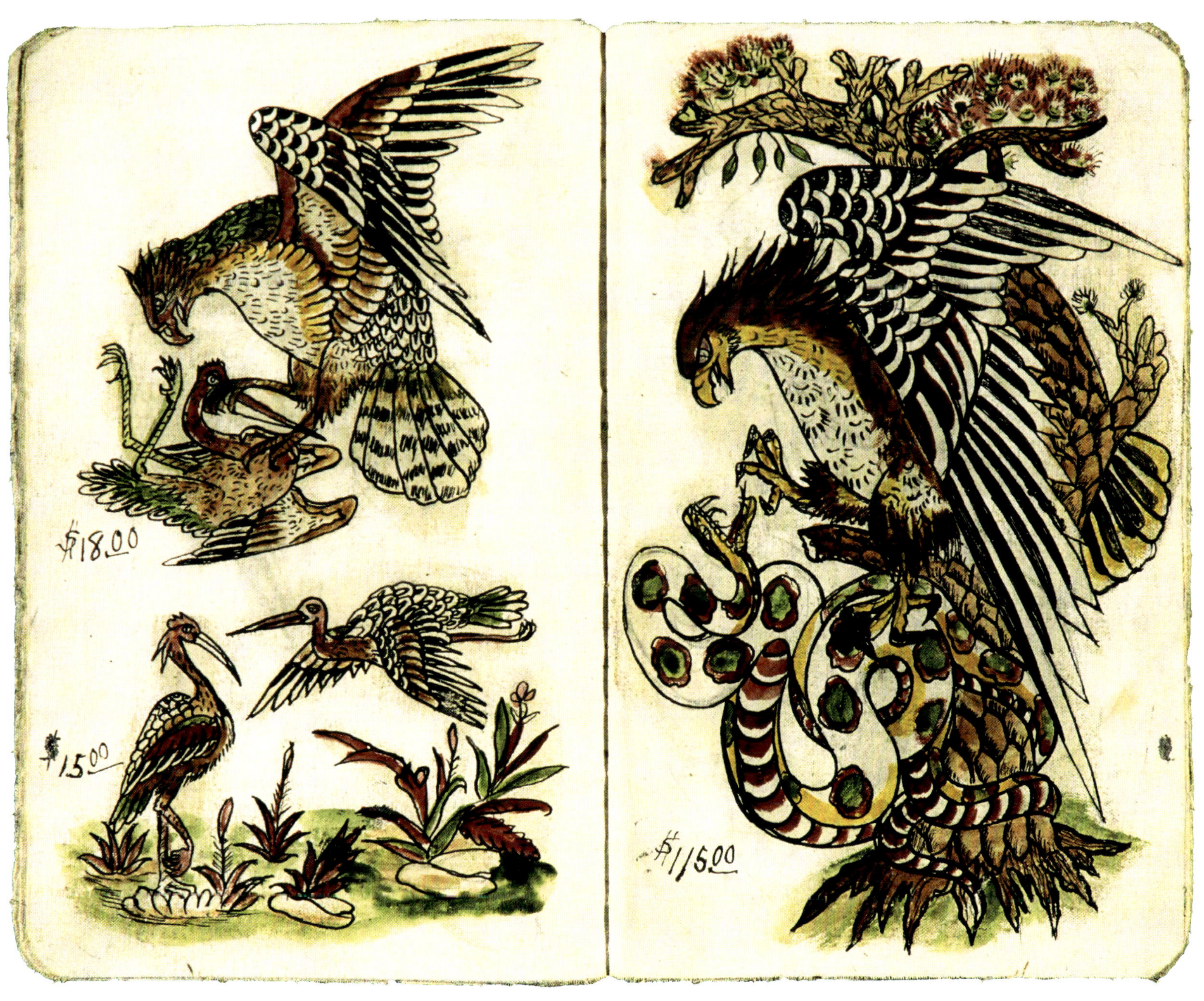
$18.00
$15.00
$11.50

GUS WAGNER'S TATTOO INSTRUMENTS

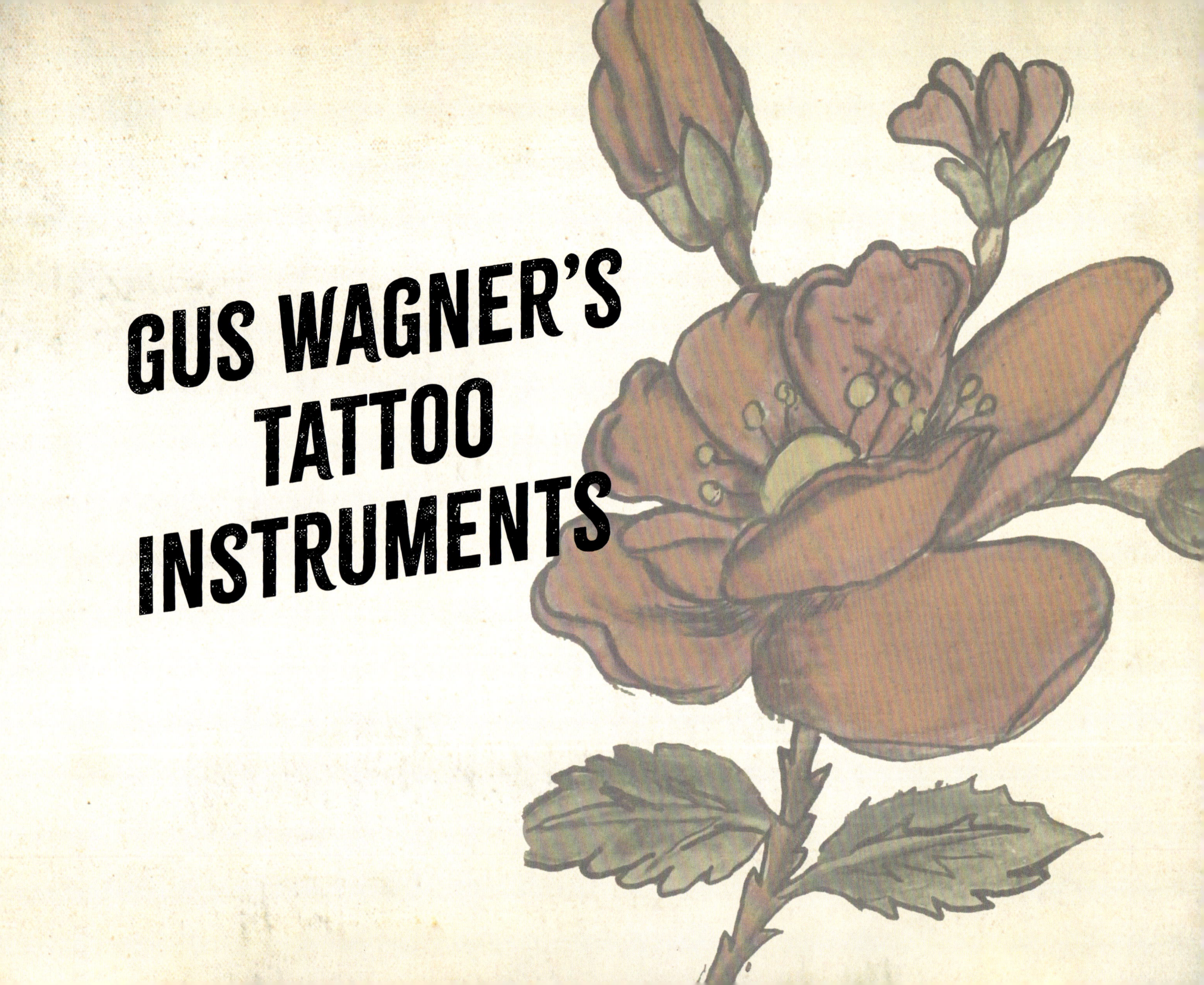

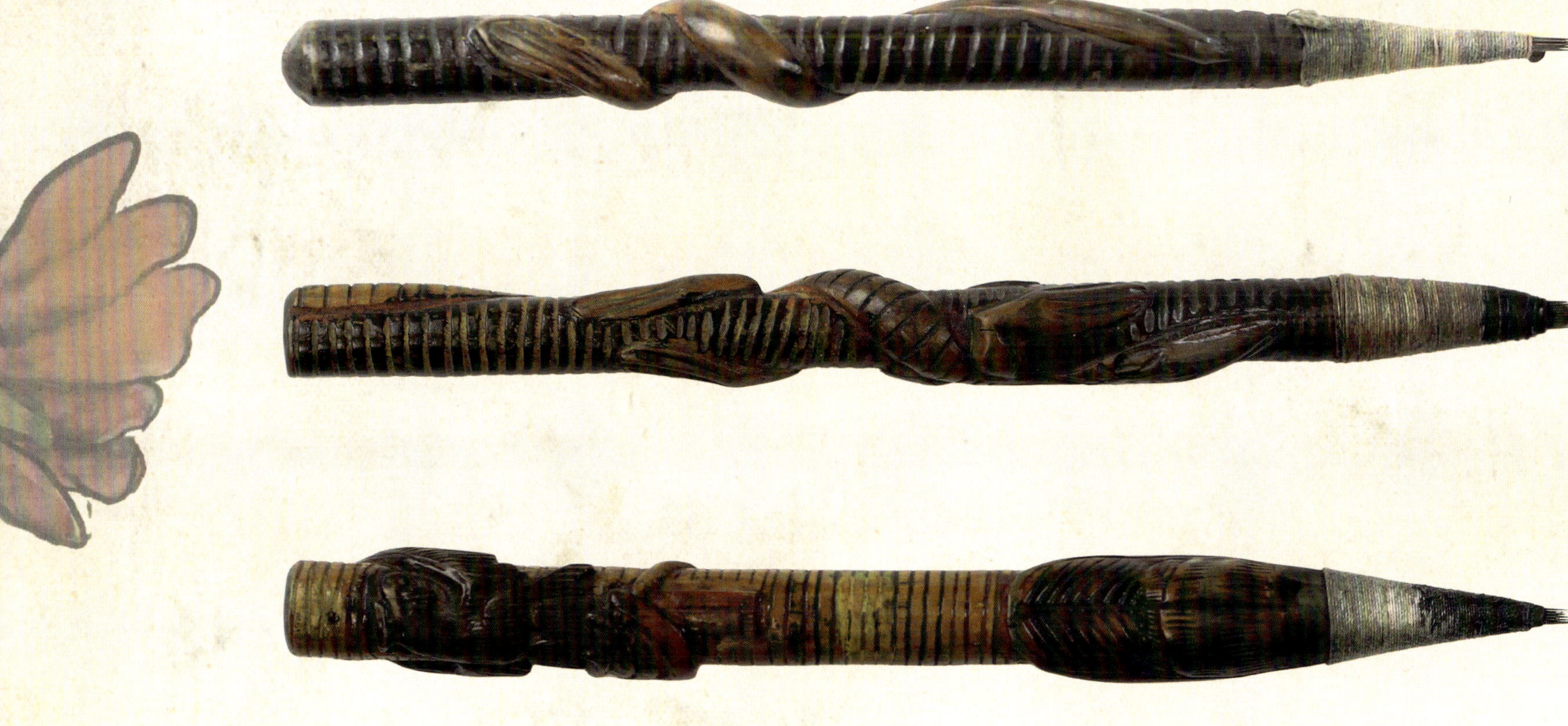

Hand-tattooing instruments carved by Gus Wagner

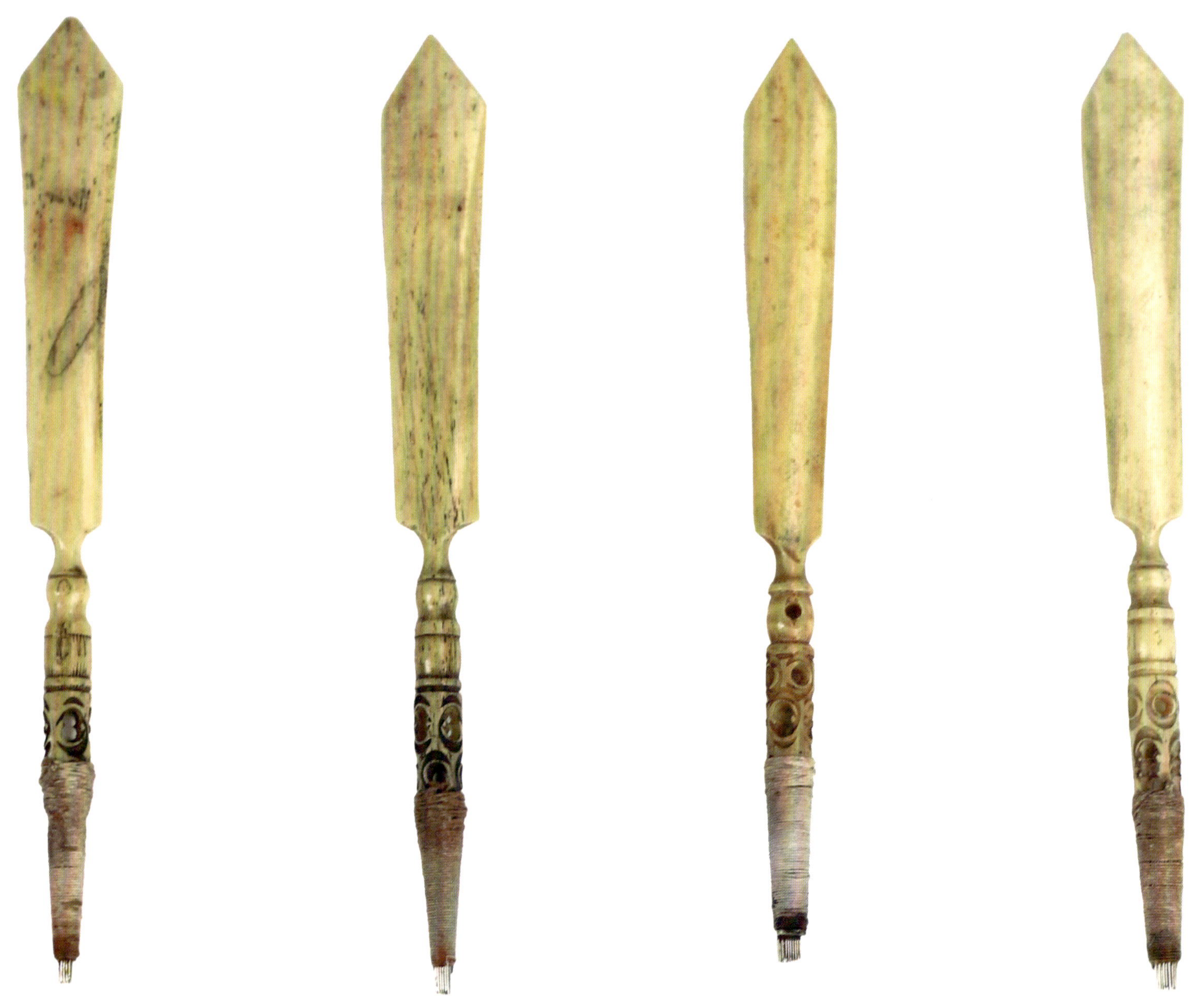

Hand-tattooing instruments carved by Gus Wagner

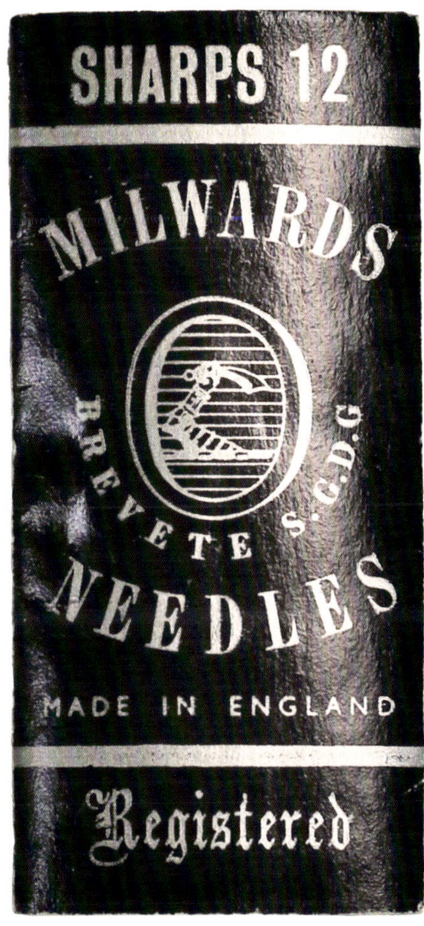

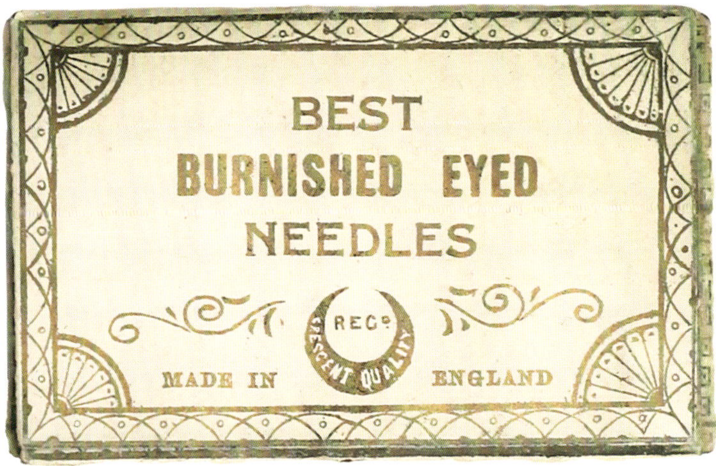

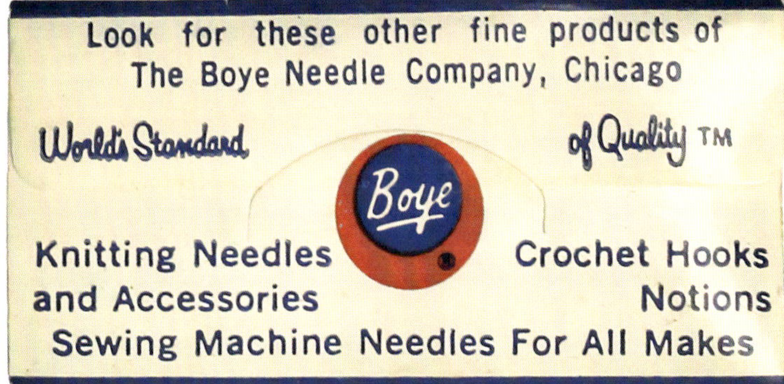

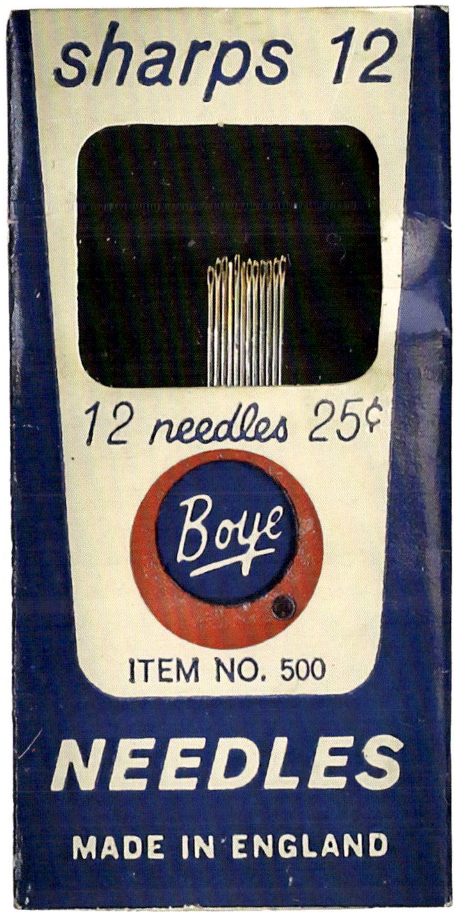

Gus Wagner's tattoo needles

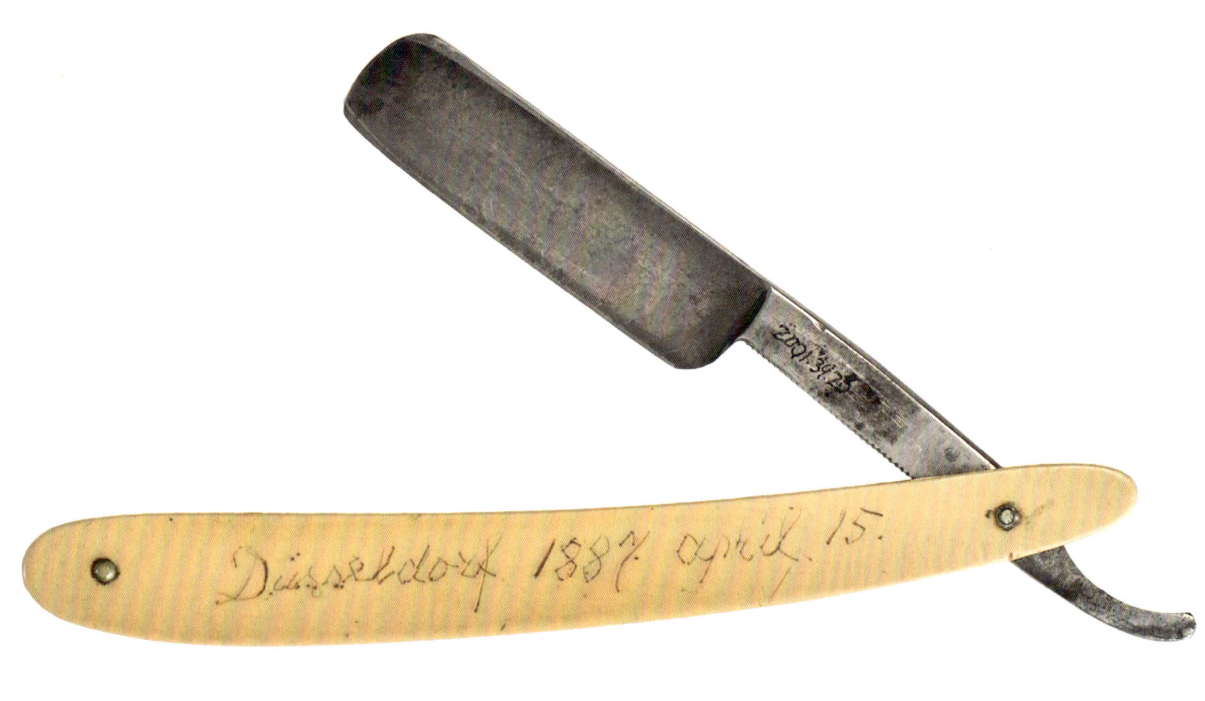

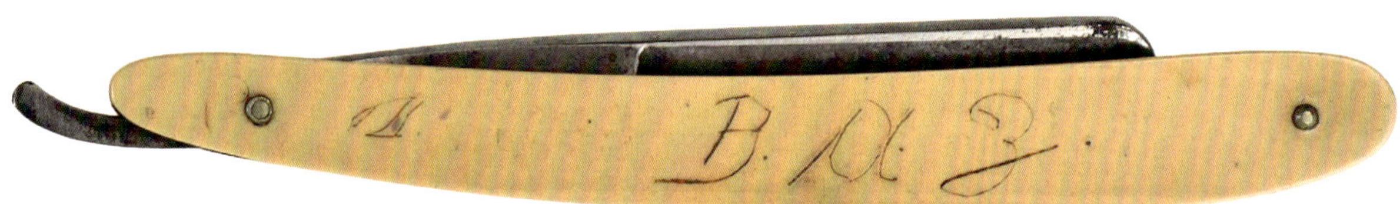

One of Gus Wagner's knives

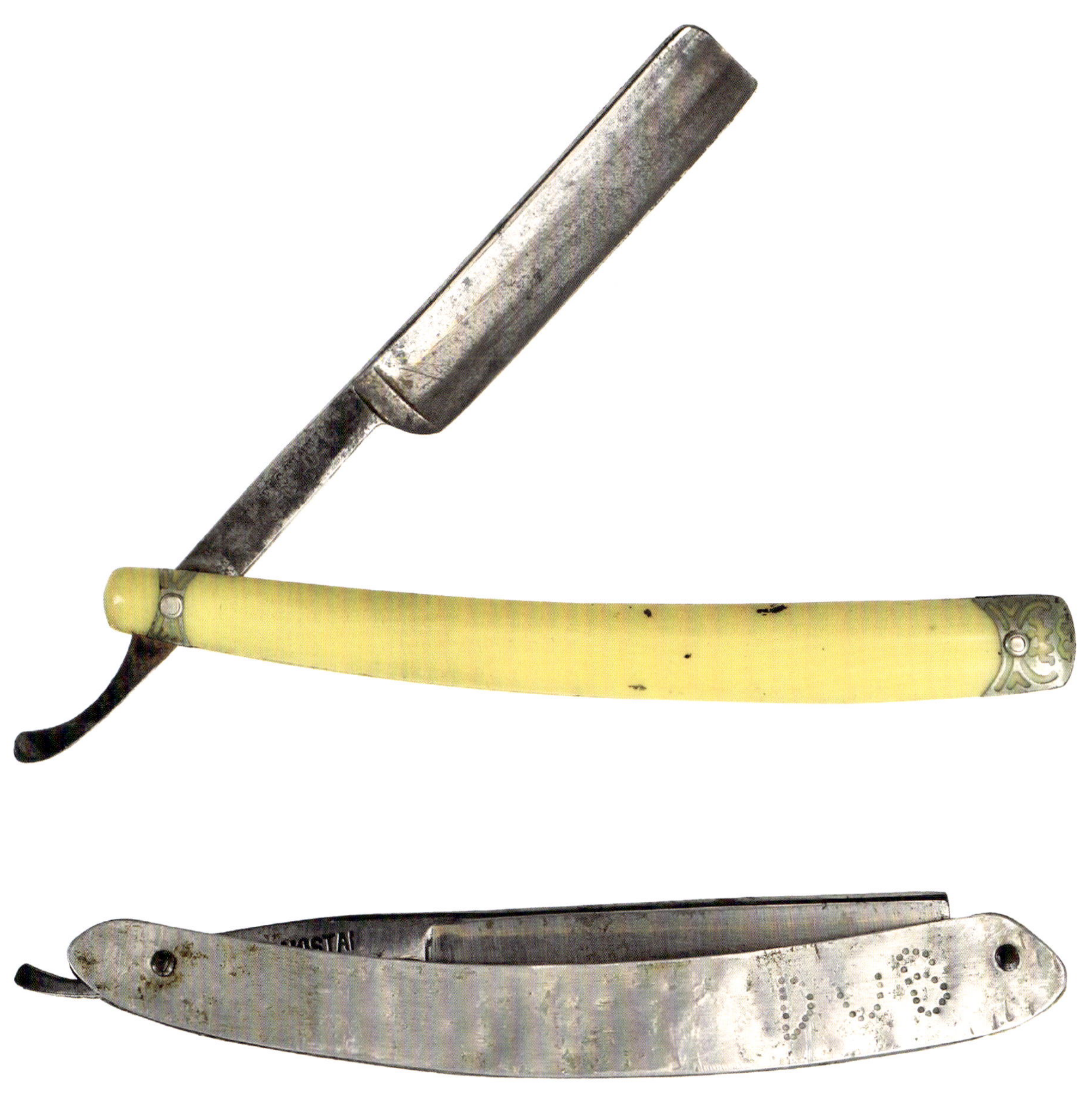

Two of Gus Wagner's knives

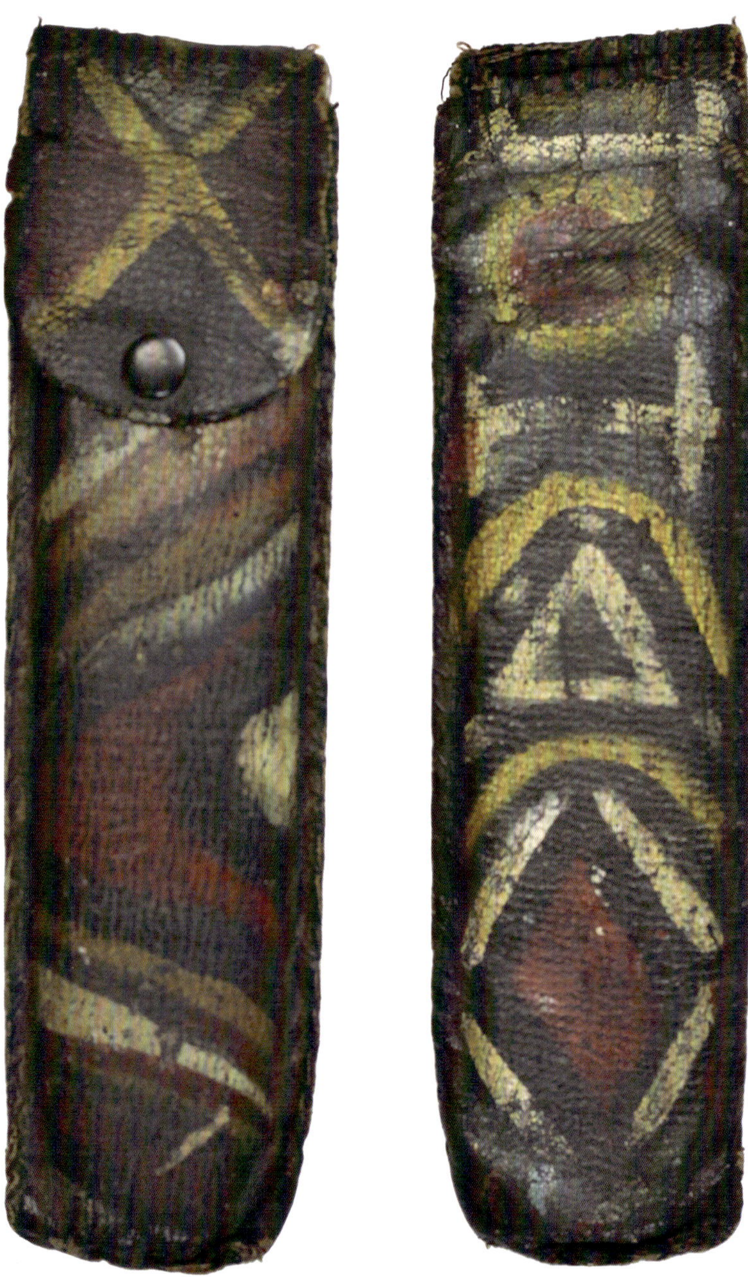

One of Gus Wagner's hand-painted sheaths

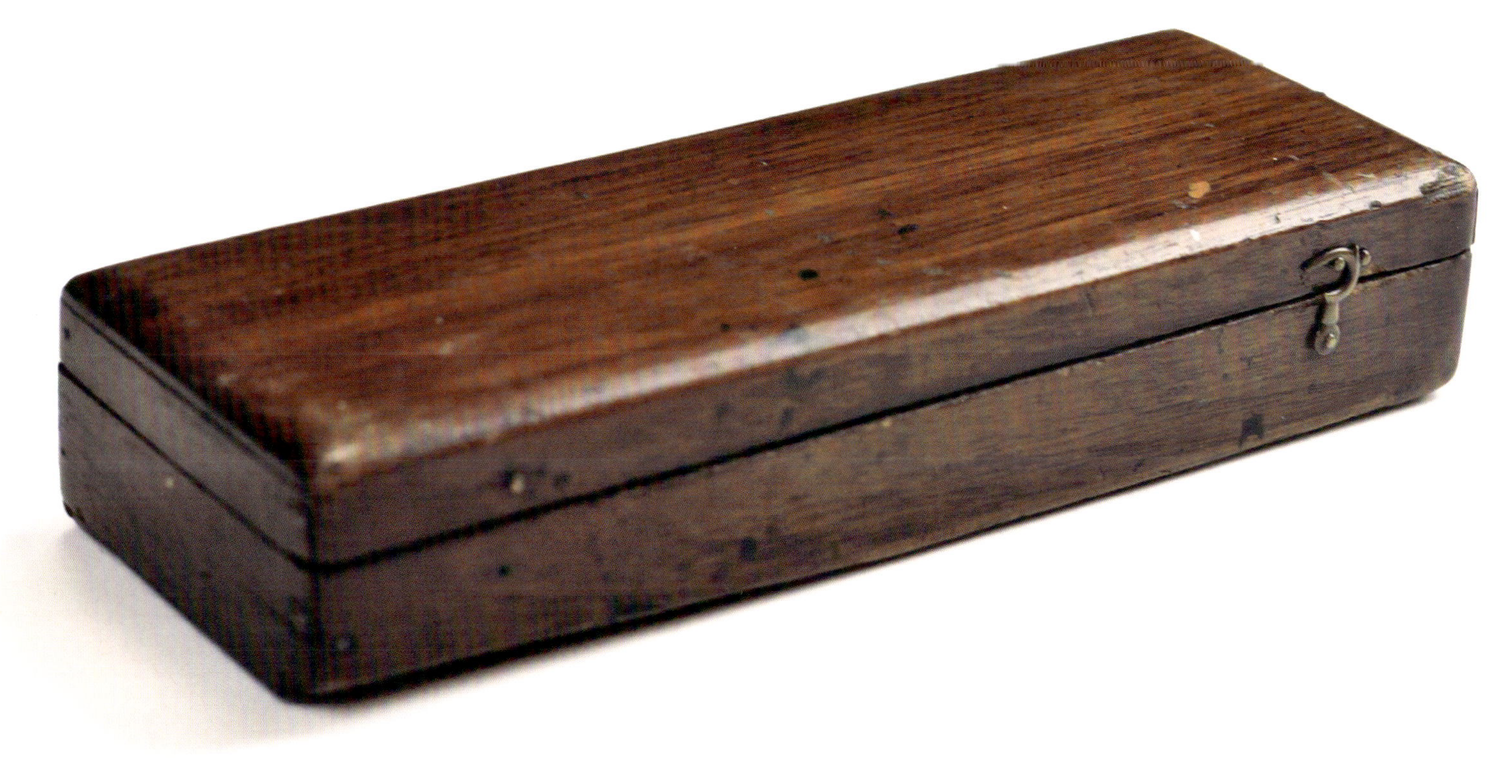

One of Gus Wagner's seaman's boxes

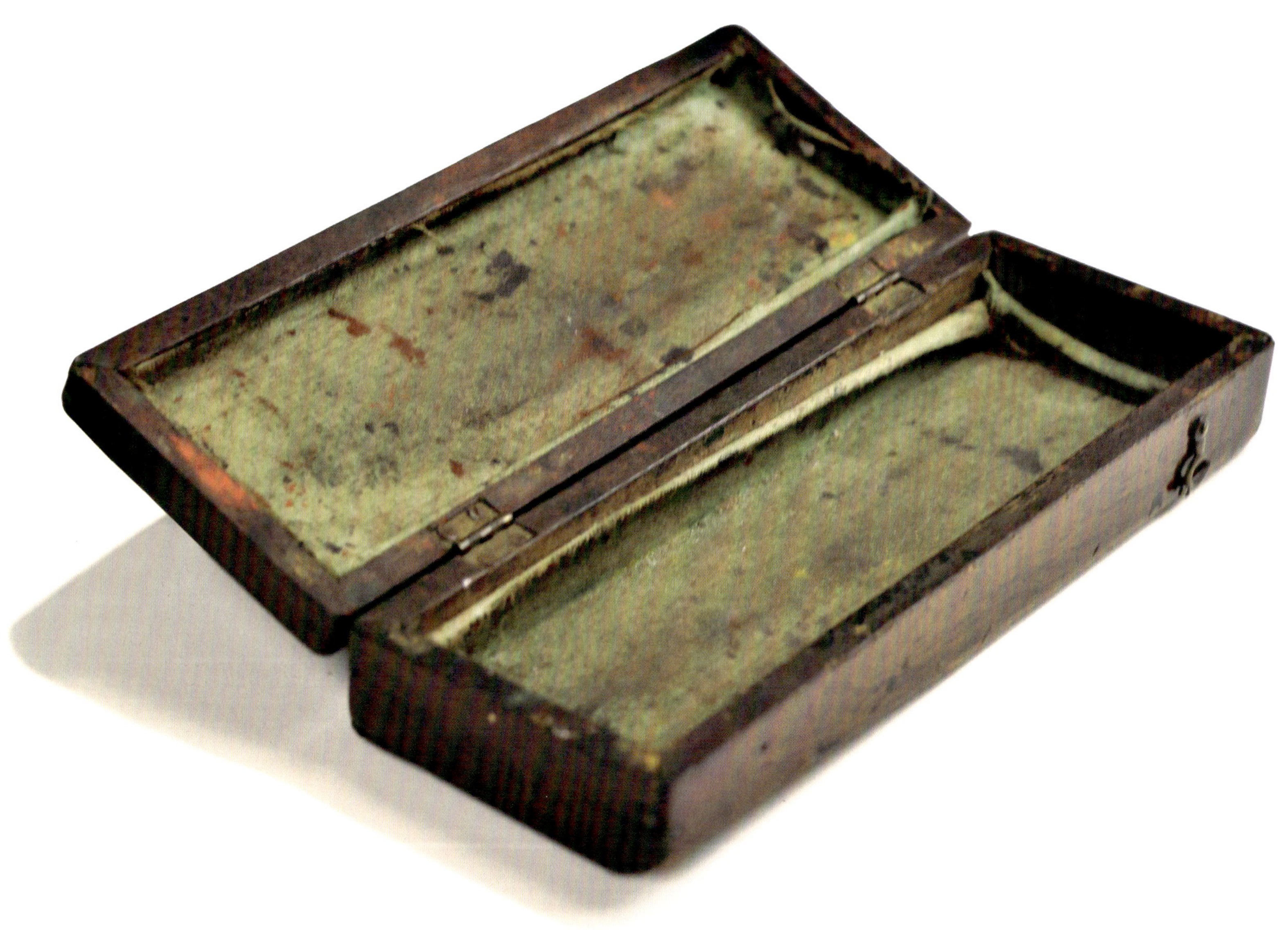

One of Gus Wagner's seaman's boxes

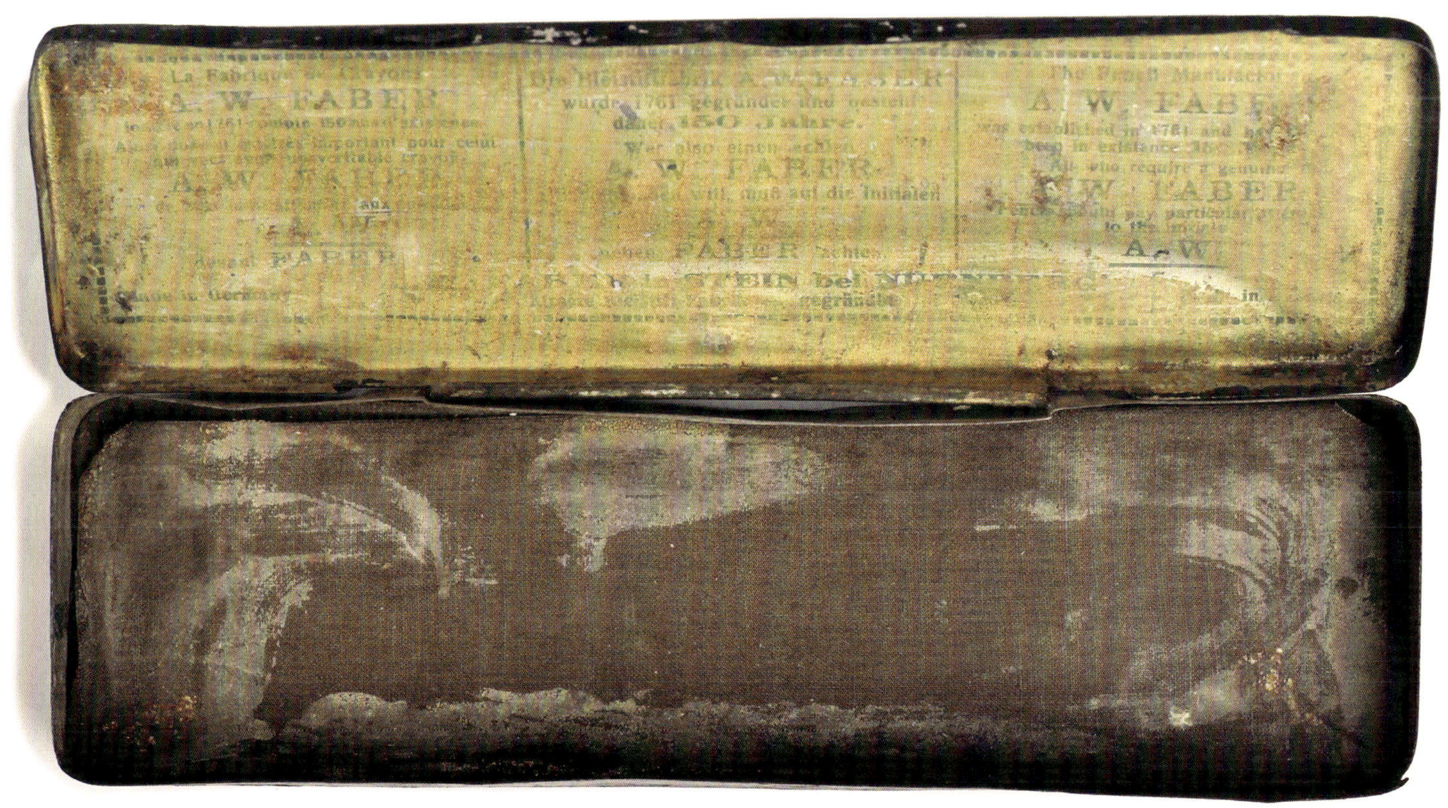
A. W. FABER
A. W. FABER
A. W. FABER
A. W.

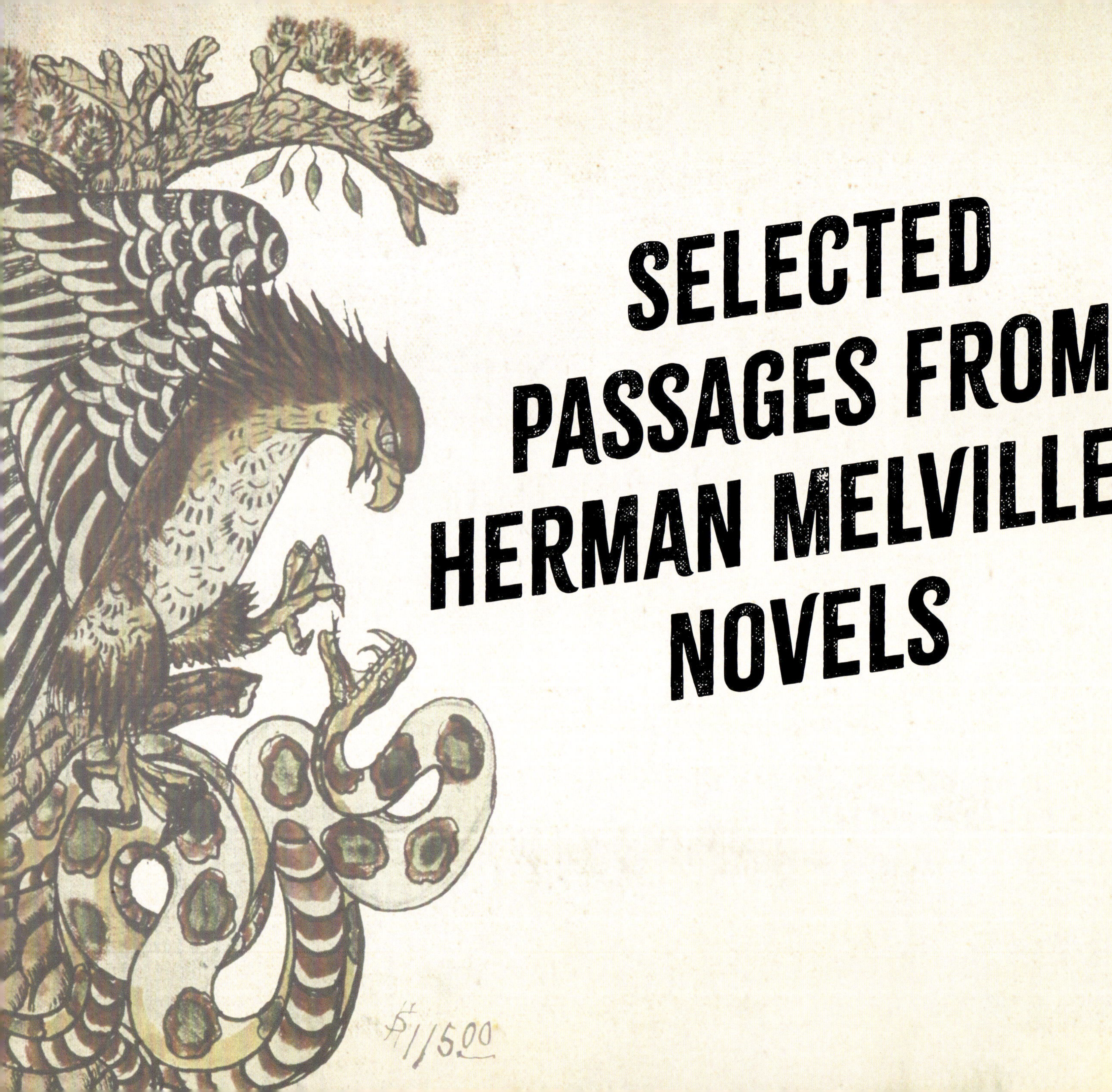

SELECTED PASSAGES FROM HERMAN MELVILLE'S NOVELS

TYPEE: A PEEP AT POLYNESIAN LIFE (1846)

EXCERPT FROM CHAPTER ONE

[The queen] singled out from their number an old salt, whose bare arms and feet, and exposed breast were covered with as many inscriptions in India ink as the lid of an Egyptian sarcophagus. Notwithstanding all the sly hints of the French officers, she immediately approached the man, pulling further open the bosom of his duck frock, and rolling up the leg of his trousers, she gazed with admiration at the bright blue and vermilion pricking thus disclosed to view. She hung over the fellow, caressing him and expressing her delight in a variety of wild exclamations and gestures.

This section of the book was removed from future editions for being too objectionable.

EXCERPT FROM CHAPTER FIVE

Ten to one, men, if you go ashore, you will get into some infernal row, and that will be the end of you; for if these tattooed scoundrels get you a little ways back into their valleys, they'll nab you—that you may be certain of. Plenty of white men have gone ashore here and never been seen any more. There was the old Dido, she put in here about two years ago, and sent one watch off on liberty; they never were heard of again for a week—the natives swore they didn't know where they were—and only three of them ever got back to the ship again, and one with his face damaged for life, for the cursed heathens tattooed a broad patch clean across his figure head.

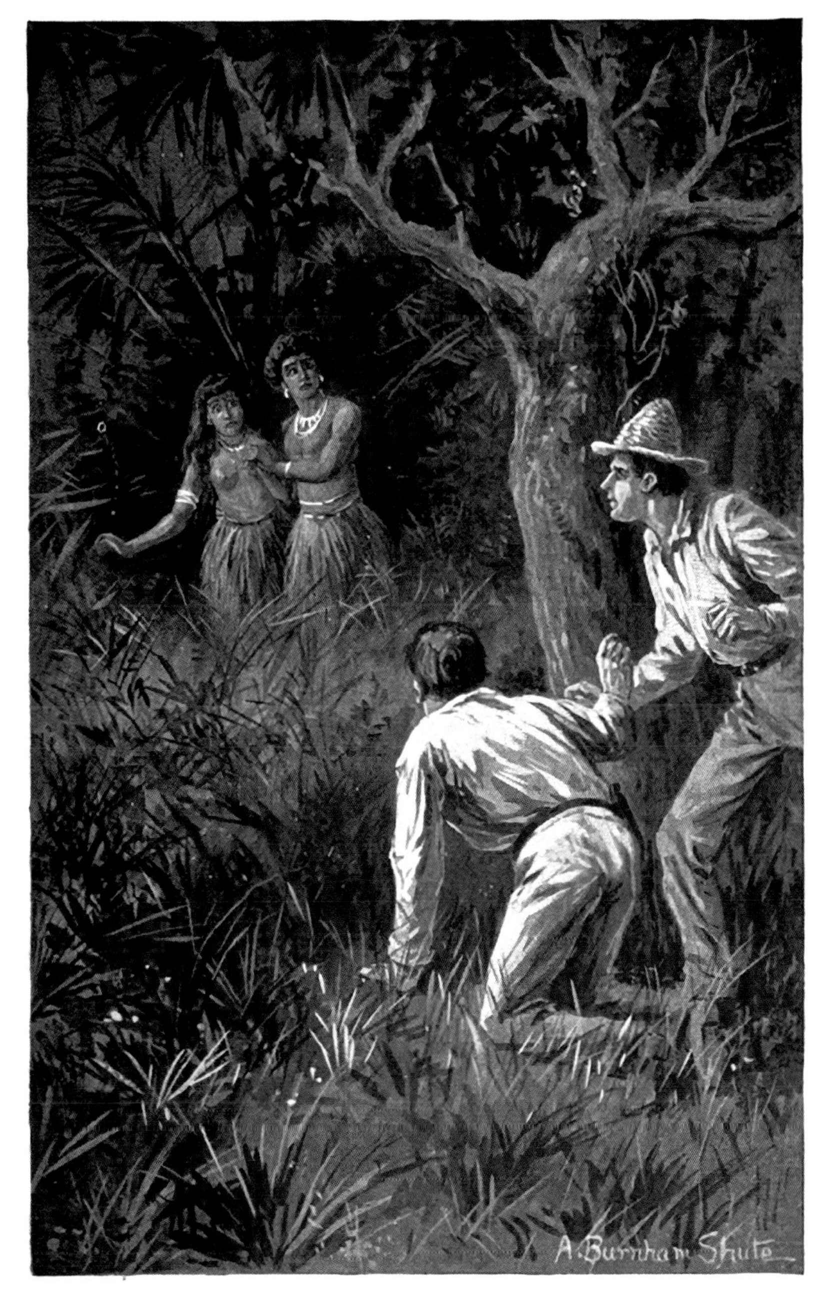

Illustration by Augustus Burnham Shute.
From the 1892 edition of the novel *Typee* by Herman Melville.

EXCERPT FROM CHAPTER TEN

But that which was most remarkable in the appearance of this splendid islander, was the elaborate tattooing displayed on every noble limb. All imaginable lines and curves and figures were delineated over his whole body, and in their grotesque variety and infinite profusion, I could only compare them to the crowded groupings of quaint patterns we sometimes see in costly pieces of lacework. The most simple and remarkable of all these ornaments was that which decorated the countenance of the chief. Two broad stripes of tattooing, diverging from the centre of his shaven crown, obliquely crossed both eyes—staining the lids—to a little below either ear, where they united with another stripe, which swept in a straight line along the lips, and formed the base of the triangle. The warrior, from the excellence of his physical proportions, might certainly have been regarded as one of nature's noblemen, and the lines drawn upon his face may possibly have denoted his exalted rank.

Kory-Kory, with the view of improving the handiwork of nature, and perhaps prompted by a desire to add to the engaging expression of his countenance, had seen fit to embellish his face with three broad longitudinal stripes of tattooing, which, like those country roads that go straight forward in defiance of all obstacles, crossed his nasal organ, descended into the hollow of his eyes, and even skirted the borders of his mouth. Each completely spanned his physiognomy; one extending in a line with his eyes, another crossing the face in the vicinity of the nose, and the third sweeping along his lips from ear to ear. His countenance thus triply hooped, as it were, with tattooing, always reminded me of those unhappy wretches whom I have sometimes observed gazing out sentimentally from behind the grated bars of a prison window; whilst the entire body of my savage valet, covered all over with representations of birds and fishes, and a variety of most unaccountable-looking creatures, suggested to me the idea of a pictorial museum of natural history, or an illustrated copy of Goldsmith's *Animated Nature*.

But it seems really heartless in me to write thus of the poor islander, when I owe perhaps to his unremitting attentions the very existence I now enjoy. Kory-Kory, I mean thee no harm in what I say in regard to thy outward adornings; but they were a little curious to my unaccustomed sight, and therefore I dilate upon them. But to underrate or forget thy faithful services is something I could never be guilty of, even in the giddiest moment of my life.

Were I asked if the beauteous form of Fayaway was altogether free from the hideous blemish of tattooing, I should be constrained to answer that it was not. But the practitioners of this barbarous art, so remorseless in their inflictions upon the brawny limbs of the warriors of the tribe, seem to be conscious that it needs not the resources of their profession to augment the charms of the maidens of the vale.

The females are very little embellished in this way, and Fayaway, and all the other young girls of her age, were even less so than those of their sex more advanced in years. The reason of this peculiarity will be alluded to hereafter. All the tattooing that the nymph in question exhibited upon her person may be easily described. Three minute dots, no bigger than pinheads, decorated either lip, and at a little distance were not at all discernible. Just upon the fall of the shoulder were drawn two parallel lines half an inch apart, and perhaps three inches in length, the interval being filled with delicately executed figures. These narrow bands of tattooing, thus placed, always reminded me of those stripes of gold lace worn by officers in undress, and which are in lieu of epaulettes to denote their rank.

Thus much was Fayaway tattooed. The audacious hand which had gone so far in its desecrating work stopping short, apparently wanting the heart to proceed.

EXCERPT FROM CHAPTER TEN

As we advanced farther along the building, we were struck with the aspect of four or five hideous old wretches, on whose decrepid forms time and tattooing seemed to have obliterated every trace of humanity. Owing to the continued operation of this latter process, which only terminates among the warriors of the island after all the figures stretched upon their limbs in youth have been blended together—an effect, however, produced only in cases of extreme longevity—the bodies of these men were of a uniform dull green colour—the hue which the tattooing gradually assumes as the individual advances in age.

EXCERPT FROM CHAPTER SEVENTEEN

The hair of Marnoo was a rich curling brown, and twined about his temples and neck in little close curling ringlets, which danced up and down continually when he was animated in conversation. His cheek was of a feminine softness, and his face was free from the least blemish of tattooing, although the rest of his body was drawn all over with fanciful figures, which—unlike the unconnected sketching usual among these natives—appeared to have been executed in conformity with some general design.

Illustration by Augustus Burnham Shute.
From the 1892 edition of the novel *Typee* by Herman Melville.

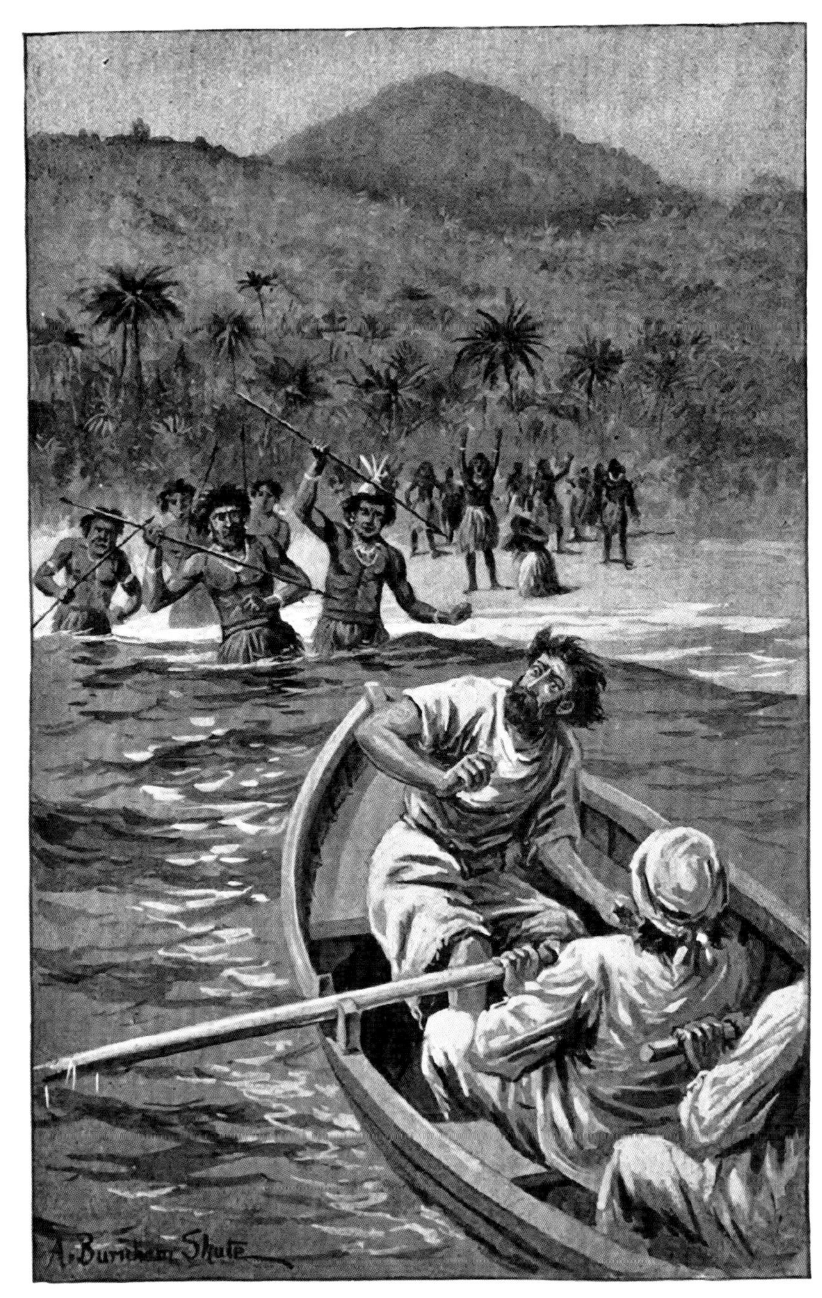

The tattooing on his back in particular attracted my attention. The artist employed must indeed have excelled in his profession. Traced along the course of the spine was accurately delineated the slender, tapering, and diamond-checkered shaft of the beautiful "artu" tree. Branching from the stem on either side, and disposed alternately, were the graceful branches drooping with leaves all correctly drawn, and elaborately finished. Indeed, this piece of tattooing was the best specimen of the Fine Arts I had yet seen in Typee. A rear view of the stranger might have suggested the idea of a spreading vine tacked against a garden wall. Upon his breast, arms, and legs, were exhibited an infinite variety of figures; every one of which, however, appeared to have reference to the general effect sought to be produced. The tattooing I have described was of the brightest blue, and when contrasted with the light olive-colour of the skin, produced an unique and even elegant effect.

EXCERPT FROM CHAPTER TWENTY-FIVE

During the second day of the Feast of Calabashes, Kory-Kory—being determined that I should have some understanding on these matters—had, in the course of his explanations, directed my attention to a peculiarity I had frequently marked among many of the females,—principally those of a mature age and rather matronly appearance. This consisted in having the right hand and the left foot most elaborately tattooed; while the rest of the body was wholly free from the operation of the art, with the exception of the minutely dotted lips and slight marks on the shoulders, to which I have previously referred as comprising the sole tattooing exhibited by Fayaway, in common with other young girls of her age. The hand and foot thus embellished, were, according to Kory-Kory, the distinguishing badge of wedlock, so far as that social and highly commendable institution is known among these people. It answers, indeed, the same purpose as the plain gold ring worn by our fairer spouses.

EXCERPT FROM CHAPTER TWENTY-NINE

In one of my strolls with Kory-Kory, in passing along the border of a thick growth of bushes, my attention was arrested by a singular noise. On entering the thicket, I witnessed for the first time the operation of tattooing as performed by these islanders.

I beheld a man extended flat upon his back, on the ground, and, despite the forced composure of his countenance, it was evident that he was suffering agony. His tormentor bent over him, working away for all the world like a stone-cutter with mallet and chisel. In one hand he held a short slender stick, pointed with a shark's tooth, on the upright end of which he tapped with a small hammer-like piece of wood, thus puncturing the skin, and charging it with the colouring matter in which the instrument was dipped. A cocoa-nut shell containing this fluid was placed upon the ground. It is prepared by mixing with a vegetable juice the ashes of the "armor," or candle-nut, always preserved for the purpose. Beside the savage, and spread out upon a piece of soiled tappa, were a great number of curious black-looking little implements of bone and wood, used in the various divisions of his art. A few terminated in a single fine point, and, like very delicate pencils, were employed in giving the finishing touches, or in operating upon the more sensitive portions of the body, as was the case of the present instance. Others presented several points distributed in a line, somewhat resembling the teeth of a saw. These were employed in the coarser parts of the work, and particularly in pricking in straight marks. Some presented their points disposed in small figures, and being placed upon the body, were, by a single blow of the hammer, made to leave their indelible impression. I observed a few, the handles of which were mysteriously curved, as if intended to be introduced into the orifice of the ear, with a view perhaps of beating the tattoo upon the tympanum. Altogether, the sight of these strange instruments recalled to mind that display of cruel-looking mother-of-pearl-handled things which one sees in their velvet-lined cases at the elbow of a dentist.

The artist was not at this time engaged on an original sketch, his subject being a venerable savage, whose tattooing had become somewhat faded with age and needed a few repairs, and accordingly he was merely employed in touching up the works of some of the old masters of the Typee school, as delineated upon the human canvas before him. The parts operated upon were the eyelids, where a longitudinal streak, like the one which adorned Kory-Kory, crossed the countenance of the victim.

In spite of all the efforts of the poor old man, sundry twitchings and screwings of the muscles of the face denoted the exquisite sensibility of these shutters to the windows of his soul, which he was now having repainted. But the artist, with a heart as callous as that of an army surgeon, continued his performance, enlivening his labours with a wild chant, tapping away the while as merrily as a woodpecker.

WHITE JACKET (1850)

EXCERPT FROM CHAPTER FORTY-TWO

Reading was by no means the only method adopted by my shipmates in whiling away the long, tedious hours in harbour. In truth, many of them could not have read, had they wanted to ever so much; in early youth their primers had been sadly neglected. Still, they had other pursuits; some were expert at the needle, and employed their time in making elaborate shirts, stitching picturesque eagles, and anchors, and all the stars of the federated states in the collars thereof; so that when they at last completed and put on these shirts, they may be said to have hoisted the American colours.

Others excelled in *tattooing,* or *pricking*, as it is called in a man-of-war. Of these prickers, two had long been celebrated, in their way, as consummate masters of the art. Each had a small box full of tools and colouring matter; and

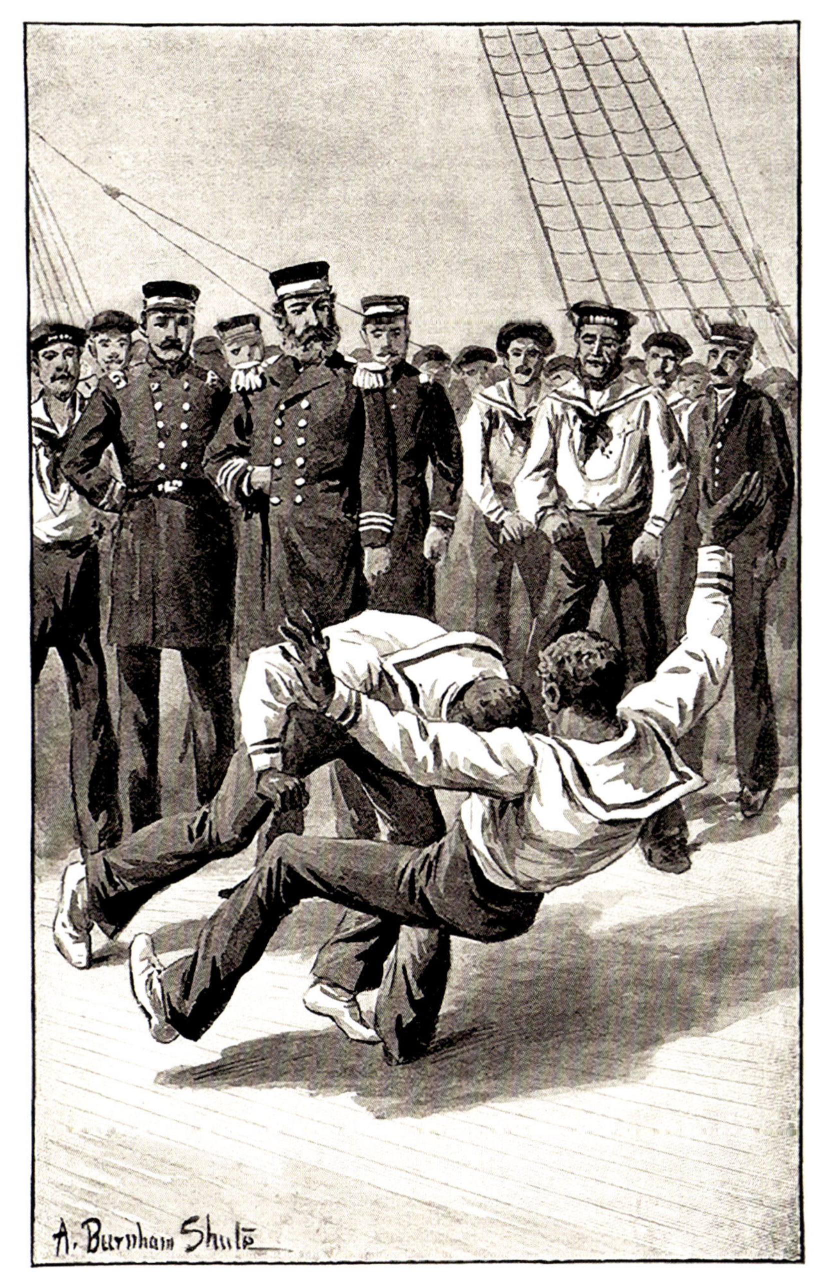

Illustration by Augustus Burnham Shute.
From the 1892 edition of the novel *White Jacket* by Herman Melville.

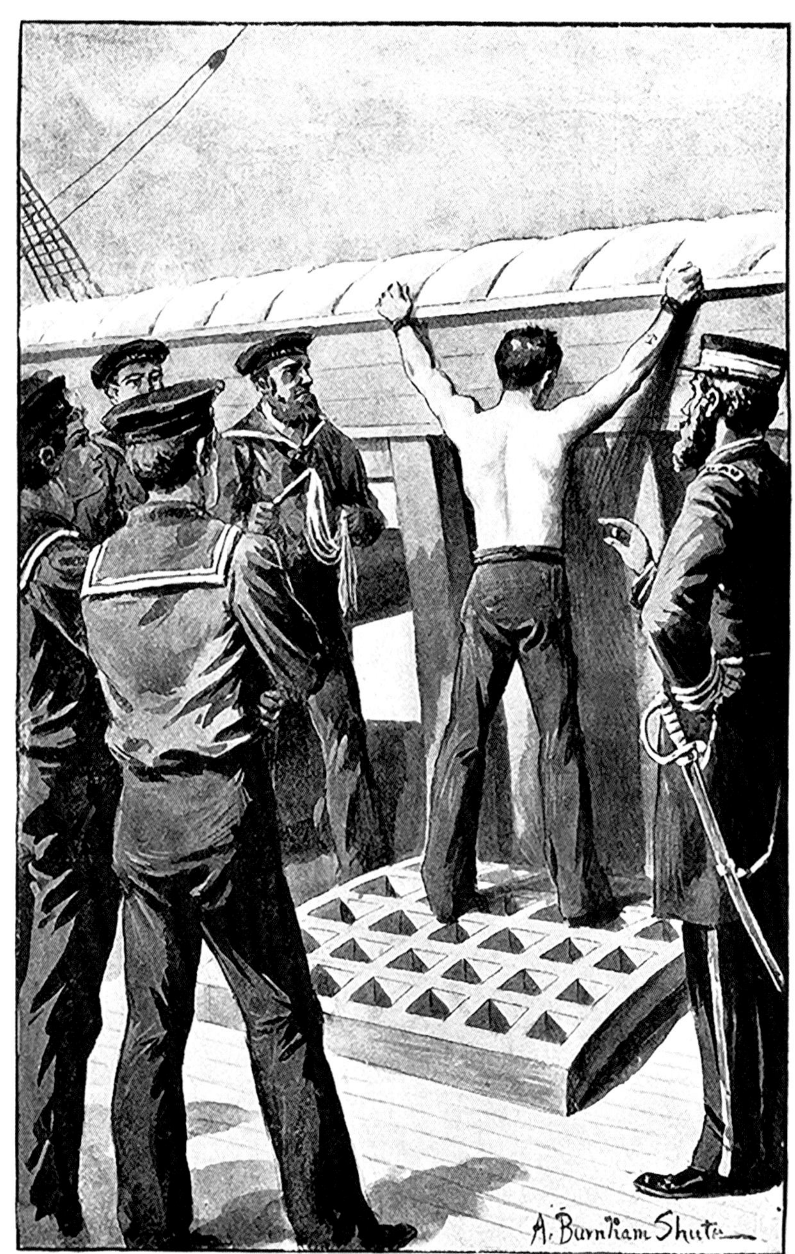

Illustration by Augustus Burnham Shute.
From the 1892 edition of the novel *White Jacket* by Herman Melville.

they charged so high for their services, that at the end of the cruise they were to have cleared upwards of four hundred dollars. They would *prick* you to order a palm-tree, an anchor, a crucifix, a lady, a lion, an eagle, or anything else you might want.

The Roman Catholic soldiers on board had at least the crucifix pricked on their arms, and for this reason: If they chanced to die in a Catholic land, they would be sure of a decent burial in consecrated ground, as the priest would be sure to observe the symbol of Mother Church on their persons. They would not fare as Protestant sailors dying in Callao, who are shoved under the sands of St. Lorenzo, a solitary, volcanic island in the harbour, overrun with reptiles, their heretical bodies not being permitted to repose in the more genial loam of Lima.

And many sailors not Catholics were anxious to have the crucifix painted on them, owing to a curious superstition of theirs. They affirm—some of them—that if you have that mark tattooed on all four limbs, you might fall overboard among seven hundred and seventy-five thousand white sharks, all dinnerless, and not one of them would so much dare to smell at your little finger.

We had one fore-top man on board, who, during the entire cruise, was having an endless cable *pricked* round and round his waist, so that, when his frock was off, he looked like a captain with a hawser coiled round about it. This fore-top man paid eighteenpence per link of the cable, besides being on the smart the whole cruise, suffering the effects of his repeated puncturings; so he paid very dear for his cable.

MOBY DICK, OR THE WHALE (1851)

EXCERPT FROM CHAPTER THREE THE SPOUTER-INN

Lord save me, thinks I, that must be the harpooner, the infernal head-peddler. But I lay perfectly still, and resolved not to say a word till spoken to. Holding a light in one hand, and that identical New Zealand head in the other, the stranger entered the room, and without looking towards the bed, placed his candle a good way off from me on the floor in one corner, and then began working away at the knotted cords of the large bag I before spoke of as being in the room. I was all eagerness to see his face, but he kept it averted for some time while employed in unlacing the bag's mouth. This accomplished, however, he turned round—when, good heavens! What a sight! Such a face! It was of a dark, purplish, yellow color, here and there stuck over with large blackish

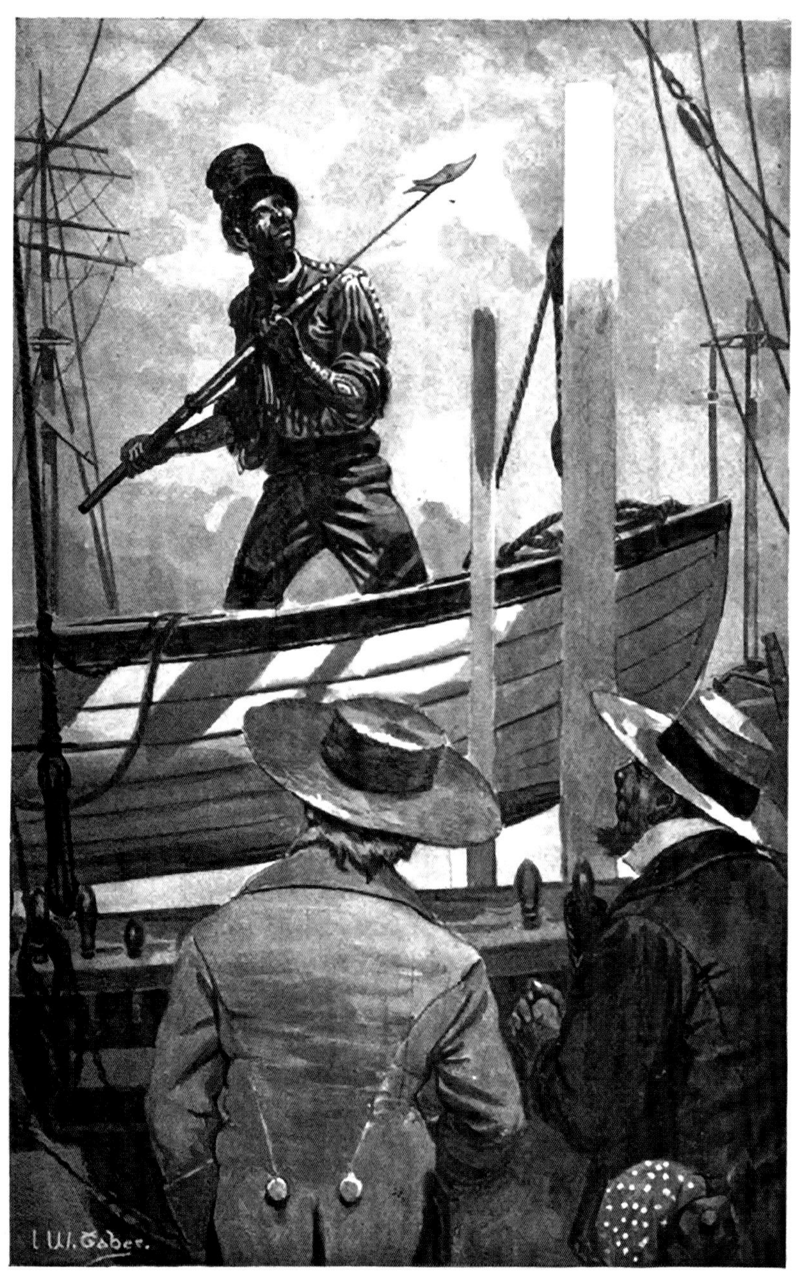

Illustration by I. W. Taber.
From the 1902 edition of the novel *Moby Dick* by Herman Melville.

looking squares. Yes, it's just as I thought, he's a terrible bedfellow; he's been in a fight, got dreadfully cut, and here he is, just from the surgeon. But at that moment he chanced to turn his face so towards the light, that I plainly saw they could not be sticking-plasters at all, those black squares on his cheeks. They were stains of some sort or other. At first, I knew not what to make of this; but soon an inkling of the truth occurred to me. I remembered the story of a white man—a whaleman too—who, falling among the cannibals, had been tattooed by them. I concluded that this harpooneer, in the course of his distant voyages, must have met with a similar adventure. And what is it, thought I, after all! It's his outside; a man can be honest in any sort of skin.

EXCERPT FROM CHAPTER EIGHTEEN
HIS MARK

"Yea," said Captain Bildad in his hollow voice. . . . "He [Queequeg] must show that he's converted. Son of darkness," he added, turning to Queequeg, "art thou at present in communion with any Christian church?"

"Why," said I, "he's a member of the first Congregational Church." Here be it said that many tattooed savages sailing in Nantucket ships at last come to be converted into churches.

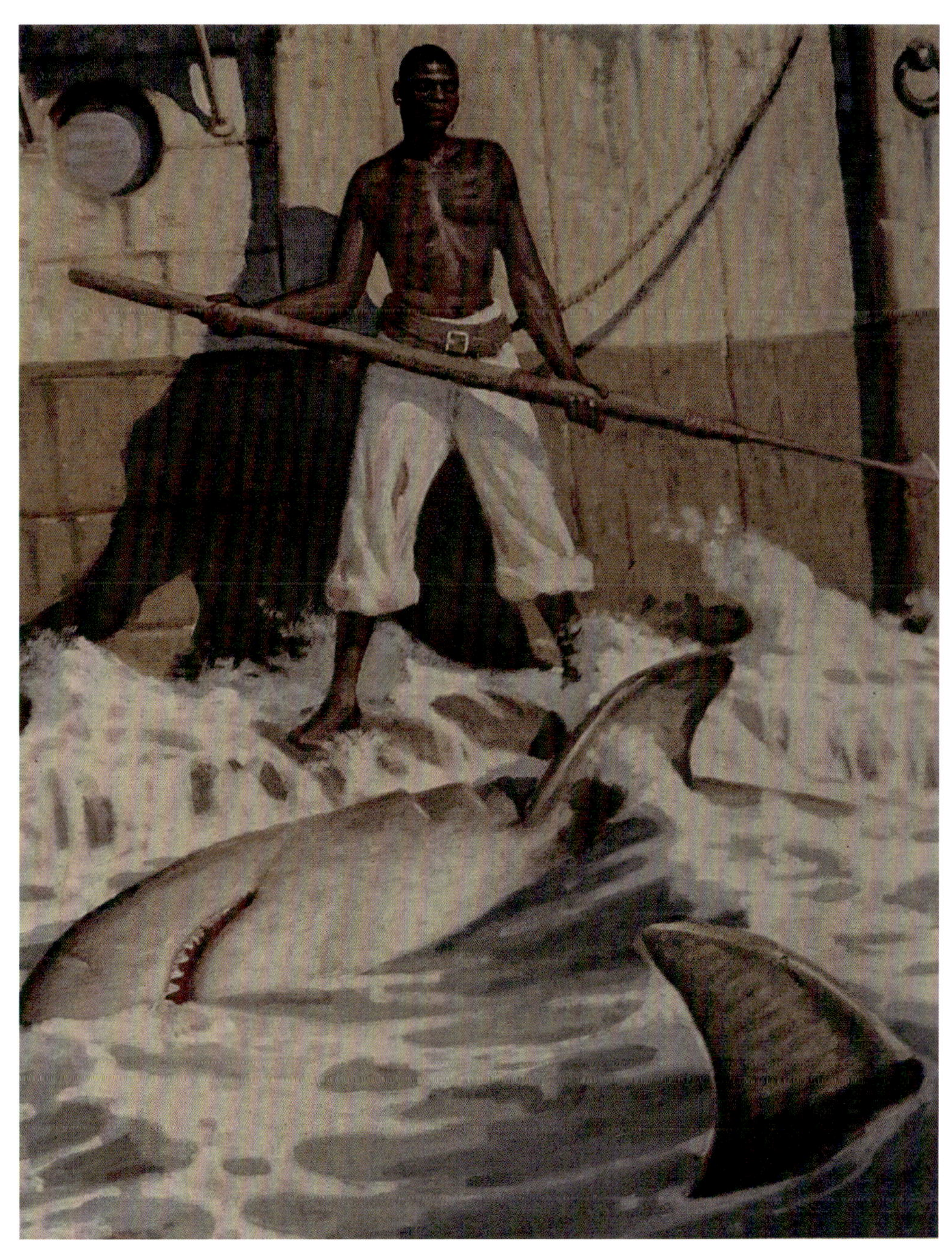

Illustration by Mead Schaeffer.
From the 1922 edition of the novel *Moby Dick*
by Herman Melville.
Courtesy of Library of Congress

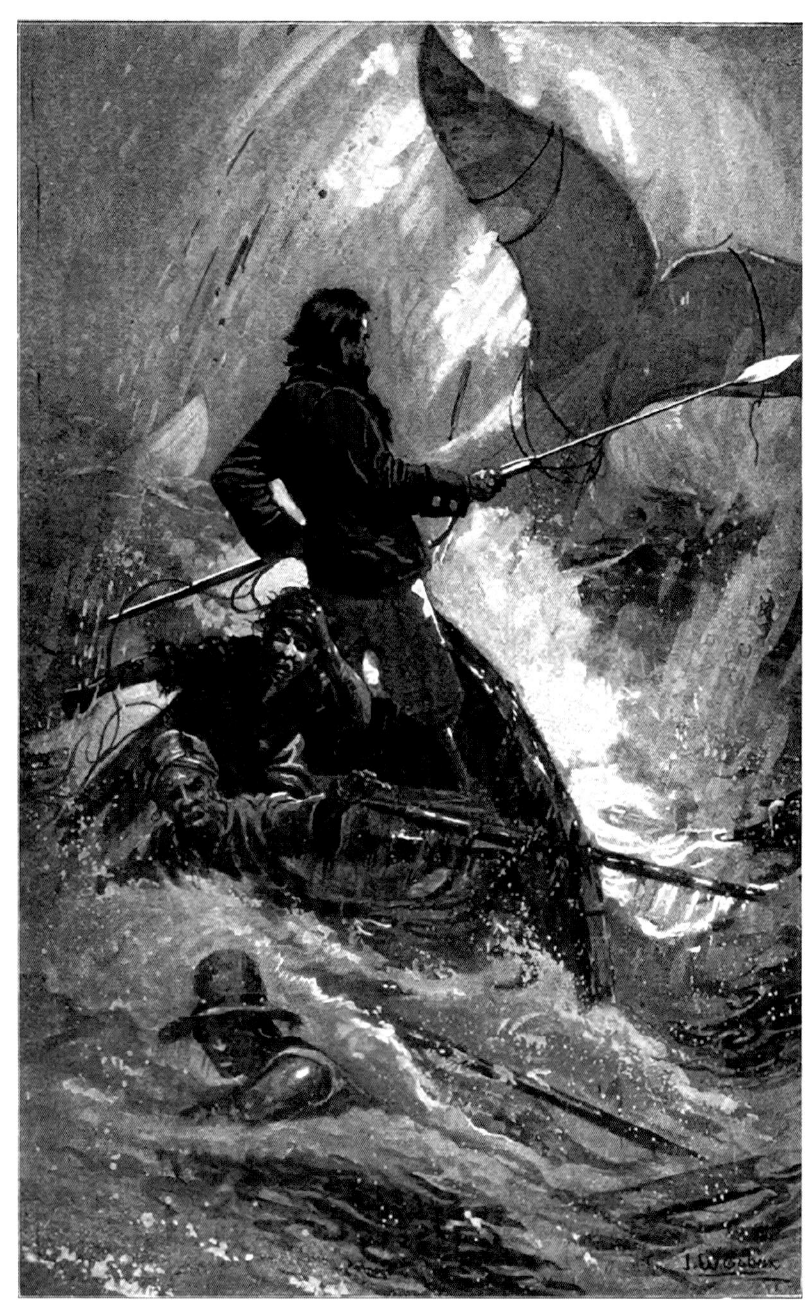

Illustration by I. W. Taber.
From the 1902 edition of the novel *Moby Dick* by Herman Melville.

EXCERPT FROM CHAPTER ONE HUNDRED AND TWO
A BOWER IN THE ARSACIDES

The [sperm whale] skeleton dimensions I shall now proceed to set down are copied verbatim from my right arm, where I had them tattooed; as in my wild wanderings at that period, there was no other secure way of preserving such valuable statistics. But as I was crowded for space, and wished the other parts of my body to remain a blank page for a poem I was then composing—at least, what untattooed parts might remain—I did not trouble myself with the odd inches; nor, indeed, should inches at all enter in a congenial admeasurement of the whale.

EXCERPT FROM CHAPTER ONE HUNDRED AND TEN
QUEEQUEG IN HIS COFFIN

With a wild whimsiness, he now used his coffin for a sea-chest; and emptying into it his canvas bag of clothes, set them in order there. Many spare hours he spent, in carving the lid with all manner of grotesque figures and drawings; and it seemed that hereby he was striving, in his rude way, to copy parts of the twisted tattooing on his body. And this tattooing had been the work of a departed prophet and seer of his island, who, by those hieroglyphic marks, had written out on his body a complete theory of the heavens and the earth, and a mystical treatise on the art of attaining truth; so that Queequeg in his own proper person was a riddle to unfold; a wondrous work in one volume; but whose mysteries not even himself could read, though his own live heart beat against them; and these mysteries were therefore destined in the end to moulder away with the living parchment whereon they were inscribed, and so be unsolved to the last. And this thought it must have been which suggested to Ahab that wild exclamation of his, when one morning turning away from surveying poor Queequeg—"Oh devilish tantalization of the gods!"

EXCERPT FROM CHAPTER ONE HUNDRED AND NINETEEN
THE CANDLES

The parted mouth of Tashtego revealed his shark-white teeth, which strangely gleamed as if they too had been tipped by corposants; while lit up by the preternatural light, Queequeg's tattooing burned like Satanic blue flames on his body.

Illustration by Augustus Burnham Shute.
From the 1892 edition of the novel *Moby Dick* by Herman Melville.

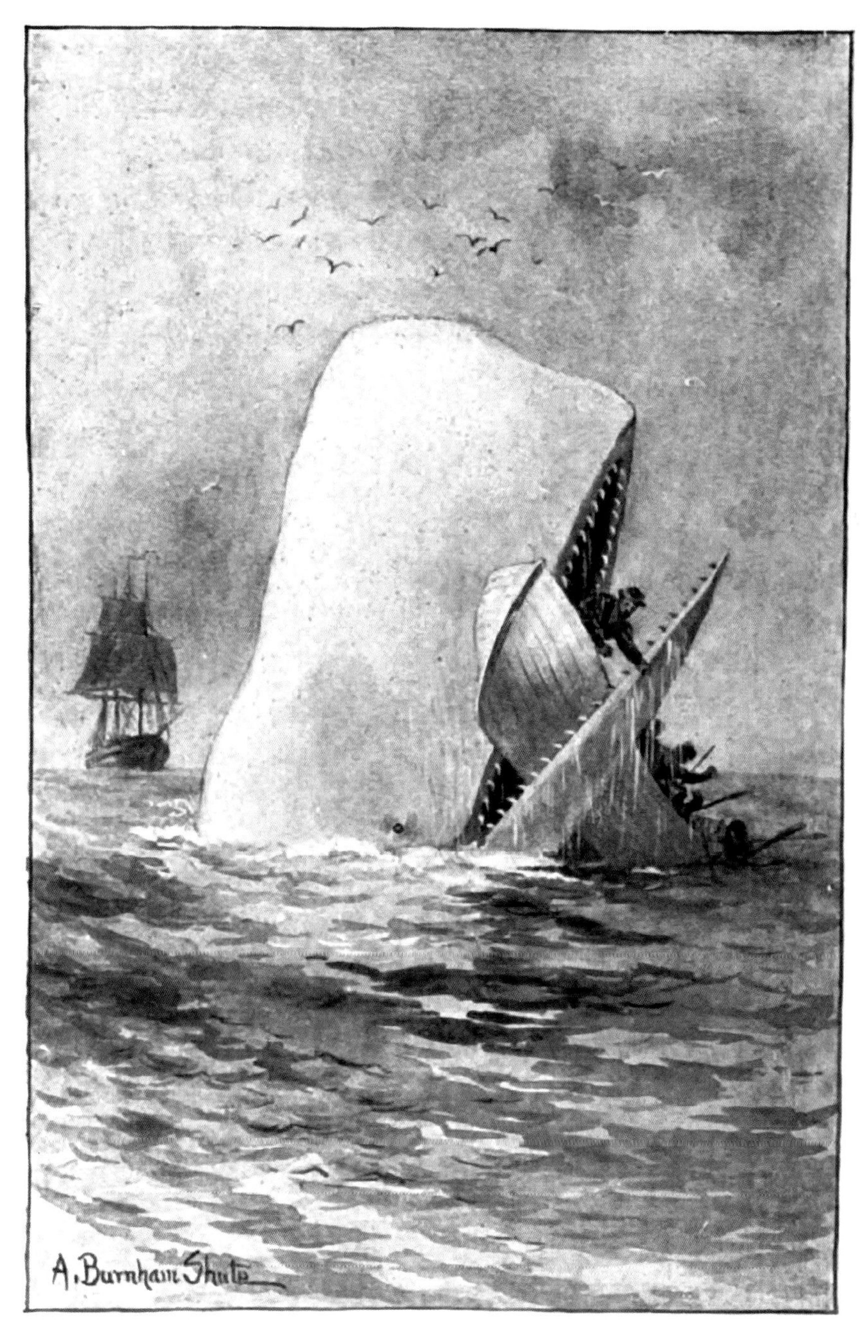

ABOUT THE AUTHOR

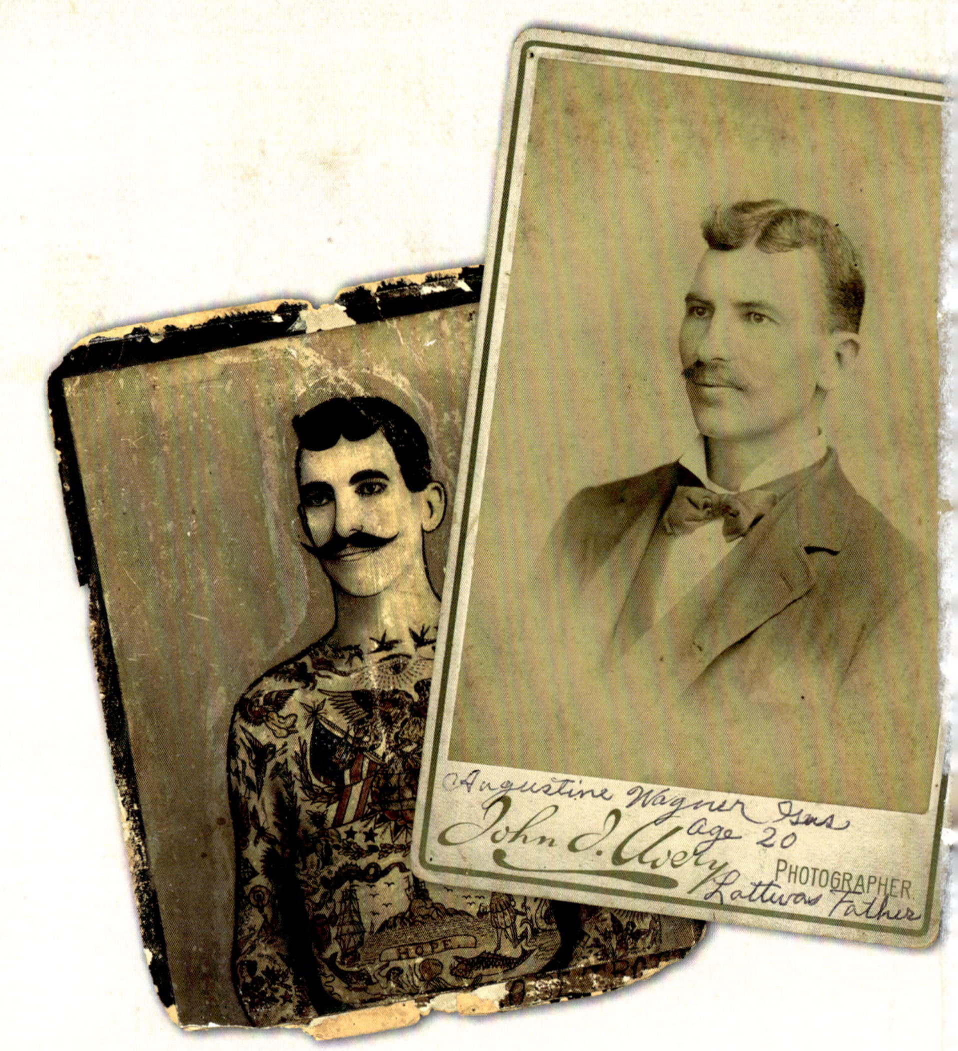

Alan Govenar is an award-winning writer, folklorist, playwright, poet, photographer, and filmmaker. He is president of Documentary Arts, a nonprofit organization he founded to advance essential perspectives on historical issues and diverse cultures. Govenar is a Guggenheim Fellow and the author of more than 35 books, including *Boccaccio in the Berkshires*, *Flash from the Past: Classic American Tattoo Designs 1890-1965*, *Beyond Skin: Ed Hardy*, *Stoney Knows How: Life as a Sideshow Tattoo Artist*, *Stompin' at the Savoy: The Story of Norma Miller*, *Everyday Music*, *Untold Glory*, *Texas Blues*, and *A Pillow on the Ocean of Time*. For more information, see www.documentaryarts.org.

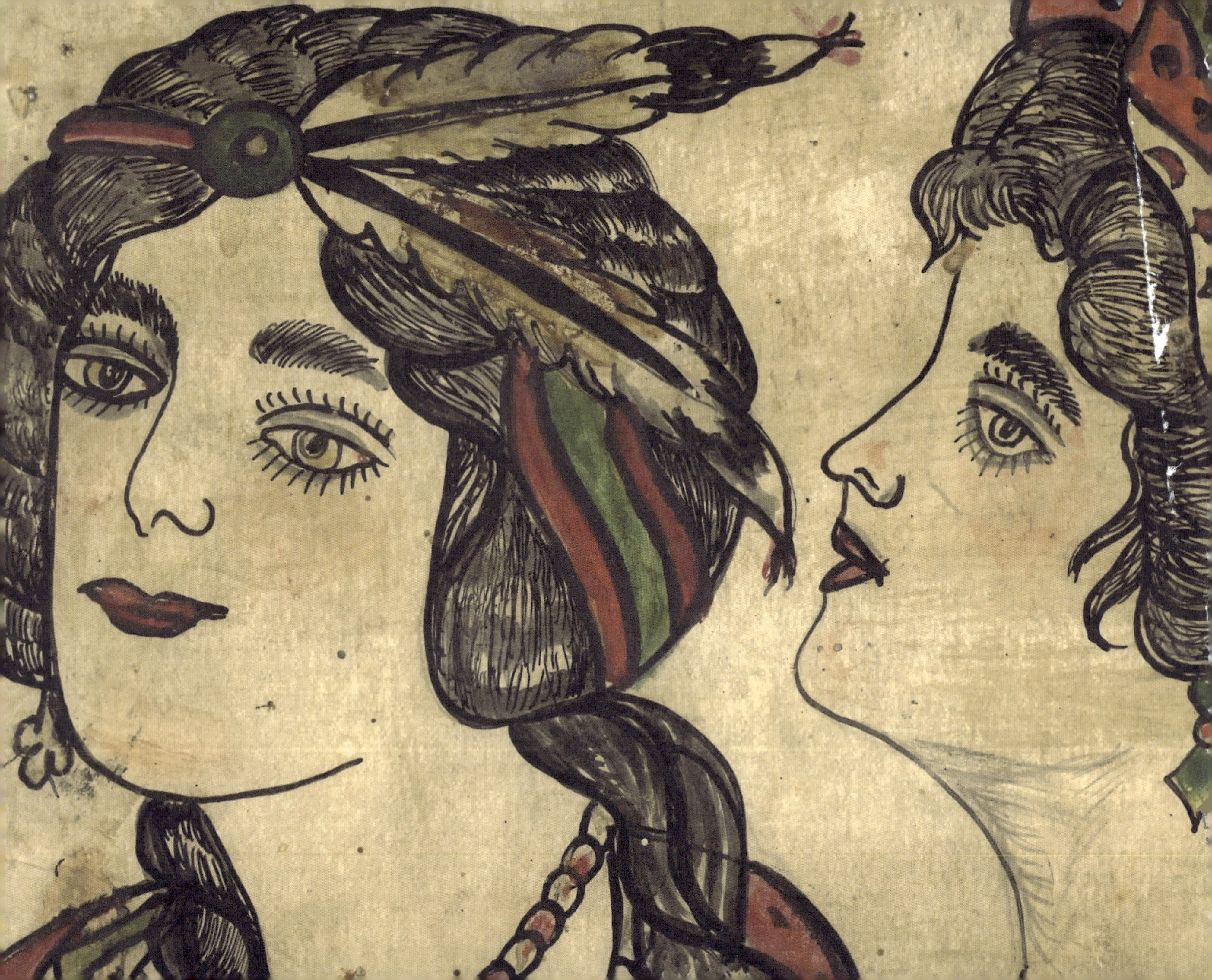